Palm Beach, Miami
& the Florida Keys

A COMPLETE GUIDE

FIRST EDITION

Palm Beach, Miami & the Florida Keys

Includes 2004 Post-Hurricane Updates

Trish Riley

The Countryman Press
Woodstock, Vermont

This book, like everything I do, is for Rachel and Bud.

We welcome your comments and suggestions. Please contact Great Destinations Guide Editor, The Countryman Press, P.O. Box 748, Woodstock, VT 05091, or e-mail countrymanpress@wwnorton.com.

Copyright © 2005 Trish Riley

First Edition

ISBN 1-58157-026-0
ISSN 1554-2696

Maps by Mapping Specialists Ltd., © The Countryman Press
Book design by Bodenweber Design
Text composition by Melinda Belter
Cover photograph of Fort Lauderdale Beach © James Randklev
Interior photographs by the author unless otherwise indicated

Published by The Countryman Press, P.O. Box 748, Woodstock, VT 05091

Distributed by W. W. Norton & Company, Inc., 500 Fifth Avenue, New York, NY 10110

Printed in the United States of America

10 9 8 7 6 5 4 3 2 1

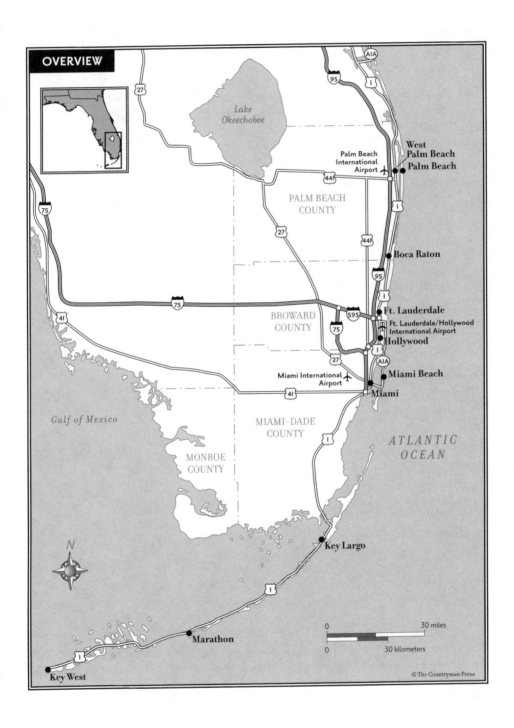

Contents

ACKNOWLEDGMENTS

Tackling a book that covers four major counties in a top tourist destination is no small task, and I surely couldn't have accomplished it without a great deal of help from those in the know. Thanks to Jean Rousseau at Berkshire House Publishing for recommending my proposal upon his retirement, and to Kermit Hummel, whose company, The Countryman Press, absorbed Jean's business and took on my book project. Thanks to Jennifer Thompson and everyone else at The Countryman Press for guidance and support through the process. Although most of the time I tried to do my research quietly and unnoticed, there were certainly occasions when I couldn't have done my job without the help of tourism and marketing professionals, property owners, and staff. My sincere thanks and appreciation to specialists Chip Armstrong and Gayle Ameche, Arnelle Kendall, Margee Adelsperger, Josie Gulliksen, Bruce Peterson, Stacey Promish, Alisah Jeffries, Jeanne Sullivan, Charles Kropke, Amanda Schinder, Kristen Vigrass, Deborah Davidson, Jeff Davis, Kelly Batson, Carrie Babich, Michael Zaidman, Christine Carney, Vivian Liberman, Sheila Thompson, and so many others who provided information about interesting places to consider for the book.

Thanks, too, to Beth Kaminstein, Hib and Martha Casselberry, Craig Palmer, Alma Bond, Elbe Burke, Janice Cacace, Lois Perdue, and everyone else who suggested favorite places for me to check out. Thanks to Chandra McMillan, who traded her time for Christmas money to spend weeks helping me organize and format the text. Thanks to Brian Rector, who helped me finish the project by running the tedious conclusive fact check, and thanks to editor Justine Rathbun for tightening everything into such a neat final package. Finally, thanks to my husband, Jim Wurster, for chauffeuring me all around the Gold Coast and the Keys and for helping to finance much of my research; my children, Rachel and Bud, who were too busy being an excellent student and a cool rock star to help me; and our sweet terrors, Christie and Teddi, for their constant supervision, companionship, and kisses.

TRISH RILEY
www.trishriley.com

Introduction

Welcome to beautiful Florida, an amazing paradise of unparalleled beauty, a place where people from all over the world go for rest and relaxation—as well as relief from winter cold spells. Florida is our American Riviera, our Mediterranean coast. Soak in the deliciously warm sunshine, breathe the sweet jasmine-scented air, and indulge yourself in bliss . . . we've got it here.

History

Although traces of native occupation in Florida date back ten thousand years, the state's first European settlements were established in the mid- to late 1800s. Native tribes such as the Tequesta and Calusa fought the early European explorers, and the Seminoles were here when the first settlements were established. A few rugged pioneers made their way to Florida by the end of the 19th century, but the real action began when the Gilded Age sparked an interest among its fathers—Rockefeller, Vanderbilt, Flagler, and friends—to chase the unknown. They developed an appreciation for warm, sunny, exotic Florida as a welcome winter getaway. Flagler made it happen for all of them by establishing rail service into the jungle wilderness, building hotel resorts as he went.

Henry Flagler, who earned a fortune as John D. Rockefeller's partner in Standard Oil of Ohio, then turned his attention and considerable financial interests to Florida. It can fairly be said that Flagler created the Florida we know today. By pushing his railroad farther and farther south all the way to Key West, he established cities along the way as resorts for those who traveled his trains; built worker towns for those who laid the rails, built the hotels,
and fed the swells; and in the process lent his financing to develop schools, postal services, and hospitals—creating infrastructure along the way to sustain the tourist trade that filled his thousand-room hotels in St. Augustine, Palm Beach, and Miami. Since the state offered him huge land grants in return for building the railroad, Flagler's realty company helped establish farming communities along the rail as well as the tourist trade. Those two industries persist today as Florida's biggest markets.

Flagler's trail finally reached Key West in 1912, with major development in St. Augustine, Palm Beach, and Miami behind him. He felt that this was his greatest achievement in life, and he died in 1913 at age 83. Flagler's gift of transportation and tourism has become the lifeblood of the state, but in some ways it's also been a double-edged sword.

Protecting Paradise

It's no secret why Florida is the number one tourist destination in the nation: we have perpetual sunshine and blue skies, a year-round average temperature of about 78 degrees, beautiful subtropical flora that lends a heavenly fragrance to the air, and delicious exotic fruits and vegetables. Almost everyone who is here today came to live because a visit wasn't enough—an estimated one thousand new residents arrive in Florida daily.

Of course, we want to share our gift of nature with the world, but we also want to protect it, so peppered throughout the book are bits and pieces of information about the environmental challenges facing our region, what we're doing to correct past mistakes and preserve the treasures before we've lost them, and how you can help. Snorkel, dive, hike the

Hurricanes in Heaven

"Hurricanes are said to cleanse the earth," said Gayle Ameche, who owns three small rentals on Singer Island, "and it's true, now the air does smell so sweet." Gayle's backyard at Southwind on Singer Island was piled with debris after Hurricane Frances and, after she'd gotten it cleaned up, Hurricane Jeanne. She's decided to keep a half dozen hunks of coral rock that were dredged out of her pool, for posterity and as a reminder of just how powerful those hurricane winds were.

"This is unprecedented, certainly, to have two hurricanes back-to-back, four in the state. There have been some devastating hurricanes come through south Florida," she said. "It goes with the turf. You have to be prepared."

Chip Armstrong agrees. "If you're here and a hurricane's coming, you need to go home. If you're coming here and a hurricane's coming, change plans." Armstrong is the president of the Singer Island Business Association and owner of Oceanside Beach Service, which rents beach supplies and offers guided tours.

"Luckily hurricanes aren't these silent killers. You get a lot of warning with a hurricane. If you do what you're supposed to do, you're not going to get caught with your pants down."

Meanwhile, Armstrong suggests that media coverage of the hurricane damage was exaggerated, saying that TV cameras focused on a building that had plywood covering window spaces. But Armstrong says the wood was part of a new balcony project, not windows blown out in a hurricane.

At the same time, Ameche, past president of the Singer Island Business Association, says that tourism officials were too quick to report that Singer Island was not damaged and was indeed ready for business, even while power companies scrambled to get power turned back on and residents were receiving bottles of water from state and federal aid trucks.

Let us not underestimate the seriousness of the conditions of south Florida post-hurricane season, however. Scientists suggest that the trend in increased hurricane storm activity will continue for the next decade, in part due to global warming, caused by pollution, of which the United States is the world's biggest offender.

In Andrew the death toll of 23 was much lower than that of some of the devastating hurricanes of Florida's past, such as those in 1928 and 1935, yet the damage cost of $34.9 billion was the highest in U.S. history at the time. Much of the damage was housing that had been hastily constructed in response to rapid development and population growth. In addition, mobile homes, a popular housing alternative for retirees and lower-income residents, are particularly vulnerable to hurricanes and are often the site of the most damage.

Florida estimates its damage from the storms of 2004 at $42 billion, with twenty-five thousand homes destroyed and 117 deaths across the state. The Gold Coast, from Palm Beach to Miami, was just at the southern tip of the affected area from Hurricanes Frances and Jeanne, so damage in Palm Beach was limited. Although some hotels suffered damage, most considered it a renovation opportunity and reopened within weeks. Just as the earth seems to recover quickly from disasters, the populace eventually follows suit, adjusting to the emotional losses and shock of the tragedy and rebuilding. But the best form of evolution is through education. If we can learn to work with Mother Nature instead of against her, our chances of living harmoniously together are certainly enhanced.

While scientists predict increased hurricane activity in the coming years to herald the changing of the seasons, don't think for a moment that the weather is going to keep us from enjoying the land of perpetual sunshine. The 871,000 Florida residents whose job it is to make sure visitors enjoy themselves will not let you down.

beach, and kayak the 'Glades. Delight in coconut palms, bougainvillea, passion fruit, papaya, and pink shrimp. There's plenty here for all of us to enjoy forever, so long as we are careful stewards of these phenomenal delights. We invite you to join us in walking softly on our sandy beaches, so that we can all diminish the size of the footprint we're leaving on the landscape.

Transportation

Florida highways parallel Flagler's railway, both along the coastline. Our main highways are I-95, which cuts right alongside or within most major cities, and Florida's Turnpike, which runs a bit farther west and costs a few bucks for tolls, but which is therefore less traveled and generally safer—the recommended choice unless it's simply out of the way.
If at all possible, avoid traveling during rush hours, and remember that south Florida is a very diverse community—some drivers can't read the street signs and are not familiar with our customs and road rights-of-way. Caution and courtesy go a long way.

The coastal highway, FL A1A, takes longer to travel, but it often provides a scenic way to enjoy the beaches and barrier islands of the Gold Coast from Palm Beach to Miami. When traveling to the Florida Keys, be aware that US 1, also called Federal Highway and the Overseas Highway (in the Keys), is the main artery from the mainland in Florida City to Key West. Travel this road with care. The site of many auto accidents, the 18-mile land bridge from Florida City to Key Largo is especially dangerous, and it will be under construction for most of 2005. It may be advisable to travel alternate Card Sound Road, for a small toll fee, from Florida City to the Keys to avoid delays.

There are major airports in West Palm Beach, Fort Lauderdale–Hollywood, and Miami, and a small one in Marathon as well as in Key West. West Palm is currently expanding, as is Fort Lauderdale, which although it was once deliciously convenient and easy has grown into a behemoth that's expensive to park at and time-consuming to navigate. Miami Airport has been overgrown and one to avoid for years, but it does have one plus: a nice rooftop restaurant and hotel with a fitness room and pool that travelers can use during layovers.

Local mass-transit systems aren't widely used—the bus routes are slow, and trains are rarely on time. These systems are currently under regional scrutiny and are due for improvement soon. Miami does offer the Metromover downtown, however, which runs in a continuous loop around the city, stopping at the Cultural Center, Bayside, Miami-Dade Community College, and other interesting destinations—and it's free. (For more information log on to www.co.miami-dade.fl.us/transit/metromover.asp.)

How to Use This Book

Rather than attempt to create a comprehensive, all-inclusive guide to the nation's most popular travel destination, this is a selective guide, filled with places I feel are of particular interest and that I can recommend. The listings included for each area represent a full range of prices, and while there are many more choices that haven't been listed here, I've tried to give a good sampling to help guide you and make your Florida visit most memorable.

Organization

This book runs geographically along the coastline, traveling north to south as much as possible, beginning in Jupiter, the north end of Palm Beach County, and ending in Key West, the southern tip of Monroe County. Each county has its own chapter—Palm Beach, Broward, Miami-Dade, and Monroe—which are further divided by separate listings for each town's lodging, dining, culture, recreation, and shopping options. Maps have been provided for each county, as well as for a few of the major cities. Please note, however, that these maps are for reference only, and we recommend that you bring along more detailed maps and atlases to help guide you on your trip.

Working geographically was especially easy in Monroe County, where all the Keys are strung together by the long overseas highway. Since mile markers are used there extensively to locate addresses, I've followed that lead in organizing the information in the Keys section of the book, providing the mile marker designation for each key in the titles and in the address of each lodging and attraction. When you've hit mile marker 4, you've found Key West.

Prices

Since prices change rapidly, I've used the following chart to give you an idea of the price ranges of lodgings, restaurants, and attractions. Please note that these prices do not include sales taxes or gratuities. The state sales tax is 6 percent, and each county and city may add additional sales tax. In addition, local tourist taxes ranging from 4.5 to 6 percent are added onto hotel bills. The total sales and lodging taxes in Palm Beach are 10.5 percent; Broward, 11 percent; Miami-Dade, 13 percent; and the Keys, 11.5 percent. A sales tax of 6 to 6.5 percent is added onto dinner bills, and watch out for gratuities of 15 to 20 percent, which may be added automatically by some restaurants. Double check before you add your tip to the bill.

Price Codes

Code	Lodging (double occupancy)	Restaurants (per entrée) and attractions (per adult)
$	up to $75	up to $10
$$	$76–$150	$11–$25
$$$	$151–$250	$26–$40
$$$$	more than $250	more than $40

Photo courtesy of Palm Beach County Convention and Visitors Bureau

1

PALM BEACH COUNTY
The Icing on the Cake

Palm Beach County caters to travelers with the most discriminating tastes. Home to some of the wealthiest families in the world, the county has restaurants, shops, and cultural opportunities that reflect the best that's available. In the triumvirate of counties that make up Florida's Gold Coast, Palm Beach is the icing. Glitz and glamour certainly aren't strangers here, but the real players are privilege and elegance. And although the county, like all of south Florida, is growing rapidly, there is still a cozy sense of intimacy in the communities from Singer Island and Palm Beach to Lake Worth and Delray Beach.

Palm Beach County is the largest in Florida, nearly 2,578 square miles with 1.1 million residents. The county has the highest per capita income in the state and the third in the nation. It has been since its inception a winter home to the "swells" of the Gilded Age: the Rockefellers, Vanderbilts, and Astors; Andrew Carnegie; J. P. Morgan; William Randolph Hearst; and, of course, Henry Morrison Flagler, the man who brought his pals to play here.

Discoverers and purveyors of all the modern conveniences of the industrial age, these scions of wealth felt that they had ascended to a higher plane of citizenry, and their opulent lifestyles and homes reflected that high esteem. A few of their palatial homes and hotels remain here, some as museums, such as Flagler's home, Whitehall, and some are even still available to us as they were to the swells, such as the Breakers Hotel, built by Flagler in 1896, and the Cloisters Inn, built by famous architect Addison Mizner and now part of the Boca Raton Resort and Club. It's incredibly fun to visit these richly appointed palaces and to imagine life among the elite of America's Golden Days.

Palm Beach is the grandfather of golf in Florida, and today it's the state's golf capital, with more courses than any other county. Many golf greats have settled in the region, and their influence is noted at many courses, which they've helped design, such as PGA National, where Jack Nicklaus and Arnold Palmer have contributed their champion styles. The first course was built by Henry Flagler at his hotel, the Breakers. He kept it small, a nine-hole course, because he believed golf would be a passing fancy of the fickle class. His vision somehow didn't extend as usual in this case.

So come for golf, or polo or croquet, or snorkel and dive the offshore reef. Or let this be your winter shopping and spa retreat—you'll find only the best of both. Come in the winter if you relish rubbing elbows with the wealthy, or in the summertime if you'd like to pretend you own the place. Palm Beach is beautiful year-round.

Jupiter: Celestial Vantage Point

Jupiter provides the most rural coastal atmosphere on the Gold Coast, thanks to much as-yet-undeveloped property along the shoreline and inland. The beach is a quiet expanse shielded from the road by protected dunes with scenic wild grasses, which make for a pastoral view as well as protect both the endangered sea oats and the beach from erosion. Low-rise apartment and condominium complexes wind along the other side of the beach highway (FL A1A), but they're a far cry from the dense condo canyons created by high-rises in other coastal communities. Just a half hour north of West Palm Beach, Jupiter is close to nightlife and cultural activity as well, so visitors can enjoy the best of both sides of Florida here. There is a very well-heeled segment of the local population that has figured that out and settled in exclusive neighborhoods in Jupiter, such as Jupiter Island; however, property values and prices are generally much better here than farther south.

DINING

Trapper's Cabin

561-743-9700
631 N. FL A1A, Jupiter 33477

Named for local legend Trapper Nelson, this rustic saloon brings to light the rugged frontier history of Palm Beach County. Nelson lived—and died—near his swampy cabin on the Loxahatchee River, unwilling to move when land developers came along. Nelson was found there with a bullet hole in his head in 1968, a mysterious and yet-unsolved crime, though authorities ruled it a suicide. Dine in his honor on all-local gator bits and frog legs, catfish,

The view at Blowing Rocks Preserve

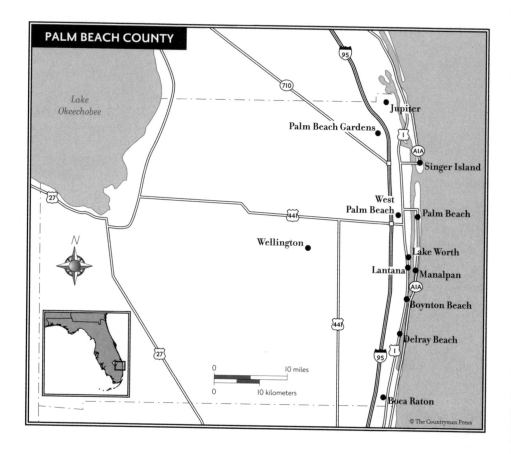

PALM BEACH COUNTY

Lake Okeechobee

Jupiter

Palm Beach Gardens

Singer Island

West Palm Beach

Palm Beach

Wellington

Lake Worth

Lantana

Manalpan

Boynton Beach

Delray Beach

Boca Raton

0   10 miles

0   10 kilometers

© The Countryman Press

shrimp, and barbecue ribs, just as he must have done. Kids love cuddling up with the 6-foot grizzly bear and other critters he might have trapped, and the artifacts and history make for a very interesting and educational dining experience for the whole family. $–$$.

ATTRACTIONS, PARKS, AND RECREATION

Blowing Rocks Preserve
561-744-6668
www.nature.org/wherewework/northamerica/states/florida/preserves
1574 S. Beach Rd., Hobe Sound 33455

This barrier island sanctuary was preserved by residents who donated the land to the Nature Conservancy to protect it from development in 1969. Anastasia limestone rocks create a very craggy shoreline, and when high seas break against it, the water is blown upward as high as 50 feet, hence the name of the preserve. The 73 acres are kept as natural as possible, protecting native species of plants and providing habitat for wild birds and animals. Guided nature walks are held on Sunday at 11 and other times, as well as work-shops and educational programs—call or check online for the schedule. Open daily 9–4:30; closed major holidays. $.

Burt Reynolds and Friends Museum

561-743-9955
www.burtreynoldsmuseum.org
100 N. US 1, Jupiter 33477

A resident of Jupiter for more than 40 years, Reynolds's fame helped put Jupiter on the map. The star helped create a theater and acting school, both now closed, which drew other celebrities to the small town over the years. The city has created a nonprofit museum to house memorabilia and souvenirs from his career, including a huge collection of auto-graphed photos of costars. Tax-deductible donations are welcome in lieu of admission. Open 10–4 Wednesday through Sunday.

Jonathan Dickinson Park

772-546-2771
16450 S.E. Federal Hwy., Hobe Sound 33455

Explore the nationally designated "Wild and Scenic" Loxahatchee River aboard the *Loxahatchee Queen II*, a 44-passenger boat that offers a two-hour tour of the river along with a bit of its history. The boat stops at the campsite of Trapper Nelson, the infamous "Wildman of the Loxahatchee," where he had built cabins, created a wildlife zoo, and planted tropical gardens. Boaters often see alligators in the river, and other animals in the park include deer, foxes, otters, endangered manatees, gopher tortoises, and Florida scrub jays. The 11,500-acre park, named for a merchant shipwrecked off the coast in 1696, has nature trails, picnic areas, camping, and fishing. Open daily 8–sunset. $.

Jupiter Beach Park

561-966-6600
1375 Jupiter Beach Rd., Jupiter 33477 (south of Jupiter Inlet)

Jupiter beaches are some of my favorite in all of south Florida. FL A1A winds along the oceanfront with very limited construction to block the view, although high dunes covered with seagrasses line the road and are about all that's visible. Nonetheless, the natural vista is much more appealing than the commercial high-rises found along the ocean almost everywhere around the state. Another plus is that dogs are welcome to join their families for a romp in the surf, which is great fun as long as owners clean up after their pets and dogs are friendly with other people and pets. Open sunrise to sunset.

Jupiter Inlet Lighthouse

561-747-6639
www.lrhs.org
Lighthouse Park, 500 Captain Armour's Way, at South Beach Rd. and N. US 1, Jupiter 33477

The Jupiter Lighthouse was surveyed by a young Robert E. Lee and built by the man who later defeated Lee's army at Gettysburg, George Meade. Meade's epitaph read that he hoped to be best remembered for his lighthouses, which line Florida's coast, rather than for his war record of defeating General Lee. The lighthouse began its service in 1860 and continues to protect and guide ships along the reef-wrapped shoreline today. The hike up the 105-step spiral staircase to the top of the tower reveals a lovely panoramic vista of the Atlantic coast and Jupiter Inlet. A local magazine proclaims it the best place to get engaged,

Jupiter Inlet Lighthouse

and area residents voted it the best attraction in Palm Beach County. Tours are given 10–4 Saturday through Wednesday. $.

The Marine Life Center at Loggerhead Park

561-627-8280
www.marinelife.org
14200 US 1, Juno Beach 33408

An education, rehabilitation, and research center specializing in the sea turtle population along the Atlantic coast, the Marine Life Center offers educational programs and holds turtle walks during turtle nesting season in June and July. The staff report that the park finds more than one thousand nests per mile, but only one in ten thousand hatchlings survives into adulthood. Storms are the greatest threat to hatchlings. Open 10–4 Tuesday through Saturday and noon–3 Sunday. No set fee; donations requested.

CULTURE

Atlantic Arts Academy

561-575-4422
www.atlanticartsacademy.com
6779 W. Indiantown Rd., Jupiter 33458

About time you learned to dance? Getting a grip on muscle control is essential to physical health. Join creative and stimulating dance classes for adults at the Atlantic Arts Academy in Jupiter. Classes run $60 an hour or $100 for two hours or more.

Lighthouse Center for the Arts

561-746-3101
www.lighthousecenterforthearts.org
373 Tequesta Dr., Gallery Square North, Tequesta 33469

Wish you'd learned to paint but never got around to it? Many arts classes for adults are offered in Palm Beach County. Painting classes run $150 to $200 for six to eight weeks at the Lighthouse Center School of Arts, but the school offers two free lessons as samplers.

The hustle and bustle of Palm Beach seems a world away at Singer Island. Rachel Rector

Singer Island: Swan Song to Paradise

Named for Paris Singer, heir to the sewing-machine fortune, Singer Island lies just north of Palm Beach, yet it's a world away. While Palm Beach is the domain of the "swells"—those with riches and fame—Singer Island is a paradise reserved for the rest of the world. Fishermen, retirees, local residents of the nearby mainland, and vacationers gather here to enjoy island living, the Atlantic Ocean, and the Lake Worth Lagoon. Accommodations are sweet, clean, and modest without undue frills or expense, and crowds are few.

But, of course, nothing stays the same—Singer Island is in the early throes of change. Marriott has already built four new condo-hotels on the south end of the beach, and a fifth is under way. Many of the older mom-and-pop units on the waterfront are facing the end of their days, and they're being bought and replaced by big, new sleek buildings, most employing the condo-hotel approach to capitalize on both markets.

While some area business owners expressed concern that there could be a clash of clientele in the multipurpose buildings, the change is seen as a positive one for the community. The multimillion-dollar condos are expected to strengthen the tax base of the area and enhance the public treasury.

Little Peanut Island, in the Lake Worth Lagoon, is a man-made island with a Coast Guard museum and the old Kennedy Bomb Shelter, now open for tours. Boats anchor at a sandbar off the island, where kids and dogs play in the shallow water. The island offers camping, and the snorkeling and fishing are particularly good in the inlet nearby.

With a claim to fame as the closest point in the continental United States to the Gulf Stream, Singer Island is considered by some to be the sailfish mecca of the world. You'll find eels, lobster, snook, tarpon, ladyfish, barracudas, and tropical fish.

A popular dive spot is under the Blue Heron Bridge at high tide, where a wealth of marine life resides. Divers can swim to the bridge from Phil Foster Park without need for a boat. Be on the lookout for sea turtles that may be drifting along with you.

LODGING

Crowne Plaza Oceanfront North Palm Beach

561-842-6171, 1-800-327-0522
www.oceanfrontcp.com
3200 N. Ocean Dr., Singer Island 33404

With classical music playing gently in the background, the lobby of this waterfront gem is as peaceful and cool as the blue sea beyond. With a two-year, $4 million renovation recently completed, the hotel, redecorated in a sleek Danish modern style, is surely the crown jewel of Singer Island. The 5-acre waterfront property is a popular wedding destination, with an open-air pavilion and dining area off the ocean, pool, and wide, clean, not-too-crowded beach. 193 rooms. $$$–$$$$.

Hilton Singer Island Oceanfront Resort

561-848-8338, 1-800-941-3592
www.hilton.com
3700 N. Ocean Dr., Singer Island 33404

Competition keeps the local standard at an optimum level. The Hilton is spotless and the service appreciable. There are 223 rooms with ocean views and a refrigerator. A business center in the lobby offers computer data ports and desks. $$–$$$.

Portside on the Inlet

561-842-1215
www.portside1.com
206 Inlet Way, Palm Beach Shores 33404

This tropical home and pool overlook the Lake Worth Inlet, with a strip of motel efficiency and one-bedroom units for more conservative travelers. It's popular with seasonal residents, who appreciate the monthly rates, the assurance of a well-cared-for and homelike setting, and friendly management. Rent by the week, by the month, or year-round. $$.

Sailfish Marina

561-844-1724, 1-800-446-4577
www.sailfishmarina.com
98 Lake Dr., Singer Island 33404

This vintage motel has efficiencies at the marina and restaurant complex. Amenities include boat rentals and charters, a pool, bikes, and a barbecue grill. Rent rooms by the night or a three-bedroom house nightly, weekly, or monthly. $$–$$$.

Snug Haven Inn

561-845-2035, 1-800-730-2156
www.snughaven1.com
2675 Lake Dr., Singer Island 33404

There are studio and one-bedroom units, or rent an entire two-bedroom house for the whole family. Dock your boat at the backyard dock on the Intracoastal Waterway—called Lake Worth in this area. Colorful and comfortable accommodations in a renovated home and vintage motel—it's easy to imagine it's more than a vacation: it's the life. $–$$.

Snug Haven Inn

DINING

Coconuts on the Beach, Hilton Singer Island

561-848-8338, 1-800-941-3592
www.hilton.com
3700 N. Ocean Dr., Singer Island 33404

Flavors from the Caribbean and Asia blend with traditional favorites such as Prime Dip and filet mignon to ensure there's something for everyone in this Hilton hotel dining room. Try jerk or Havana chicken or voodoo shrimp for something different—all are served as small appetizers, so sampling is simple. A nice wine selection and interesting desserts (such as Mango Pango Cake with mango mousse and coconut) round out the meal. $–$$.

Hurricane Café

561-630-2012
14050 US 1, Juno Beach 33408

This cozy café is owned by Scott Philip and his wife, Virginia, who is also sommelier at the Breakers's L'Escalier restaurant. Grilled blueberry streusel and a cinnamon pecan corn muffin are tasty and unusual choices to start the day, or perhaps choose raspberry white chocolate pancakes. For lunch try a club sandwich, grouper fingers, calamari, or falafel, and for dinner, pizza, pasta, or seafood—such as the macadamia-nut-crusted grouper with mango butter. A generous wine list (naturally) is paired with reasonable prices in this casual, gourmet café. $$.

Johnny Longboats

561-882-1333
2401 Ocean Ave., Singer Island 33404

This rustic island pub is a popular hangout for locals and tourists alike and has indoor and patio dining. With the bigger-than-life-size shark hanging from the ceiling, a sailor climbing the ropes nearby, and a

Johnny Longboats

skeleton in the wings, this place is a relic of Florida Cracker style. The house special, grouper in a brown paper bag, is a popular choice: more than one hundred thousand have been sold in 20 years. Alas—or perhaps for the best—the building that houses the restaurant and a few waterfront shops across from the public Riviera Beach are slated for the wrecking ball. But fear not: planners are plotting to keep Johnny Longboats, so hopefully it'll survive the change and make it back in new, fresh digs. $$.

The Lobby Bar and Flagler's Oceanview Grille at the Crowne Plaza Oceanfront North Palm Beach

561-842-6171, 1-800-327-0522
www.oceanfrontcp.com
3200 N. Ocean Dr., Singer Island 33404

The sleek lobby bar and restaurant serve buffet brunch, evening libations, and seafood as well as traditional fare. $–$$.

Panama Hattie's

561-627-1545
www.panama-hatties.com
11511 Ellison Wilson Rd., N. Palm Beach 33408

On the Intracoastal Waterway just southeast of the PGA Boulevard Bridge, Panama Hattie's offers vodka rigatoni, Mojo Pork Roast, and Key lime pie. Sunday brunch. $$.

Sailfish Marina Restaurant
561-844-1724
www.sailfishmarina.com
98 Lake Dr., Singer Island 33404

This is the hot spot on Singer Island for Sunday brunch. Join travelers from all along the Atlantic seaboard who dock their million-dollar yachts here while enjoying the area. Grab a "Grouper Dawg" on the dock (a hot dog!), or sit down to eat in the large, loud dockside dining room and enjoy dinners of Caribbean crab nachos (with black beans, mango, jalapeño, and cream cheese), ceviche tropicale (lime-juice-marinated shrimp and fish with fruit salsa), Atlantic sea bass, yellowtail, grouper, dolphin, or Florida paella, a one-dish blend of fresh fish, chicken, and sausage with rice and peas. The Thursday-night Sunset Celebration features artists displaying their work along the docks as well as musicians, making for a pleasant evening stroll. $$–$$$.

The Waterway Café
561-694-1700
2300 PGA Blvd., N. Palm Beach 33410 (on the Intracoastal Waterway just southwest of the PGA Bridge)

Pull your boat up to the floating round bar in the Intracoastal Waterway—that's the one with the life jackets conspicuously stowed over the bar—and enjoy a cool refreshment during your day on the water. Or arrive by land for seafood specials and the water view. $$.

ATTRACTIONS, PARKS, AND RECREATION

John D. MacArthur Beach State Park
561-624-6950
www.macarthurbeach.org
10900 FL 703 (FL A1A), N. Palm Beach 33408

This wonderful 174-acre preserve of Florida uplands can be explored by rented kayak or by guided tour. Explore the William T. Kirby Nature Center, hike the forested trails, or enjoy the natural (unguarded) beach and consider what Florida looked like before we all arrived. The park conducts regular nature-based activities from bird-watching, butterfly gardening, and beach cleanups to barbecues and live music events. It's very popular with nesting sea turtles from May through August; join a ranger-led turtle walk in June or July. Open daily 8–sunset. $ per car (maximum eight people).

Oceanside Beach Service
1-888-826-9046
www.beachservice.com
1165 E. Blue Heron Blvd., Singer Island 33404

This islandwide company will help ensure that your visit includes all the recreational activities you can dream of enjoying on the ocean or the Intracoastal Waterway. They'll set up your day at the beach with lounge chairs, umbrella, and cabana ($30), just the chair for $10, a kayak or bike for $40, or snorkeling gear for $30. They sell sunscreen and bikinis and conduct sailing, snorkeling, and diving tours.

Palm Beach Water Taxi
561-683-8294
Sailfish Marina, 98 Lake Dr., Singer Island 33404

Cruise all around the Lake Worth Lagoon, explore Peanut Island, tour the Kennedy Bomb Shelter, or enjoy a sunset cruise. $–$$.

Phil Foster Park, Riviera Beach
561-966-6600
900 E. Blue Heron Blvd., Singer Island 33404

Currently being revitalized to provide more recreational opportunities for boaters and water lovers, this little park wedged between the Blue Heron Bridge and the Intracoastal Waterway is a popular spot for fishing and boat launching. A picnic area has barbecue grills and a playground. Open sunrise to sunset. Free.

Palm Beach Gardens: Golfer's Greens

LODGING

PGA National Resort and Spa
1-800-633-9150
www.pga-resorts.com
400 Avenue of the Champions, Palm Beach Gardens 33418

This expansive resort is surrounded by the peaceful greens it's dedicated to: as the street name indicates, this is the home of golf's champions. Guests, whether they stay in a

Golf: The Green Game

Golf courses can be a model of environmental responsibility. In spite of their appearance and the obvious impression that such perfection can be achieved only by artificial means, such as pesticides, herbicides, and fertilizers, golf courses provide huge chunks of habitat to wildlife and plants across Florida. With such wide expanses of greens to manage, it would be cost prohibitive to maintain them using the poisons popular for lawns. Greenskeepers become experts at spot-treating problem areas and finding ways to extend natural resources. Audubon International provides Sanctuary Certification to courses that meet its eco-requirements by conserving resources, avoiding poisons, and protecting habitat. PGA National in Palm Beach Gardens has earned the Audubon Certification.

Photo courtesy of Palm Beach County Convention and Visitors Bureau

standard room, a cottage, or the presidential suite, are well cared for in a sophisticated, active atmosphere. The on-site world-class spa, Waters of the World, offers mineral baths and has indoor and outdoor pools. Enroll in the Academy of Golf, or enjoy activities on the 26-acre recreational lake. $$$$.

Dining

Off the Vine

561-799-6655

5530 PGA Blvd., Palm Beach Gardens 33418

This delightful little lunch and dinner spot offers cozy indoor and patio dining and delicious gourmet fare. $$.

Eco-Friendly Homes at Evergrene

Evergrene, a WCI Community in Palm Beach Gardens, is an Audubon International Cooperative Sanctuary Development, thanks to the protective layout of the housing development, which maintains wild habitat preserve for creatures and implements many innovative eco-features throughout the 365-acre community. About one thousand homes are clustered around a 36-acre lake, and the community includes 80 acres of nature preserve, with twelve hundred trees transplanted rather than razed during construction. No homes back up to the lake, keeping it a centerpiece for community involvement, with fishing, kayaking, and educational programs available to residents through the clubhouse.

Home buyers can select upgrades ranging from a solar water heater and nonchlorine pool to dual-flush toilets and motion-sensor water faucets. Buyers can choose floors of bamboo; cork; marmoleum, a biodegradeable, antibacterial composite material; or carpets made from recycled soda bottles.

A jumble of flowering bushes and fragrant herbs cluster around the walkways—which aren't solid, but crisscross with pavers spaced a half inch apart and lined with tiny stones so rainwater runs back into the ground instead of into the sewer, collecting pollutants along the way. Composters hide in the bushes, and rain barrels capture runoff from the gutter. A tiny crystal suspended from the ceiling glistens in the sunlit foyers (a bit of feng shui thrown in for luck). Bamboo floors gleam with the richness of wood, and gentle fiber-optic lighting lends a colorful ambience to the kitchens. The air is fresh, unpolluted by off-gassing synthetic building and décor materials and filtered through the latest purification system designed to capture dust and zap mold spores with ultraviolet light.

Without sacrificing comfort or luxury, the Evergrene model is the greenest production home in Florida, according to the Florida Green Building Council, which offers a checklist for builders, designers, and homeowners to assess a building's environmental integrity. But do home buyers and citizens in general even care about being environmentally correct?

Sales staff at Evergrene say it's a chance to educate many buyers about environmentally friendly housing alternatives, a welcome choice for buyers who are energy conscious and for those with allergies or asthma. Perhaps most don't bother to think about it, assuming environmentalism is the arena of alarmists. Yet everyone wants the advantages of fresh water and clean air. We enjoy the gentle beauty butterflies lend to the landscape, and we take for granted availability of limitless fuel to heat our homes and transport us through our busy lives. Forward-thinking scientists—and builders—want us to be able to continue to enjoy the luxurious lifestyles we've become accustomed to.

ATTRACTIONS, PARKS, AND RECREATION

The Champion Course at PGA National Resort and Spa

561-627-2000, 1-800-858-1904
www.pga-resorts.com
400 Avenue of the Champions, Palm Beach Gardens 33418

This historic course is one of five championship courses at this golfer's paradise.

SHOPPING

The Gardens of the Palm Beaches Mall

561-775-7750
www.thegardensmall.com
3101 PGA Blvd., Palm Beach Gardens 33410

Here you can shop at Saks Fifth Avenue, Bloomingdale's, and Burdines-Macy's, as well as 150 other shops and restaurants. Nordstrom is expected to open in early 2006. Open 10–9 Monday through Saturday and noon–6 Sunday.

West Palm Beach: Worker's Retreat

Originally built as a town for workers by Flagler when he needed builders for his railroad and hotels, West Palm evolved into its own city, establishing a middle-class middle ground with retail growth that captures some of the flow of wealth from the east, although it continues to be a bit of a foil, and worker resource, for rarefied Palm Beach, the barrier island just over the Royal Palm Way (Okeechobee Boulevard) and Royal Poinciana Way bridges. There's a sparkle and shine to West Palm Beach, with an exciting downtown area with shops, restaurants, and nightclubs as well as family parks, a fountain that begs kids to play in it, and a library on the banks of the Intracoastal Waterway. A vibrant cultural life emanates from Kravis Center, and in recent years City Place, a festival marketplace hosting trendy and upscale shops, has helped to revitalize the downtown area. The surrounding older, Mediterranean-style neighborhoods have been all the rage among those with an eye for the potential of the charming bungalows in the past few years, with real estate values skyrocketing and catching the attention of investors from the sophisticated north. But do be aware that the trendy zone is still a bit rough around the edges.

LODGING

Hibiscus House

561-863-5633, 1-800-203-4927
www.hibiscushouse.com
501 30th St., W. Palm Beach 33407

The first licensed bed & breakfast in Palm Beach County, Hibiscus House in Old North-wood was the home of the town's mayor David Dunkle in 1922, who developed the now-historic neighborhood. Owners Colin Rayner and Raleigh Hill rescued this gem from a fate as a crackhouse in 1986 and have completely restored it. Today Rayner boasts that 78 of their guests have bought homes in the emerging trendy neighborhood. Richly decorated rooms feature four-poster beds and private terraces overlooking tropical gardens in this highly rated, romantic bed & breakfast. $$–$$$.

Hibiscus House Downtown

561-833-8171, 1-866-833-8171
www.hibiscushousedowntown.com
213 South Rosemary Ave., W. Palm Beach
33401

The latest venture of successful Hibiscus House owners Colin Rayner and Raleigh Hill, this is just a block off Clematis Street, within a walk of downtown shopping and nightlife. Rooms are a mix of old and new in this pair of historic homes, outfitted to match today's discriminating standards. Colorfully decorated and furnished with antiques, the bed & breakfast is fresh, comfortable, and beautiful. Plan a steamy night of romance in the Red Room, or choose the upstairs suite for a week's power stay. Rooms and suites include Internet access. $$–$$$$.

Hilton Palm Beach Airport

561-684-9400
www.hilton.com
150 Australian Ave., W. Palm Beach 33406

With easy access to the airport, this is a good selection for a business trip, but there are better choices for vacation. The rooms and suites are well kept. $$$.

Hotel Biba

561-832-0094
www.hotelbiba.com
320 Belvedere Rd., W. Palm Beach 33405

This 43-room historic motor lodge that was reinvented as a sleek, hip hotel is on the fringes of the downtown scene of West Palm Beach. Coolest of cool décor and amenities include glass tiles—mosaics and terrazzo—Egyptian cotton linens, Aveda bath products, bamboo bead doors, and burlap headboards. The candle-lit wine bar, decorated with colorful silk, is the subject of wide acclaim, and I think the Biba has the coolest package on the Gold Coast: surf lessons with your room (call for prices). $$–$$$.

DINING

Bellagio

561-659-6160
600 Rosemary Ave. at City Place, W. Palm Beach 33401

The aroma of delicious northern Italian comfort food greets you as you enter this fountainside eatery at City Place. Try sautéed artichokes and mushrooms, or save your appetite for a main dish of chicken dressed with spinach and mozzarella in a cognac cream sauce. $$.

Brewzzi

561-366-9753
www.brewzzi.com
700 S. Rosemary at City Place, W. Palm Beach 33401

Take a break from shopping at this City Place brewery, where you can sit upstairs or on the open-air patio and look down upon the less-savvy shoppers. Try the award-winning brew, as well as the Gorgonzola chips, a huge Brewzzi salad, meat loaf, Farfalle à la Vodka, crusted snapper, Angus steaks, or pizza—there's something here for everyone. $–$$.

Café Mediterraneo

561-837-6633
200 Clematis St., W. Palm Beach 33401

Northern Italian cuisine is served in a casual yet elegant atmosphere, with patio dining and a pleasant view of Centennial Square across the street. Sample Pasta Filetto di Pomodoro, your choice of home-made noodles with a fresh tomato sauce; or Gnocchi Sorrentina, fresh potato dumplings tossed with tomatoes and fresh mozzarella cheese. Later on the place evolves into a nightclub with an upstairs lounge. Open until the wee hours for dancing on Friday and Saturday. $$.

E. R. Bradley's Saloon

561-833-3520

www.erbradleys.com

104 Clematis St., W. Palm Beach 33401

This saloon was named for a Florida dandy who struck a deal with Henry Flagler to build and run a beach club alongside Flagler's hotel. Bradley became known as the world's luckiest gambler when his adopted homeland became the subject of Flagler's railway and glitterati of the Gilded Age. The saloon is the perfect way to keep his memory alive, and it does so with hallways lined with newspaper and magazine accounts from Bradley's day. The restored waterfront home is a lovely place to sit outside for views of the Intracoastal, or inside after dark the barroom turns into a dance hall. Delicious soups and seafood are served, with fresh homemade pretzels served with lunch instead of bread. Open until the wee hours for dancing. $$.

Leila

561-659-7373

120 S. Dixie Hwy., W. Palm Beach 33401

At this tiny spot south of City Place, you'll find a casual atmosphere and fragrant, sensuous, and tasty fare. I love the curries and falafel, Mediterranean salads, and heady Lebanese specialties. The moderately sized portions make it fun to try several dishes at once. Choose a few or a sampler. $$–$$$.

Montezuma Restaurant

561-586-7974

5607 S. Dixie Hwy., W. Palm Beach 33405

What's the best sign that a Mexican restaurant is authentic? The salsa, but more importantly, the clientele. Montezuma is just such a place. Even the babies are spoon-fed spicy beans and rice at this unassuming café, which caters to the strong local population of Mexican farm workers. The small gift shop and grocery of Mexican imports is interesting and has friendly service. $.

391st Bomb Group

561-683-3919

3989 Southern Blvd., W. Palm Beach 33406

Convenient before or after a flight, this cozy restaurant on the runway at Palm Beach International Airport has comforting fireplaces and an outdoor patio in a cottagelike building. Kids can put on headphones at the table and listen in on air-traffic-control transmissions while they watch planes coming and going. Sunday champagne brunch. $$.

Tsunami

561-835-9696

www.tsunamirestaurant.com

651 Okeechobee Blvd. at City Place, W. Palm Beach 33401

From its black-as-night wood bar and two-story granite walls to the 30-foot floor-to-ceiling fuzzy drapes and shimmering pink chopsticks, Tsunami is a study in contrasts. The menu of this highly acclaimed and exciting restaurant follows suit. In keeping with its Asian promise, the sushi bar will not disappoint, but the mix of dried tomatoes, sake, cilantro, lime, and naan gives hint to the fact that traditions of all cultures have fallen from the stony heights, gone forever. The flavor blends are garnering accolades from all corners of the world. An experience. $$$.

ATTRACTIONS, PARKS, AND RECREATION

Lion Country Safari

561-793-1084
www.lioncountrysafari.com
2003 Lion Country Safari Rd., Loxahatchee 33470

This wildlife park presents one thousand animals as exotic as white rhinoceroses and African elephants living in natural habitats, and though they're fenced in, they are free to roam within their large areas as if they were wild. Visitors drive along 5 miles of paths through the 500-acre park, crossing from one species' zone to the next. Amazingly, Lion Country Safari was able to open a week after Hurricane Jeanne came through in October 2004. One animal died in the storm, and another was born (they named her Jeanne). To protect the animals—and the community—park staff housed many of the animals, usually allowed to roam in wide-open fenced areas, in concrete and steel cages. Opened in 1967, this is a favorite stop for residents and visitors alike. Open daily 9:30–5:30. $$.

National Croquet Center

561-478-2300
www.croquetnational.com
700 Florida Mango Rd., W. Palm Beach 33406

Is that fun '50s backyard game croquet your calling? Learn everything there is to know about it at the National Croquet Center, and then play a few rounds if you like. The National Croquet Center is a club, complete with pro shop. Visitors are welcome to try their hand on the 10 acres of croquet courts—rolling lawns—or to observe professional competitions from the clubhouse veranda. Free croquet offered 10–noon on Saturday. Open daily. $$.

Palm Beach Yacht Club Marina

561-655-1944
www.pbyachtclub.com
800 N. Flagler Dr., W. Palm Beach 33401

Established in 1911, the Palm Beach Yacht Club is private, but sport fishing charters ($750 a day) are available at the marina. The vintage yacht *Lady Patricia* is available for dinner cruises during the winter.

Black Cloud

A memorial garden is under way at Tamarind Avenue and 25th Street in West Palm Beach, 2 miles north of downtown, in a vacant lot that has been neglected for years. Area residents may have forgotten that the lot is the site of a mass burial of victims of the Hurricane of 1928. Coming ashore near the Jupiter Inlet Lighthouse, just a few miles from where both Hurricane Frances and Hurricane Jeanne came ashore in 2004, the storm blew through West Palm Beach and inland to Lake Okeechobee, flooding farmers' shacks as the powerful winds caused the lake to surge over the man-made barrier of soil.

Palm Beach Zoo

561-533-0887
www.palmbeachzoo.com
1301 Summit Blvd., W. Palm Beach 33405

Located in Dreher Park, this 23-acre tropical habitat is home to more than nine hundred animals from around the world, including jaguars, giant anteaters, and tapirs. Recovering from the hurricanes of 2004, the zoo closed for cleaning for a month, but it's now open again daily 9–5. $.

The South Florida Science Museum

561-832-1988
www.sfsm.org
4801 Dreher Trail N., W. Palm Beach 33405

High-tech meets history at this kid's holiday hideout full of exploratory opportunities. Find out what scientists know about Mars, and visit ancient Egyptian tombs to learn about the past. Open 10–5 Monday through Friday, 10–6 Saturday, and noon–5 Sunday. $.

CULTURE

Ballet Florida, Inc.

561-659-2000, 1-800-540-0172
www.balletflorida.com
500 Fern St., W. Palm Beach 33401

Founded by the exquisite Marie Hale in 1973, Ballet Florida's students and company members have performed around the country, including in New York City. But its main base is Kravis Center, where each year the company performs Marie Hale's *Nutcracker*, her special twist on the traditional ballet. Dance classes are available here by the hour, with discounts when you purchase several hours at a time. Tickets $$–$$$$.

Kravis Center of the Performing Arts

561-832-7469, 561-966-3309
701 Okeechobee Blvd., W. Palm Beach 33401

West Palm Beach's million-dollar performance center is the cultural nucleus of dance, music, and arts in the city. $$–$$$$.

Mounts Botanical Garden

561-233-1757
North Military Trail, W. Palm Beach

This 13-acre paradise opened in the mid-1950s and offers more than two thousand varieties of plants growing in several south Florida habitats, including citrus, cactus, herb, organic, and poisonous gardens. The double whammy of Hurricanes Frances and Jeanne caused significant damage to the gardens; however, a massive cleanup and replanting effort is under way. Volunteers welcome. $; small donation requested.

An exhibit at the Norton Museum of Art Norton Museum of Art

Norton Museum of Art

561-832-5196
www.norton.org
1451 S. Olive Ave., W. Palm Beach 33401

A force in Palm Beach County's cultural scene, the Norton's permanent collection includes Chinese art from the Ming (1368–1644) and Qing (1644–1911) dynasties and ancient pieces from as far back as 1450 B.C. Also represented are American, European, contemporary, and photographic arts, along with a continuous flow of traveling exhibits. Picasso, Renoir, Degas, Cezanne, and Mapplethorpe are on permanent display here. Open 10–5 Monday through Saturday and 1–5 Sunday; closed on major holidays and on Mondays May through October. $.

The Robert and Mary Montgomery Armory Art Center

561-832-1776
www.armoryart.org
1703 Lake Ave., W. Palm Beach 33401

This art center offers visual arts, sculpture, and ceramics classes, as well as workshops and lectures, to more than three thousand students of all ages. Scholarships are available at the Armory Art Center, as at many arts schools.

Sound Advice Amphitheatre

561-793-0445, 1-800-759-4624
www.soundadviceamp.com
601 Sansbury's Way, #7, W. Palm Beach 33411

This outdoor concert venue in a field with rolling hills has some stadium seats, but when they fill up there's plenty of blanket space. Tickets $$–$$$$.

SHOPPING

City Place

561-366-1000
www.cityplace.com
700 S. Rosemary Ave., W. Palm Beach 33401

Some of the treasures at City Gems, City Place

This festival shopping market, which opened in 2000, has 78 retailers, restaurants, and movie and performance theaters in a two-story indoor/outdoor group of buildings that reflect an Italianate architectural structure. The 72-acre multiuse project includes apartments built on the perimeter of the shops. The result is a modern mob scene with some of the best choices in mainstream shopping (Worth Avenue excluded, of course). In addition to standbys Burdines-Macy's, Ann Taylor, and Gap, there is a nice assortment of small, shops—some independent. I like Lauren Adams Fine Arts Gallery, which had a display of tiny netsukes and cloisonné treasures in the window; Handmade Gallery, filled with furnishings and accessories imported from Colombia; Artisans, with colorful glassware and other art objects small enough to be accessible gifts; and the exclusive gifts of Murano and Oggetti glass sculpture and vases at

City Gems, which also sells estate jewels. Colorful Lime Tree carries handmade jewelry, Lilly Pulitzer jewelry, and other fun, artful accessories.

West Palm Beach Green Market
561-659-8003
Narcissus Ave. and Second St., W. Palm Beach

Take a morning stroll through vendor tents (you may want to begin at the gourmet coffee booth) to select fresh flowers to perk up your hotel room and fresh vegetables to snack on during your visit. Create a picnic, or if your accommodations include a kitchen, you may wish to go all out and select fresh, locally grown ingredients for your vacation feast. Fresh fish, herbal teas, breads, prepared foods, and potted plants are also sold. Open 7–1 Saturdays from October through March. Free admission.

Fresh flowers abound at the West Palm Beach Green Market.

Palm Beach: Candy Canes and Sugared Scones

Dubbed Palm Beach thanks to an 1878 shipwreck whose cargo of coconuts took root all along the coast of the barrier island protecting the mainland, Palm Beach was home to a few of the most adventurous early settlers in the late 1800s. When Henry Flagler brought his train to town, however, the town was marked as a retreat for the wealthiest scions of Gilded Age society, and so it remains.

Palm Beach is candy colored, a sugar confection created by the wealthiest Americans in the first decades of the 20th century, and it's still the fourth most popular vacation getaway for those with incomes of $200,000 or more. The rest of us might feel a little uncomfortable here at times—not for lack of graciousness, for the most part, but simply because living in such opulence can be inconceivable to those who regularly choose between a night on the town or making the mortgage payment on time.

When you come to town, bring plenty of pink and green and pastel clothes, the uniform at this island retreat. Make time to shop both Worth Avenue, where the finest couture houses in the world reside, and the consignment shops, where you can find original designer gowns for much-reduced prices because they've already been worn to galas in town. And galas are it: Palm Beach is a charity mecca. The charity balls draw an international crowd stunningly attired in elaborate gowns destined to find their way to the famous consignment shops before the next season. But Palm Beach is not necessarily the domain of old money and its aged earners. In recent years more and more families have been traveling together; more kids are joining their parents on business trips or just for fun.

The whole town is elegant without being stuffy, and prices are surprisingly reasonable. Celebrities like to come here because they're unlikely to be bothered. You got it: put away the pens and cameras; this is not the place to collect autographs. Save that for South Beach.

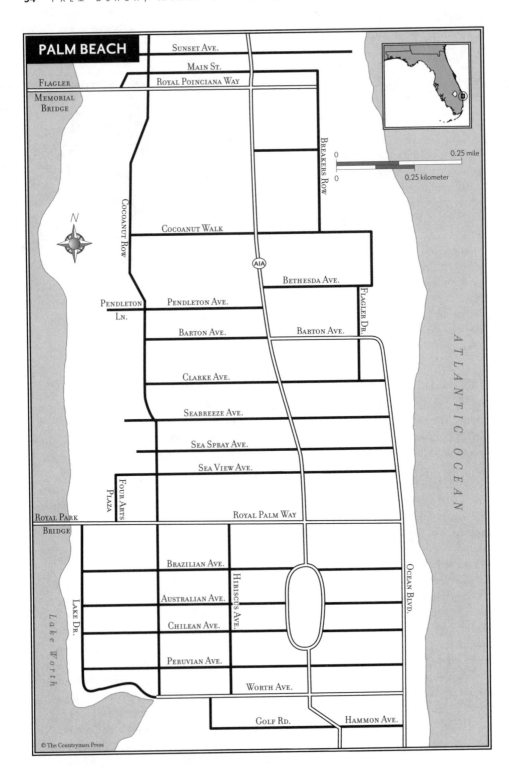

© The Countryman Press

You Deserve the Breakers Today

The Palm Beach Inn was built in 1896 as an addition to Flagler's Royal Poinciana, which opened in 1894 with 1,100 rooms accommodating 1,750 guests and hallways longer than 3 miles. Sitting on the oceanfront, the new addition became known as the Breakers by its patrons. The hotel burned down in 1903, but it was rapidly rebuilt and reopened in 1904, with 425 rooms. (Back then the rooms started at $4 a night—today's prices are one hundred times the original fee.) The hotel burned down again in 1925, and Flagler's heirs again scrambled to reconstruct this paragon of America's wealthy. The new hotel took just 11 1/2 months to build and was far more grand than its predecessors, with Italian Renaissance decor suitable for kings and queens. Still standing today, the hotel, now called the Breakers, continues to set an unmatched precedent of beauty and excellence, and it is still independently owned by Flagler's heirs.

The grand main lobby at the Breakers The Breakers Palm Beach

LODGING

The Bradley House Hotel

561-832-7050, 1-800-822-4116
www.bradleyhousehotel.com
280 Sunset Ave., Palm Beach 33480

Founded by Florida pioneer and Flagler contemporary E. R. Bradley, this hotel is a remnant from the days when Bradley ran the Beach House, an entertainment venue and casino adjunct to Flagler's hotel. Bradley won the reputation of "Mr. Lucky," the greatest gambler that ever lived. Today's hotel has 31 suites, from studios to penthouse, each with kitchen facilities. $$–$$$$.

The Breakers

561-655-6611, 1-888-BREAKERS
www.thebreakers.com
1 S. County Rd., Palm Beach 33480

A AAA five-diamond resort, the Breakers is simply incomparable to any other Gold Coast property. Originally built in 1896 and twice reconstructed because of fires, the hotel was created for the wealthiest Americans of the Gilded Age. While most remaining properties created during that time of opulence and luxury have become museums, the Breakers remains in full use, still serving the crème de la crème and giving the rest of us a glimpse at the good life, too, should we choose to accept it. Speaking from experience, my advice is this: treat yourself right. Everyone deserves to find out what it's like to live at the height of luxury. You may just be surprised to discover that the place is filled with people like you. From the 220-foot-long lobby to the carved and painted ceilings, this hotel is filled with luscious beauty. Patterns and colors combine everywhere—striped upholstery and diamond-patterned carpet and floral curtains and polka-dotted linens. Perhaps it's the pastel colors that make it all work so well, but it is simply richly gorgeous. Then there are the marble baths, glass-walled shower, and the balcony overlooking the sea. There is

The Chesterfield Palm Beach The Chesterfield Hotel

a world-class spa, pools, and golf, and beach activities include guided trips to the offshore reef. A children's labyrinth garden and the chef's herb garden contribute to the award-winning grounds, all combining to give the feel of a grand estate—more like a stately home than a hotel. $$$$.

The Chesterfield Palm Beach
561-659-5800
www.chesterfieldpb.com
363 Cocoanut Row, Palm Beach 33480

Enjoy a coziness akin to Grandma's cottage at the shore at this lush and plush little treasure a block off the beach. Built in the early 1920s, the hotel combines European elegance with Palm Beach luxury to create a charming hideout for visiting dignitaries, celebrities, and families. Throughout the hotel is a "wild" theme reminiscent of Africa, and the animal-print patterns somehow work perfectly with the high-style stripes and brocades. In the library you can enjoy sherry upon arrival, as well as afternoon tea or a cigar and cognac. Make it a spa weekend, or plan to catch a couture trunk show. $$–$$$$.

The Colony
561-655-5430, 1-800-521-5525
www.thecolonypalmbeach.com
155 Hammon Ave., Palm Beach 33480

A few steps from Worth Avenue, the Colony offers simple, unpretentious finery. This luxurious Euro-style boutique hotel has rooms and villas (available by the month during the season). $$$–$$$$.

Four Seasons Resort
561-582-2800
www.fourseasons.com/palmbeach
2800 S. Ocean Blvd., Palm Beach 33480

This oceanfront resort brings a new sense of luxury to Palm Beach, with carefully appointed full-service rooms and suites, a

Intimate alfresco dining with a view at the Four Seasons Resort The Four Seasons Resort Palm Beach

spa, water sports, and golf. This is a good place for the ultimate luxury vacation, with fine dining and relaxation the only concerns on the agenda. Make it a romantic getaway, or bring the whole family and take a four-bedroom suite, with work spaces, sitting areas, and oceanfront balconies. $$$$.

Hilton Palm Beach Oceanfront Resort
561-586-6542
www.hilton.com
2842 S. Ocean Blvd., Palm Beach 33480

Offering mainstream luxury for the rest of us, the Hilton provides the chance to enjoy the nation's premiere luxury vacation spot without feeling the least bit conspicuous. And why not? You'll be paying just as much as the high rollers, but while your treat is every bit as lovely as your neighbor's, there is a certain old-money air missing from the scene. $$$–$$$$.

The elegant Leopard Lounge and Restaurant at the Chesterfield Palm Beach The Chesterfield Hotel

DINING

Bice
561-835-1600
www.biceristorante.com
313 Worth Ave., Palm Beach 33480

Northern Italian fare is served in this family-owned chain of a growing list of about 24 restaurants around the world. Try tuna tartare before shopping on holy Worth Avenue or while reviewing your finds afterward. Bice has a pleasant, open feeling; a light dining room; and colorful, tropical patio dining. $$$.

Café Boulud at the Brazilian Court
561-655-6060
301 Australian Ave., Palm Beach 33480

Celebrated chef Daniel Boulud's restaurant, a Palm Beach institution, features luscious, world-renowned, French-inspired food. Boulud combines fresh local fare with worldly flavors to create dishes both traditional and trendy, such as grilled swordfish with fennel and mango in a curry sauce, or braised short ribs with mushrooms and watercress. Top it off with a delicious chocolate soufflé paired with pistachio ice cream. $$.

Café Merryl's
561-296-7300
235 Sunrise Ave., Palm Beach 33480

Walking into this delicious setting is like walking through the looking glass and back in time. Recovering instead of replacing the rich early décor, hosts Merryle and Gary Israel have re-created the charm of the past off the lobby of the Palm Beach Hotel, preserving much of the beautiful furnishings, including the lovely blue velvet banquettes. While atmosphere is queen at Café Merryl's, the food keeps up with the style. Begin your meal with a creamy lobster bisque or macadamia-nut-encrusted goat cheese salad, and follow with tender Florida snapper, citrus-marinated scallops, or a grilled New York steak. $$.

Echo
561-802-4222
www.echopalmbeach.com
230A Sunrise Ave., Palm Beach 33480

My favorite cuisines are Asian offerings, and at Echo, they're all on the menu—it's not fusion, it's variety. I was tempted by the Phuket curry shrimp, but my waiter urged me to try the banana-leaf-wrapped sea bass, one of Chef Dieu's signature favorites. The recommendation was perfect. Served on a bed of glass noodles with scallions and red pepper, and with a black bean and peppercorn sauce, the dish was out of this world—a blend of subtle earthy flavors, though from the sea. The chef uses certified organic banana leaves from local Indian River farms to wrap and cook the dish, one of those things you'll never repeat at home. My dining partner had crispy yellowtail snapper in a red spicy sauce that he talked about for months afterward. Echo is a dark place with well-placed halogen lamps, a good place to wear glittery diamonds and gold. It's a bit loud—the music makes conversation difficult—but who wants to talk when the fare is so delectable? $$–$$$$.

Leopard Lounge and Restaurant

561-659-5800, 1-800-243-7871
The Chesterfield Palm Beach, 363 Cocoanut Row, Palm Beach 33480

Predinner, post-show, and late-night music and dancing are offered at this elegant, wildly eclectic lounge. Light and full menus of fresh, gourmet cuisine are available, perfect for a snack or a full dinner. Try the seared tuna with grilled asparagus. Live music and dancing nightly. $$–$$$.

L'Escalier

561-655-6611, 1-888-BREAKERS
www.thebreakers.com
The Breakers, 1 S. County Rd., Palm Beach 33480

The signature restaurant of the venerable hotel. L'Escalier's chef, Matthew Sobon, prepares a number of French-inspired dishes. L'Escalier's award-winning cuisine includes classic French dishes as well as traditional favorites, such as the signature dish, Tournedos Rossini. Sommelier Virginia Philips carefully provides a wine list to complement the menu, with selections from the Breakers's award-winning wine cellar, which includes a twenty-thousand-bottle collection. $$–$$$$.

Ta-boo Restaurant and Bar

561-835-3500
www.taboorestaurant.com
221 Worth Ave., Palm Beach 33480

With a British colonial elegance, warm wood fireplace, and tropical décor, Ta-boo has been a popular place for Palm Beachers to relax since its founding in 1941. Celebrity sightings include Deepak Chopra, local resident Rod Stewart, Kathleen Turner, and, in days past, Gloria Swanson, Joe Kennedy, and the Duke and Duchess of Windsor. A lunch favorite is the Island Chicken Salad, with mango chutney and hints of curry and pepper, but the menu runs the gamut from elegant to express, lobster tail to pizza. The restaurant's signature dish is sesame-seared tuna served with wasabi, rice, and vegetables. $–$$$.

CULTURE

Flagler Museum

561-655-2833
www.flaglermuseum.us
1 Whitehall Way, Palm Beach 33480

Henry Morrison Flagler built this palatial home for his third wife, Mary Lily Kenan, as a bridal gift. Although it was converted into a hotel during the Depression, Whitehall was reclaimed by Flagler's granddaughter, Jean Flagler Matthews, who renovated it and opened it as a museum in 1960. Open 10–5 Tuesday through Saturday and noon–5 Sunday. $.

Whitehall

The Society of the Four Arts

561-655-7227
2 Four Arts Plaza, Palm Beach 33480

Founded in 1936 to meet the cultural needs of the growing resort community, this organization has an auditorium and small library, and it hosts arts classes, concerts, lectures, films, and performances. $–$$$.

ATTRACTIONS, PARKS, AND RECREATION

Dragonfly Expeditions

1-888-992-6337
1825 Ponce de Leon #369, Coral Gables 33134

Ride past the Kennedy estate and Revlon mansion and tour Flagler's mansion Whitehall—now the Flagler Museum—on this guided 7-mile tour for groups of 15 to 20. Tours by appointment. $$$–$$$$.

Golf at the Breakers

561-655-6611, 1-888-BREAKERS
www.thebreakers.com
1 S. County Rd., Palm Beach 33480

Henry Flagler built the first Florida golf course at the Breakers—only nine holes because he thought it was surely a passing fancy—and the Breakers keeps the tradition alive. The revitalized Ocean Course offers the best in vintage golf. Open daily 7 AM–7:30 PM. $$$$.

Historical Bike Tours

www.visitpalmbeach.com

These two- and three-hour tours explore upper-crust Palm Beach Island from a vantage point no motorized vehicle has ever achieved. The famous Lake Trail was established by Henry Flagler to accommodate the rickshaw-style chairs used in his day because he forbade cars on the path. The trail winds around the perimeter of the island, along the oceanfronts of the mansions of the rich and famous, and through the most exclusive neighborhood in the country. The longer tour includes a few stops and a snack break. Tours depart from the Society of the Four Arts (see above) and run several times each month on weekends. $$$.

Bike Tours

Henry Flagler built a promenade along the lakefront for his guests to enjoy, but he didn't allow motorcars on the island, so little bike chairs similar to rickshaws were employed for those who chose not to walk. The Lake Trail is still exclusive to bicycles, bladers, walkers, and joggers. There are 3-, 5-, and 10-mile paths that circle around the north end of the island of Palm Beach, with water to one side and mansions on the other. Ride with a tour guide, who can point out some of the famous homeowners, or rent a bike and ride on your own.

Palm Beach Bicycle Trail Shop
561-659-4583
223 Sunrise Ave., Palm Beach 33480

Bike rentals and tours. Open 9–5:30 Monday through Saturday and 10–5 Sunday. $$.

Palm Beach Municipal Park
561-838-5450
325 S. Ocean Blvd./FL A1A, Palm Beach 33480

This small park features a wide, freshly sanded and palm-specked beach with lifeguard service during open hours (sunrise to sunset). No concession or facilities. Free.

SHOPPING

Classic Book Shop
561-655-2485
310 S. County Rd., Palm Beach 33480

This small, independent bookstore is a good place to stop for reading material for your days at the beach. There's a selection of popular titles as well as a collection of rare books. Open 9–9 Monday through Saturday and 10–5 Sunday.

Fiore Fine Men's Wear Consignment
561-655-9965
116 N. County Rd., Palm Beach 33480

It wouldn't be fair to offer the deals only to the ladies, would it? Fiore is full of new and used clothing, shoes, and accessories for discriminating men. Open 10–5 Monday through Saturday.

Palm Beach Affair
561-833-9908
114 N. County Rd., Palm Beach 33480

It's great fun to peruse the castoffs of those who buy the best in designer clothing but can only be seen in it once. Palm Beach has many consignment shops, and the deals are great, but don't expect Goodwill prices! A sampling from a recent visit yields Escada shoes, $180; Chanel suits, $550; and Marc Jacobs, Armani, Versace, and Dana Buchman starting at $110. Open 10–5 Monday through Saturday.

Publix Supermarket
561-655-4120
265 Sunset Ave., Palm Beach 33480

This makes for some fun shopping—it's the only Publix in the country with valet service.

Worth Avenue
(shops line Worth Avenue from Cocoanut Row to the ocean)

From Bvlgari and Cartier to Dana Buchman, Giorgio Armani, Chanel, and Christian Dior—if you're looking for fine couture, you'll find it here. Worth Avenue offers simply the best shopping in the world.

Lake Worth: Evenings on the Avenue

A peaceful strip of city edging on the waterfront, Lake Worth is a small community of consignment shops, antiques shops, and restaurants surrounded by a quaint village. The main drag consists of two parallel streets, Lucerne and Lake Avenues, which come together as they head west into Lake Worth Road, perpendicular to I-95. The two avenues create a village atmosphere between the highway and the Intracoastal Waterway (Lake Worth), with quaint and hot-to-renovate residential communities to the north and south. It seemingly has not yet been discovered by the high rollers: I spotted a riverfront home built in the '30s that apparently hasn't been touched since. I priced the place a few years ago at $255,000, and today it's on the market again, this time for $649,000. This place, like so much of Florida's waterfront, is begging for big spenders to come along, raze the vintage structure, and create a sleek, new high-rise with multiple units. Maybe. Two other condo projects in Lake Worth are facing legal challenges that may halt "progress" and preserve the past and the ambient air of the present. But chances are, this being Florida, sooner or later money will win out.

LODGING

The GulfStream Hotel

561-540-6000, 1-888-540-0669
www.thegulfstreamhotel.com
1 Lake Ave., Lake Worth 33460

Rumored to be haunted, this gorgeous relic of the past is well preserved and well loved. Patrons from around the world keep this elegant waterfront hotel filled to the gills. Built in 1924 and beautifully restored in 1999, it offers charm, class, coziness, and creativity. DIGS restaurant serves wings, shrimp, and lemongrass chicken in the cool, comfortable lounge. $$–$$$$.

ATTRACTIONS, PARKS, AND RECREATION

John Prince Memorial Park

561-966-6600
2520 Lake Worth Rd., Lake Worth 33461

Just west of I-95, this great family park has more than 300 acres of game fields, tennis courts, campgrounds, and a lake with canoe, kayak, and paddleboat rentals. There are also picnic areas, nature walks, an exercise trail, and wheelchair-accessible activities. Free admission.

Lake Worth Municipal Beach

561-533-7367
10 S. Ocean Blvd., Lake Worth 33460

Lake Worth's beach, located off FL A1A at the end of Lake Worth Bridge, offers fun in the sun for all ages. Enjoy the pier, playground, picnic areas, and restaurant. A favorite local spot. Open daily sunrise to sunset; lifeguards are on duty daily 9–5. Free admission.

CULTURE

The Bamboo Room

561-585-BLUE
www.bamboorm.com
25 S. J St., Lake Worth 33460

This is the place where music is king, an extremely cool nightclub venue created by Russell Hibbard and featuring some of the most interesting musicians to come through south Florida. Enjoy the relaxing atmosphere without the frenetic dance and dating scene. $$.

Lake Worth Playhouse

561-586-6410
713 Lake Ave., Lake Worth 33460

Opened in 1924 as a silent-film house, the renovated Lake Worth Playhouse retains its 1920s art deco style and feel, which lend both charm and glamour to an evening at the theater. In addition to traditional theater, the playhouse also hosts dance and poetry performances and conducts acting classes and playwriting workshops. $$.

SHOPPING

Hoffman's Chocolate Factory

561-433-GIFT
5190 Lake Worth Rd., Greenacres 33463

Opened in 1973, Hoffman's has become a bit of a local institution. Counters are filled with truffles and white chocolate bark, chocolate-covered cherries, orange peel, and pecans and peanuts. Select your own delicacies, or choose from among many boxed and packaged gifts. You're likely to find a line of chocolate lovers at the checkout, and if you're lucky, you'll be able to observe the confection in the making—the glass-walled showroom overlooks the chocolate factory.

Boynton Beach: Sleepy Slice of Paradise

Boynton Beach is a tiny, 16-square-mile community sandwiched among several small towns between West Palm Beach and Fort Lauderdale. The town seems to be just waking up to the surge in optimistic development and tourism taking place throughout south Florida. Signs of joining the trend are minimal—the beachfront is still quiet and lined with residential property, and the downtown area is still business oriented rather than lined with gift shops and restaurants—but a new marina is planned, which is expected to boost the leisure crowd in the area.

SHOPPING

The Crystal Garden
561-369-2836
www.thecrystalgarden.com
2610 N. Federal Hwy., Boynton Beach 33435

In need of a mandala or psychic reading? All things spiritual are at this book and gift store, and there are always interesting classes, from yoga and meditation to astrology and numerology. Occasionally you can even have a photo of your aura taken! Open 11–8 Monday through Thursday, 11–6 Friday and Saturday, and 11–3 Sunday.

Past Perfect Florida History
561-742-7822, 1-888-828-7822
www.past-perfect-florida-history-books.com
640 E. Ocean Ave., Boynton Beach 33435

Find Florida interesting enough to want to learn a bit more? Look no further than Past Perfect Florida History for books about Florida: history, fiction, nature, children's, travel, biography, cookbooks, Florida postcards, maps, and prints. Open 10–5 Monday through Friday and by appointment.

Delray Beach: Atlantic Avenue Action

Founded by a group from Michigan, this town also had a settlement of Japanese farmers who raised pineapples until Flagler's railway brought Cuban competition. The town then turned to tomato growing and became known for its ketchup. The downtown ketchup factory was said to emit a distinct odor of vinegar and spices, much different from the sweet pineapple of the past. Now a fast-growing and popular area for the arts, fine dining, and casual entertainment, Delray Beach's Atlantic Avenue is usually the site of all the activity. As in Lake Worth, the main drag runs due east from I-95 to the Intracoastal Waterway (called Lake Worth here), with residential communities north and south of the commercial corridor.

LODGING

The Colony Hotel and Cabaña Club
561-276-4123
525 E. Atlantic Ave., Delray Beach 33483

Built at the height (and nearly the end) of Florida's grand land boom in 1926, the Colony is a study in grace and charm right on Delray Beach's Atlantic Avenue—still the hotbed of excitement. A fun alternative to highway-side modern trend hotels, the Colony has all the amenities and luxuries. The Boughton family, who are founding members of the Green Hotel Association, a group of hoteliers committed to improving environmental practices in the hospitality industry, have owned the Colony since 1935. All rooms in both Colony hotels in Delray Beach and Kennebunkport, Maine, adhere to green qualities, with 100 percent nonsmoking rooms; using recycled paper; recycling newspapers, cans, glass, and plastics; purchasing in bulk to reduce packaging (and costs); and eliminating the use of toxic materials in their hotels. $$.

Crane's Beach House

561-278-1700, 1-866-372-7263
www.cranesbeachhouse.com
82 Gleason St., Delray Beach 33483

Cool and breezy, colorful and creative, Crane's Beach House hosts an artist in residence and has original artwork—such as murals, hand-painted glassware, and linens—woven into the décor, all of which are also sold here. The hotel is unique, trendy, and comfortable, and it's just a block from the beach. Rooms have private patios and balconies. $$–$$$$.

Delray Beach Marriott

561-274-3200
www.delraybeachmarriott.com
10 N. Ocean Blvd., Delray Beach 33483

Located at the beach end of trendy Atlantic Avenue, the Delray Beach Marriott is a popular choice for travelers seeking waterfront sports and sunny relaxation plus sophisticated shopping, dining, and nightlife. It's a great family location. Complimentary breakfast for two, free in-room movie. $$$–$$$$.

Ritz-Carlton Palm Beach

561-533-6000
www.ritz-carlton.com
100 S. Ocean Blvd., Manalapan 33462

This primo destination took a few potshots from the 2004 hurricanes that ripped into the land at the Palm Beach shoreline, but after several weeks the hotel reopened, ready to welcome customers. The Ocean Cafe & Bar serves light lunch items (I love the gazpacho), and the Lobby Lounge features high tea during the day and light bites and a live pianist later in the day. $$$$.

Wright By The Sea

561-278-3355
1901 S. Ocean Blvd., Delray Beach 33483

Sporting much the same design and atmosphere as it has for the past 50 years, Wright By The Sea is a throwback to the old days, a place where you can go to imagine nothing has changed since childhood, except that now you're paying the bill instead of dear old Dad. If you don't mind the out-of-date furniture, these bargain-priced, spacious suites have ocean views, and the grounds and the beach have the atmosphere of a private club. $$.

DINING

De La Tierra at Sundy House

561-272-5678
www.sundyhouse.com
106 S. Swinton Ave., Delray Beach 33444

Built in 1902, this gem is the historic home of the first mayor of Delray Beach, John Sundy, who served eight terms. Now an inn as well as a restaurant, De La Tierra has an acre of lush gardens that surround the dining and lodging areas to create an intimate tropical experience. Continental breakfast is served all day every day, but the Sunday brunch is a special treat, complete with everything from waffles to shrimp and salmon, roast beef and ham, and mimosas

Dining in a tropical setting at De La Tierra at Sundy House

Ellie's '50s Diner

and juice. Eleven garden apartments open out into the Taru Gardens, and a suite features a fireplace and Jacuzzi. $$.

Ellie's '50s Diner

561-276-1570

2410 N. Federal Hwy., Delray Beach 33483

A throwback to the past, Ellie's is the place for Mom's comfort food, when you're yearning for home-cooked meat loaf or apple pie. Soothe your longings for the past with Great Balls of Fire Chili or a Sweet Pea steak and cheese. Ellie's also has a fish fry, roast turkey and dressing, prime rib, and sugar-free pies. But it pays to remember that Ellie's is cash only—just like in the '50s. $.

J&J Raw Bar

561-272-3390

632 E. Atlantic Ave., Delray Beach 33483

Fresh and succulent is the rule at this tiny bar with big-city atmosphere. The slender bar/dining room seats all takers for seafood delights such as shrimp, clams, and oysters. Dishes are fresh and colorful, featuring a nice mix of worldly flavors and styles, including Caribbean spices, jerk sauce, bourbon barbecue, Asian wasabi, and pickled ginger. Try mushroom and crab strudel, pecan-crusted swordfish, or a spinach and sausage personal pizza. A wide selection of hot sauces is available—J&J even bottles its own peppery blend. Premium drafts and an international wine list complement the meal. $$.

Jimmy's Stone Crabs and Grille

561-278-0036

411 E. Atlantic Ave., Delray Beach 33483

Seafood is the big catch here, especially stone crabs during the mid-October to mid-May season. $$.

Mano a Mano Tapas Bar and Restaurant
561-276-3666
8 E. Atlantic Ave., Delray Beach 33444

Dark and colorful inside, but open to the sidewalk with wide windows and outdoor tables, this restaurant specializes in Spanish cuisine. My server brought delicious fresh garlic aiello—homemade mayonnaise with olive oil, garlic, and egg—to dip the bread in as I perused the menu. I couldn't get enough of it. The seared tuna was excellent (how Spanish is that? It's everywhere these days, and for good reason), as was the simple salad of fresh mango and avocado slices. $$.

Old Calypso
561-279-2300
900 E. Atlantic Ave., Delray Beach 33483

Creole and Caribbean flavors are combined with fresh Florida seafood and steaks at this friendly spot. Enjoy waterfront dining on the Intracoastal Waterway. $$.

The Old Key Lime House Restaurant
561-533-5220
300 E. Ocean Ave., Lantana 33462

A renovation project surprised the owner when peeling back the layers of paneling and flooring applied over time revealed this to be the second-oldest house in Lantana. Today the rambling structure provides a fitting Cracker atmosphere for delicious Key lime pie and fresh seafood dishes. With waterfront seating and a boat dock, this is as unpretentious as it is inexpensive and delicious. Sunday brunch. $$.

Pineapple Grille
561-265-1368
800 Palm Trail, Delray Beach 33483

This little gem offers a colorful setting, a cheerful, easygoing island atmosphere, a tantalizingly fruity menu, and friendly service. The Pineapple has an outdoor terrace covered with a blue awning and edged with festive, tiny twinkling lights. Roasted

The Old Key Lime House Restaurant Jim Wurster

rack of lamb with plum mint sauce and a veal chop are rumored to be good, but I was torn between the curried shrimp with Caribbean rice and a nightly special of cashew-crusted Keys pink fish with dried cherry pico de gallo, which included bits of apple, mango, and onion. It all turned out to be delicious. Closed Sunday. $$.

Sol Kitchen

561-921-0201
4 E. Atlantic Ave., Delray Beach 33444

This is a sunny spot for fresh Floridian, Latino, and American Tex-Mex cuisine. This means tacos and taro chips, flan, and—surprise!—Jamaican ginger beer. $.

Sol Kitchen

ATTRACTIONS, PARKS, AND RECREATION

The AOS International Orchid Visitors Center and Botanical Garden

561-404-2000
www.orchidweb.org
16700 AOS Lane, Delray Beach 33446

This American Orchid Society showroom and education center provides inspiration and instruction to the floral-minded. $.

Atlantic Dunes Park

561-243-7352
1600 S. Ocean Blvd., Delray Beach 33483 (1 block north of Linton Blvd.)

A marvelous oceanside picnic spot, this little park, which is sandwiched between serious oceanfront property owners, is a gem that should last forever, but enjoy it while it lasts. Tree canopy; lifeguard on duty daily 9–5. Free.

Delray Municipal Beach

561-243-7352
Ocean Blvd. at Atlantic Ave., Delray Beach

Named one of the best beaches in the country by *Travel Holiday* in 2003, Delray Beach continues to attract family beachgoers, snorkelers, and those seeking a pleasant, safely guarded day at the seashore. Lifeguard on duty daily 9–5. Free.

Gulfstream Park

561-966-6600
4489 N. Ocean Blvd., Gulf Stream 33483

This slice of oceanfront property preserved for public enjoyment has grills and a lifeguard. Park open from sunrise to sunset; office open 8–5. Lifeguard on duty daily. Free.

Morikami Museum & Japanese Gardens

561-495-0233

www.morikami.org

4000 Morikami Park Rd., Delray Beach 33446

Delray was settled by Japanese pineapple farmers, and although their settlement never took hold, one of its most enduring residents was George Morikami, who generously left his land to Palm Beach County to preserve as a garden. Today visitors can learn about the Japanese historical connection to Palm Beach County and stroll in the peaceful gardens. There's also a bonsai garden and sushi restaurant. Closed Monday. $.

Morikami Museum & Japanese Gardens   Morikami Museum and Japanese Gardens

CULTURE

Cornell Museum

561-243-7922

www.oldschool.org

51 N. Swinton Ave., Delray Beach 33444

This multimedia art collection and showcase galleries have been housed in the restored Delray Elementary School, circa 1913, for more than a decade. The museum is one of several cultural institutions housed at Old School Square, where the restored Delray High School of 1925 serves as the intimate Crest Theatre, with just 323 seats. The 1926 high

Cornell Museum

school gymnasium has been restored and is used for public meetings and parties, and an open pavilion completes the square. The museum is closed on Mondays and major holidays October through April and on Sundays and Mondays during the summer. $.

Delray Beach Playhouse
561-272-1281
950 N.W. Ninth St., Delray Beach 33444

Located west of town and overlooking Lake Ida in Lake Ida Park, this small, local, non-profit theater has been serving the community for nearly half a century. In addition to performances, there are acting classes and children's programs. $$.

The Palm Beach Photographic Centre
561-276-9797; fax 561-276-1932
www.workshop.org
55 N.E. Second Ave., Delray Beach 33444

A museum showcasing the finest in photographic work, the photographic center also provides training for those who wish to join the ranks of professional photographic artists. A wide range of courses are available, culminating in the annual Foto Fusion conference, which brings in nationally known professionals to lend their skills to those hungry to learn. There are classes for amateurs and professionals alike, covering everything from black-and-white photography to digital imaging. Classes run from $145 for a six-week evening course for beginners to $1,200 for intensive weeklong seminars with master photographers. Museum hours are 9–6 Monday through Saturday. $.

SHOPPING

The Boys Farmers Market

561-496-0810

14378 Military Trail, Delray Beach 33484

Much more than a roadside stand, this market, which has been in business for years, has fresh fruits, vegetables, meats and seafood, and baked goods. Treasures abound.

House of Vintage in Delray Beach

561-276-7477

www.myhouseofvintage.com

123 S. Swinton Ave., Delray Beach 33444

After browsing the Betsey Johnson pseudo retro gear, you can get a retro hairdo at the Color Parlor in the back. There's also a vintage kitchen full of cook's supplies, a men's room, and my favorite—the designer show rack. Owner Michelle Parparian wants you to have fun!

Love Shack

561-276-7755

137 E. Atlantic Ave., Delray Beach 33444

This store is an offshoot of the Snappy Turtle (see below), with more pink and green monogrammed belts, hats, bags, pajamas, et cetera.

There's lots to browse at the House of Vintage.

Murder on the Beach Mystery Bookstore

561-279-7790

273 Pineapple Grove Way (N.E. Second Ave.), Delray Beach 33444

More than just a place to buy books, Murder on the Beach is a favorite haunt of mystery lovers. Hosting frequent author signings and celebrations of new books from local authors, this independent bookstore helps nurture the writing community with mystery book discussion groups, parties, and participation in conferences.

The Snappy Turtle

561-276-8088

www.snappy-turtle.com

1038 E. Atlantic Ave., Delray Beach 33483

This little shop, which is the self-proclaimed "original pink and green preppy chic store," has all sorts of accessories, and just about everything can be monogrammed. Although I thought Lilly Pulitzer might be the one responsible for the popular Palm Beach colors, I must agree that this is certainly a chic boutique.

Boca Raton: Little Pink Houses and Pink Cadillacs

Boca Raton is known as the pink city, with more pastel pink buildings and homes than you're likely to see anywhere else in Florida—or anywhere, for that matter. The color seems to express a sort of luxurious gentility: Boca is a wealthy, suburban sort of upper-middle-class community wedged between Palm Beach and Fort Lauderdale, financially as well as literally.

The town is the site of some outstanding architecture by Addison Mizner, a self-taught architect who worked in Palm Beach designing the manses the swells called "cottages" before moving to Boca Raton to gain fame through his stuccoed Mediterranean tile-roofed mansions. Mizner designed the Cloister, an inn still in use today as part of the Boca Raton Resort & Club, although it flourished for only a single season under Mizner's management. A flamboyant character who wore silk pajamas around town and enjoyed walking with his exotic pet monkeys and macaws, Mizner died bankrupt after the crash of the Florida land boom in 1933.

John and Lillian Pederson helped put Boca Raton on the map by developing Africa USA, the epitome of Florida in the '50s, a wild animal park that thrived in the city for eight years until 1961, when development pushed the jungle attraction into extinction.

Although many people wonder about the name of this city, which is said to translate to "mouth of the rat" in Spanish, city officials try to dispel that rumor, saying the name has something to do with an inlet. Smells like a swamp rat to me.

LODGING

Boca Raton Resort & Club
561-447-3000
www.bocaresort.com
501 E. Camino Real, Boca Raton 33431

Expanded from the original 1926 Cloister Inn built by Addison Mizner, which is still in use, the current configuration is a product of Arthur Vining Davis, the CEO of ALCOA who became a developer after retirement, creating much of Boca Raton and Weston in Broward County as well as many other communities in Florida with his company Arvida. Today the club has 1,041 guest rooms, suites, and villas in five different buildings. The Cloister is quaint, the tower sleek as any modern condo, the beach club very tropical in feel, and the yacht club sophisticated and exclusive. There are golf villas for those who are more interested in sports than cush; some have kitchens. There are two championship golf courses, 30 tennis courts, a spa, a marina, and much more. Past celebrity guests have included Oprah Winfrey, Robert Redford, Bill Cosby, and John Travolta. $$$–$$$$.

Radisson Bridge Resort
561-368-9500, 1-800-333-3333
www.radisson.com
999 E. Camino Real, Boca Raton 33432

Perhaps a bit nicer than many in the Radisson chain, this high-rise looms over the Intracoastal Waterway at the Camino Real bridge in Boca. Nice views; short walk to the beach. $$–$$$.

DINING

Bong
561-368-3338
www.bongdining.com
150 E. Palmetto Park Rd., Boca Raton 33432

Thai, Mandarin, and Vietnamese flavors are blended to perfection at this Asian fusion restaurant, voted Boca Raton's best new restaurant by *Boca Magazine* in 2004. Closed Monday. $$–$$$.

Carmen's at the Top of the Bridge
561-750-8354
999 E. Camino Real, Boca Raton 33432

Famous for its view as well as its cuisine, Carmen's, at the Radisson Hotel, has live music Thursday through Saturday. Try the chef's favorite, escargot and caviar served with tomatoes, garlic, and basil on pasta, or try the Florida snapper or rack of lamb. Dinner and music Thursday through Saturday; Sunday brunch. Closed Monday through Wednesday. $$–$$$.

La Tre
561-392-4568
249 E. Palmetto Park Rd., Boca Raton 33432

The Vietnamese fare served in this small yet elegant dining room makes visitors loath to leave. In addition to the exotic dinners, diners enjoy the personal service and friendly atmosphere. I loved the lemony mousse dessert suggested by my waiter. $$.

Petrossian
561-394-2237
Boca Town Center, 6000 Glades Rd., Boca Raton 33431

Located on the third floor of Bloomingdale's, this is the place to take a break from shopping and have a snack of champagne and caviar. What a way to shop! $–$$.

ATTRACTIONS, PARKS, AND RECREATION

The Gumbo Limbo Environmental Complex and Nature Center at Red Reef Park
561-338-1473
www.gumbolimbo.org
1801 N. Ocean Blvd., Boca Raton 33432

I'm not usually too enthusiastic about places where sea creatures are kept in tanks for public display, but these tanks are part of serious research projects, and the creatures are not here for exploitation. This nonprofit, 20-acre research center benefits from wonderful hardwood hammock, an Indian shell midden from early occupation, and 5-mile beachfront. Open 9–4 Monday through Saturday and noon–4 Sunday. Free, with nominal fees for special events, such as turtle walks.

Palm Beach Polo Club

561-793-1440, 561-798-7000
www.palmbeachpolo.com
11199 Polo Club Rd., Wellington 33414

International headquarters for tournament polo, this club hosts the major tournaments and the most renowned players, including His Royal Highness Prince Charles and his late wife, Princess Diana of Wales. The Equestrian Club is said to be the best in the country, with year-round events and the National Horse Show. There's also championship golf and tennis for members and their guests. Polo matches are open to the public, however, with complimentary seating.

Red Reef Park

561-393-7974
1400 N. Ocean Blvd., Boca Raton 33432

This 67-acre oceanfront park is composed of hardwood hammock, beach, the Gumbo Limbo Nature Center, boardwalk, pier, and picnic facilities and grills. Snorkelers swim from the south end of the beach to explore Red Reef, where many tropical fish can be found. Lifeguards are on duty 9–5. No pets or alcohol allowed. Open 8 AM–10 PM daily. $.

Royal Palm Polo Club

561-994-1876
www.boca-polo.com
18000 Jog Road, Boca Raton 33496

Recognized as one of the finest polo clubs in the world, the Palm Beach Polo Club polo fields and stadium have hosted champions of this sport from around the world. Events are held weekly. Tickets to attend tournaments ($ and up) are available by calling the office. Open January through April.

South Beach Park and Pavilion

561-393-7810
400 N. Ocean Blvd., Boca Raton 33432

This natural beach area and 25 preserved acres are unpolluted by development or beach amenities, just the way nature made them—with the exception of a picnic area. Open daily sunrise to sunset; lifeguard on duty daily 9–5. $.

Spanish River Park

561-393-7810
3001 N. Ocean Blvd./FL A1A, Boca Raton 33431

This large park is bordered by the Intracoastal Waterway and FL A1A, with tunnels leading to the beach on the Atlantic Ocean. Hardwood hammocks, palms, and a lagoon provide natural habitats for small animals and birds and make for fun exploring along the nature trail and observation tower. Playground, picnic areas, and boat dock. Lifeguards on duty 9–5. Open daily 8–sunset. $.

CULTURE

Boca Raton Historical Society

561-395-6766
www.bocahistory.org
71 N. Federal Hwy., Boca Raton 33432

The museum, located in Boca's gold-domed town hall, houses a collection of historical documents, maps, and artifacts that reflect the development of the community, including architectural paraphernalia and photos from the days of Addison Mizner's work in the area. In addition, the museum hosts traveling historical exhibits and conducts tours of significant properties in town, including the Boca Raton Resort & Club. Open 10–4 Tuesday through Friday. Free.

Boca Raton Museum of Art

561-392-2500
www.bocamuseum.org
Mizner Park, 501 Plaza Real, Boca Raton 33432

A rapidly growing cultural institution, the museum moved to a new 44,000-square-foot facility in Mizner Park, a shopping and dining plaza, in 2001. There are interactive children's exhibits, art classes, and a permanent collection that includes Picasso, Matisse, and Klee as well as pre-Colombian art. Open 10–5 Tuesday, Thursday, and Friday; 10–9 Wednesday; and noon–5 Saturday and Sunday. Closed Mondays and holidays. $–$$.

Caldwell Theatre Company

561-241-7432
www.caldwelltheatre.com
7873 N. Federal Hwy., Boca Raton 33487

The only professional theater company in Boca, this award-winning nonprofit company has been in business since 1975. While it currently showcases its contemporary plays in the shopping-plaza theater, a capital funding campaign is under way to build a permanent home for the company. The theater also hosts a popular play-reading series, which provides playwrights with an audience and critical review. Tickets $$–$$$$.

Children's Museum

561-368-6875
498 Crawford Blvd., Boca Raton 33432

This hands-on, inspirational, creative museum, in one of the town's oldest pioneer homes, is a fun place for kids. It takes them from prehistoric times to the future of the universe with activities that range from a fossil dig to a historic town with post office and grocery to space exploration. Each exhibit lets kids play while they learn—the best way to help them remember what they learned. Open noon–4 Tuesday through Saturday. $.

SHOPPING

King's Italian Market

561-368-2600

1900 Military Trail, Boca Raton 33431

This one-of-a-kind market satisfies its loyal customers by providing the very finest of everything culinary. From gourmet deli items, fresh fish and seafood, and meats and poultry to the finest wines, cheeses, and baked goods, King's deserves its reputation as the best in Palm Beach County. Open 7 AM–9 PM Monday through Friday and 7 AM–7 PM Saturday and Sunday.

Mizner Park

561-362-0606

www.miznerpark.org

430 Plaza Real, Boca Raton 33432

Although this gem is combined of all the elements popular today in shopping and entertainment complexes, this lovely, open-air Italianate plaza beckons with an air of sophistication and privilege that unfortunately eludes modern-day festival marketplaces. Features fashion, footwear, and food, as well as art galleries and an amphitheater. Open 10–9 Monday through Saturday and noon–5 Sunday.

Town Center Mall

561-368-6000

6000 Glades Rd., Boca Raton 33431

The nation's finest department stores are located in the suburbs of Boca: Saks Fifth Avenue, Bloomingdale's, and Nordstrom, as well as specialty shops and restaurants. Valet parking. Open 10–9 Monday through Saturday and noon–6 Sunday.

WEEKLY AND ANNUAL EVENTS

Thursday

Clematis By Night

www.clematisbynight.net

Clematis St., Centennial Square, W. Palm Beach

This downtown fountainside concert series features local rock, rhythm and blues, reggae, soul, and swing music. 5:30–9 PM. Free.

Sunset Celebration

561-844-1724

www.sailfishmarina.com

Sailfish Marina, 98 Lake Dr., Singer Island 33404

Artists display their work along the docks and musicians play, making for a pleasant evening stroll. You can buy "Grouper Dawgs" (hot dogs) on the dock or have dinner at the Sailfish Marina restaurant. 6–9 PM. Free.

Friday
Lake Worth "Evening on the Avenues"
561-582-4401
The Cultural Plaza near M Street, downtown Lake Worth

Every first and third Friday of the month there is music, crafts, food, classic cars, and lots of shopping from 6–10 PM.

Saturday
Boca Raton Greenmarket
Royal Palm Place southwest parking lot, at the corner of Federal Hwy. and Mizner Blvd., Boca Raton

Local produce, plants, and prepared foods; arts and crafts; activities. 8–1.

Delray Beach Greenmarket in the Park
150 E. Atlantic Ave., downtown Delray Beach, Worthing Park

Take advantage of this open-air marketplace to patronize local farmers for the freshest produce available. Open 8–1 October through April.

West Palm Beach Green Market
561-659-8003
Narcissus Ave. and Second St., W. Palm Beach

Take a morning stroll through vendor tents (you may want to begin at the gourmet coffee booth) to select fresh flowers to perk up your hotel room and fresh vegetables to snack on during your visit. Create a picnic, or if your accommodations include a kitchen, you may wish to go all out and select fresh, locally grown ingredients for your vacation feast. There's also fresh fish, herbal teas, breads, prepared foods, and potted plants. Open 7–1 October through March.

January
Fotofusion 2005
561-276-9797
www.fotofusion.org
Downtown Delray Beach at various locations

Sponsored by the Palm Beach Photographic Center, this annual international festival of photography and digital imaging features exhibitions of top photographers from around the world. $–$$$.

March
The Honda Classic
561-514-6999, www.pgatour.com
561-624-7555, www.mirasolclub.com
The Country Club at Mirasol in Palm Beach Gardens, 11300 Mirasol Blvd., Palm Beach Gardens 33418

Nongolfers might giggle at the thought of chasing a little ball around through pastures and forests and by sand dunes and lakes, but to those in the know, it's serious stuff and mighty big business. The Honda Classic, sponsored by the automaker for more than two decades, is an annual weeklong tournament during which players claim their turf to benefit Florida children's charities. Free daily passes Monday and Tuesday, $$–$$$ Wednesday through Sunday; many advanced amenity options available.

April
Delray Affair
1-800-304-9702
www.delrayaffair.com
Atlantic Ave., downtown Delray Beach

This 10-block-long arts and crafts festival has showcased the arts community for more than 40 years. It's held the week after Easter to celebrate local and national artists, food purveyors, and fun lovers. Free admission.

May
Cinco de Mayo
561-276-3396
Old School Square, N. Swinton Ave. and N.E. Second St., downtown Delray Beach

This celebration of Mexico's independence in 1862 features music, traditional foods, piñatas, and dancing. $.

Sunfest
561-659-5980
www.sunfest.com
Downtown W. Palm Beach

Florida's largest waterfront music and arts festival has been held over five days around the first weekend of May for the past two decades. More than three hundred thousand people attend the event, which features more than 50 concerts, many with national artists. $$–$$$.

July
Summer Nights on the Avenue
Atlantic Ave., Delray Beach

Live music, local fare, and shopping fun. 7–10 PM Fridays July through August. Free.

August
Boca Festival Days
www.bocaratonchamber.com

The chamber of commerce hosts a month of events to raise money for local nonprofit organizations from hospitals to the Humane Society. Rock-a-thon, chamber music, art shows, historical and hospital tours, wine tastings, and a martini night—there's something going on somewhere every day or night in August in Boca.

Historical Walking Tours of Boca Raton Resort & Club

561-395-6766

www.bocahistory.org

Boca Raton Historical Society, 71 N. Federal Hwy., Boca Raton 33432

Visit historic homes and the architectural wonders of Addison Mizner, including the Cloister at the Boca Raton Resort & Club. Available Tuesday; $$ donation.

November

Delray Beach Garlic Festival

www.dbgarlicfest.com

Old School Square, N. Swinton Ave. and N.E. Second St., downtown Delray Beach

Celebrate all things garlic, from breads and pastas to marinara, garlic wine, garlic art, and even a garlic university. Voted 2004 Best Festival by *New Times Magazine*. Free admission.

100-Foot Tree Lighting

561-279-1380

Old School Square, N. Swinton Ave., Delray Beach

Santa arrives and the helps light the tallest tree in the world! Free.

December

Boca Raton Holiday Boat Parade

C-15 canal to Intracoastal Waterway

Sponsored by the Boca Raton Chamber of Commerce, the parade provides a fun opportunity for boat owners to decorate their decks in support of charity, as the event collects for Toys for Tots. Spectators can view the colorful parade along the Intracoastal Waterway. Free.

Chris Evert Tennis Pro-Celebrity Tennis Classic

561-394-2400

www.chrisevert.org

7200 W. Camino Real, Suite 310, Boca Raton 33433

Whether you wish to invest $20 to watch the games or $2,500 to play a round with Chrissie herself, you can help provide for children through this wildly popular and successful benefit event that has raised more than $12 million for children's charities. The long list of celebrity participants includes George H. W. Bush, Donald Trump, Whitney Houston, Dionne Warwick, and many more. Tennis matches and events are held at the Delray Beach Tennis Center and at the Boca Raton Resort & Club.

Delray Beach Boat Parade

561-732-9501

Along the Intracoastal Waterway from Boynton Inlet south to the C-15 canal

Boats of all sizes decked in holiday finery. Free.

First Night New Year's Eve Celebration
561-279-1380
Downtown Delray Beach

Visual and performing arts and nonalcoholic venues are part of a national movement to create New Year's Eve fun without the dangers of alcohol-infused reveling. Free.

Holiday Boat Parade of the Palm Beaches
561-845-9010
www.pbboatparade.com
Sea Tow Palm Beach, 1509 Avenue C, Riviera Beach 33404

The merry parade of boats decorated for the holidays makes its way from Peanut Island northward for 10 miles up the Intracoastal Waterway to Jonathan's Landing, just north of Donald Ross Road in Jupiter. The volunteer parade committee collects donations for Toys for Tots from participants and spectators. Recommended viewing sites are Phil Foster Park off the Blue Heron Bridge, North Palm Beach Country Club Golf Course, and Juno Park. Free.

EMERGENCY NUMBERS

In an emergency, dial 911.
Poison information: 1-800-222-1222

HOSPITALS

Boca Raton Community Hospital
561-395-7100
800 Meadows Rd., Boca Raton 33486

Delray Medical Center
561-498-4440
5352 Linton Blvd., Delray Beach 33484

Glades General Hospital
561-996-6571
1201 S. Main St., Belle Glade 33430

Good Samaritan Medical Center
561-655-5511
1300 N. Flagler Dr., W. Palm Beach 33402

Jupiter Medical Center
561-744-4409
1210 S. Old Dixie Hwy., Jupiter 33458

Palm Beach Gardens Medical Center
561-622-1411
3360 Burns Rd., Palm Beach Gardens 33410

St. Mary's Hospital
561-622-1411
901 45th St., W. Palm Beach 33407

West Boca Medical Center
561-488-8000
21644 FL 7, Boca Raton 33428

NEWSPAPERS

The Palm Beach Post
561-820-4100
www.palmbeachpost.com
2751 S. Dixie Hwy., W. Palm Beach 33405

TRANSPORTATION

Airport shuttle
561-233-0500

The Super Shuttle is available at Palm Beach International Airport. Look for the representatives in the baggage-claim area wearing yellow Super Shuttle shirts.

Alamo Rent-a-Car, Palm Beach International Airport
1-800-327-9633

Palm Beach International Airport
561-471-7420
1000 Turnage Blvd., Palm Beach 33406

Tri-Rail stations
www.tri-rail.com
1-800-TRI-RAIL

Boca Raton station (601 N.W. 53rd St., Boca Raton 33487)
Boynton Beach station (2800 High Ridge Rd., Boynton Beach 33426)
Delray Beach station (345 S. Congress Ave., Delray Beach 33445)
Lake Worth station (1703 Lake Worth Rd., Lake Worth 33460)
Mangonia Park station (1415 45th St., W. Palm Beach 33407)
West Palm Beach station (203 S. Tamarind Ave., W. Palm Beach 33401)

TOURISM CONTACTS

Greater Boca Raton Chamber of Commerce

561-395-4433
1800 N. Dixie Hwy., Boca Raton 33432

The Palm Beach County Convention and Visitors Bureau

561-233-3000
www.palmbeachfl.com
1555 Palm Beach Lakes Blvd., Suite 800, W. Palm Beach 33401

Palm Beach County Cultural Council

561-471-2901, 1-800-882-ARTS
www.pbccc.org
1555 Palm Beach Lakes Blvd., W. Palm Beach 33401

VISIT FLORIDA

850-488-5607
www.flausa.com
661 E. Jefferson St., Suite 300, Tallahassee 32301

2

BROWARD COUNTY
Developed Delight

Broward County, home of Fort Lauderdale, is like the sweet cake filling, the middle between the sugary icing of Palm Beach and the spicy, tart crust of Miami. It's white-bread land, where grandmas live and people pretend to lead normal lives, basking in the glory of the perpetual sunshine and days much too beautiful to spend lingering long at the desk. Fort Lauderdale was launched to fame by Marilyn Monroe and *Where the Boys Are,* the happy little film that spawned the spring break frenzy. It was fun while it lasted, but the spring break shenanigans were eventually squelched due to excessive debauchery and replaced with wholesome fun for the whole family.

In addition to a wealth of museums and attractive walking areas, such as Riverwalk along the New River and Las Olas Boulevard, Fort Lauderdale's legendary beaches are indeed beautiful. Broward County's beaches have been recognized with the Blue Wave award, a voluntary program that ensures that beaches are well maintained and regularly tested for dangerous conditions, including rip tides and pollutants, problems that can pose dangers for swimmers. Beaches at Delray Beach, Deerfield Beach, Pompano Beach, Fort Lauderdale, Dania Beach, and Hollywood have been named Blue Wave beaches.

With 9.4 million visitors in 2004, and a projected residential growth of 46 percent over the next 20 years, Broward County's officials are actively working to meet the demands of increased population and a strong tourism industry. Broward County mayor Kristin Jacobs has announced that 2005 is the Year of the Environment. Jacobs, a proponent of environment-friendly smart planting that conserves water and cools communities, plans to establish more "greenways" throughout the county. Jacobs is also working on a mass-transit plan for the south Florida region, as well as working with more than a thousand citizens to create and implement a regional plan called VisionBROWARD, a cooperative effort of local government and citizens that will help ensure that Fort Lauderdale continues to offer the best possible options for visitors as well as residents.

The Broward County Office of Urban Planning projects population growth of almost 1 million in the next 25 years, with all land used by 2015. Planners are grappling with infrastructure ramifications, urging development of "smart" cities and urban redevelopment, the protection of beaches and older neighborhoods, and the creation of growth-management strategies and transportation solutions.

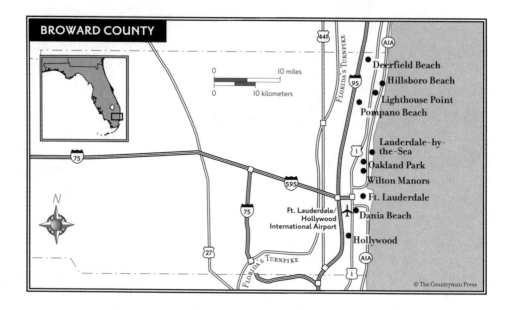

Deerfield Beach: Books and the Beach

Developed in the early 1900s by pioneers who scraped together livings as farmers, traders, explorers, hunters, and sailors, Deerfield Beach comprises only 13 square miles and accommodates about 75,000 residents, about half of each gender with a median age in the mid-40s and a median income about the same. The city's 3-mile white-sand beach, said to be one of the best in south Florida, was chosen for the set of the movie *In Her Shoes,* starring Cameron Diaz and Shirley MacClaine, which is coming to theaters in late 2005. There are a few interesting things to explore in this quiet community.

LODGING

Deerfield Beach/Boca Raton Hilton

954-427-7700, 1-800-624-3606
www.hilton.com
100 Fairway Dr., Deerfield Beach 33441

This modern luxury hotel serves business travelers and those seeking easy access to south Florida cities. Located just off I-95 between Fort Lauderdale and Boca Raton, the Hilton is 2 miles west of the beach. $$.

Embassy Suites Resort

954-426-0478, fax 954-360-0539
950 S.E. 20th Ave., Deerfield Beach 33441

This all-suites resort provides a quiet getaway on a peaceful beach nestled between Boca Raton and Fort Lauderdale. Suites feature one bedroom, a living room with sleeper sofa, and two baths. Oceanfront or poolside dining; airport shuttle available. $$$.

ATTRACTIONS, PARKS, AND RECREATION

Deer Creek Golf Club

954-421-5550
www.deercreekflorida.com
2801 Country Club Blvd., Deerfield Beach 33442

Designed in 1993 by architect Arthur Hills, and redesigned by Hills again in 2004, this championship par-72 course was voted as one of the top two courses in south Florida by *Golf* magazine. It's too soon to tell what the latest improvements will bring. $$$–$$$$, depending on tee time.

Deerfield Island Park

954-360-1320
www.broward.org/parks
1720 Deerfield Island Park, Deerfield Beach 33441

Located in the middle of the Intracoastal Waterway, this park is accessible only by boat. Bring your own (25 feet or smaller only) or catch the free shuttle, which runs every Sunday from Sullivan Park (on Riverview Road at the Intracoastal Bridge) on the hour 10–3. Trails will take you through the small island habitat of turtles and raccoons. It's a nice oasis of green in an urban environment. Reservations required; closed Monday and Tuesday. Free.

Quiet Waters Park

954-360-1315
401 S. Powerline Rd., Deerfield Beach 33442

Quiet Waters Park is particularly popular with kids for its Splash Adventure, a water park that helps people keep their cool on hot summer days. The park also has several lakes, a swimming beach, a campground, and nature trails. $.

CULTURE

Deerfield Beach Historical Society

954-429-0378
380 E. Hillsboro Blvd., Deerfield Beach 33441

The historical society oversees several sites from Deerfield Beach's early days in the 1920s that are now on the National Register of Historic Places. They include the 1920 Old Deerfield School, renovated by the city and open for tours; the 1920 Butler House, now a museum and office for the historical society; the 1926 Deerfield School, today the Deerfield Beach Elementary School; and the 1926 Seaboard Coastline Railway Station, now serving as the area's Tri-Rail station. The historical society also manages the 1930 Kester Cottage. Visit and tour the Butler House Museum ($), built in 1923 by James and Alice Butler, 9–4 Monday through Friday and 10–2 the first and third Saturday of the month.

Tubten Kunga Center for Wisdom Culture
954-421-6224
www.tubtenkunga.org
665 S.E. 10th St., Suite 202, Deerfield Beach 33442

This Tibetan Buddhist center offers classes and is a gathering place for meditation and learning. Classes $–$$.

SHOPPING

Reading Etc.
954-360-0909
www.readingetc.com
3201 S.W. 15th St., Deerfield Beach 33442

An opulent store for those who love the written word, this custom-designed Egyptian-themed shop has writing implements, books, portfolios, desks, handmade paper—everything a writer or reader might covet. But there's so much more. This shop is an offshoot of HCI Publishing—the folks who publish the Chicken Soup for the Soul books—and they offer tours of the publishing and printing facilities at 10:30 and 3 Monday through Friday. Free, but reservations are required. Open 10–6 Monday through Friday.

Beach Renourishment

At Hillsboro Inlet, sand that naturally washes away from the coastline and moves southward is caught by the jetties, and it's then perpetually pumped by a barge in the inlet from the north side of the jetties underwater to the south side of the inlet, where it forms the beach. This avoids the need for the popular practice of beach renourishment, which is constantly used in much of Florida in an attempt to replenish the beaches. The usual procedure involved dredging sand from the far-off ocean bottom and piping it to the shore. (Some sand has come from as far as the Bahamas to land on Florida beaches.) In addition to being very expensive, dragging the ocean bottom disrupts the sea life that lives there, creating breaks in the food chain that all life—including humans—depends upon. Using the jetties and barge pump system, Hillsboro has found a simple solution to recapture and reuse the sand from its own northern beaches.

According to the MIAMI HERALD, Broward County has put 7.7 million cubic yards of sand on its beaches over the past 30 years. The state of Florida plans to spend $200 million to resupply beaches with sand in the wake of the 2004 hurricanes.

Beach erosion is a constant problem in Broward County.

Lighthouse Point: Historic Hillsboro

Adventurers were drawn to the nation's last frontier during the second half of the 1800s and began establishing small communities along the coastline. Forging a living from the wilderness and working cooperatively with the local Seminole Indians, these rugged pioneers laid the framework for the cities and towns here today. Without rail service or autos, mail was delivered from Palm Beach to Miami by carrier, who hiked and paddled 136 miles to perform the service every three months for seven years. The service came to an end when one of the mailmen was killed en route, probably by an alligator while crossing the Hillsboro Inlet, which he had to swim because someone had used his boat, leaving it on the wrong side of the inlet. A memorial statue of the "Barefoot Mailman," Ed Hamilton, stands at the Hillsboro Lighthouse.

The "Barefoot Mailman"

DINING

Cap's Place

954-941-0418
www.capsplace.com
2765 N.E. 28th Ct., Lighthouse Point 33064

A National Historic Site, Cap's Place is a small seafood restaurant afloat in the Intracoastal Waterway, accessible only by boat. (The restaurant provides a motor launch.) Cap's has been serving dinner to the famous, infamous, and the rest of us since the 1920s, when a few enterprising souls tied a few shacks to a barge and floated them from Miami to this small island, creating a casino and rum-running drop point during Prohibition. Party animals such as Al Capone and Meyer Lansky have passed time at the joint, as have Franklin Roosevelt, Winston Churchill, Vanderbilts and Rockefellers, George Harrison, and Mariah Carey. The award-winning dinners of fresh seafood, island chicken, filet mignon, and hearts of palm salad aren't quite as exciting as the boat ride and historic ambience. Reservations recommended. Open daily at 5:30 December through May; closed Mondays June through November. $$–$$$.

ATTRACTIONS, PARKS, AND RECREATION

Butterfly World

954-977-4400
www.butterflyworld.com
Tradewinds Park South, 3600 W. Sample Rd., Coconut Creek 33073

When's the last time a few butterflies alighted on your hands and head? It could happen here, where thousands of butterflies live in several aviaries that create various habitat ecosystems. Visitors walk through the series of misty rooms, amazed at the sizes and colors of so many winged creatures. An outdoor area attracts wild specimens to the show, and a

Hillsboro Lighthouse

I e-mailed the Hillsboro Lighthouse Preservation Society (HLPS) for information about the Hillsboro Lighthouse and the tour schedule, and I received a phone call promptly from Mr. Hibbard "Hib" Casselberry, president of the HLPS, inviting me to come for a private tour since public events are scheduled only periodically. We made a date for the following Saturday. Hib called me at about eight that morning, saying he thought it would be okay to come ahead, in spite of the fact that the threat of tropical storms had turned into a hurricane warning overnight. Hurricanes can take days to arrive, and Hib said he didn't think they'd be closing the bridge and evacuating the barrier island where the lighthouse is in Lighthouse Point until about noon. A little unnerved by the impending storm, I decided to reschedule and spent the morning securing my home by nailing plywood sheets over the windows for the third time that year. Hurricane Jeanne made landfall at Hutchinson Island, 80 miles north of the lighthouse, late that night.

We met Hib at the lighthouse the following Saturday. He and a few HLPS members were cleaning up the beach area around the lighthouse, as there was quite a bit of debris, tree limbs, and things stirred up from the sea. A dock was broken down, its pilings gone, and some exotic trees had been uprooted. "They're those Australian pines," Hib said. "We've been wanting to replace them, but at least their roots kept the earth from washing away." He led us to the lighthouse, a rickety-looking construction that looked like it was made from rusty Tinker Toys. Appearances can be deceiving. This architectural wonder was constructed of iron and steel in 1907, and it has withstood numerous hurricanes, including the three in 2004. Built to reduce the shipwrecks on the reef that lines south Florida's coast, the lighthouse used very expensive technology—a Fresnel lens—that is still in use today and is regarded very highly for its complex design and ability to multiply the magnification of a weak kerosene light.

Hib suggested that he follow me up the 174-step spiral staircase to the top of the tower so he could catch me should I miss my step along the way. Saying he made the climb regularly, he advised me to rest at each landing and open the window for a breath of fresh air and to enjoy the view a moment. At each stop he told me a bit more of the structure's history and pointed out the exclusive club below, the Coast Guard cottages, the beach erosion, and the barge in the inlet steadily moving sand from one side to the other.

Hib and his wife, Martha, have lived in Lighthouse Point since 1965, and he is a Florida native. The central Florida town of Casselberry is named for his parents, who lived there when the main road, now a six-lane highway, was 15 feet wide.

"I've been through quite a number of hurricanes, including three in the north Atlantic. Hurricane Donna went through Lake Wales when I lived there, and these last three went through Lake Wales, too. We had four this year; last year we didn't have any. So what's the average? We had an upsurge, that's all. Look at this lighthouse; it's been standing here for nearly one hundred years."

small museum room provides information about bugs, butterflies, and birds. You can buy books and butterfly-attracting plants in the gift shop and nursery. Log on to the Web site for discount coupons. Open 9–5 Monday through Saturday and 1–5 Sunday. $$.

Fern Forest Nature Center

954-970-0150
www.broward.org/parks
201 Lyons Rd. S., Coconut Creek 33063

This small, peaceful, low-key park has a boardwalk through native forests, yoga classes (held at 6 PM on Thursday; adults only), astronomy meetings, and a nature center. This is a nice place for a walk, but not for a picnic. Open 8–6 daily. $.

Hillsboro Lighthouse Tours

954-942-2102
www.hillsborolighthouse.org
The Sands Marina, 125 N. Riverside,
Pompano Beach 33062

In operation since 1907, the Hillsboro Lighthouse continues to protect ships from running aground along the shoreline near the Hillsboro Inlet. Maintained by the Coast Guard, the lighthouse has occasional tours conducted by the Hillsboro Lighthouse Preservation Society. Charter bus tours leave from the Pompano Beach city parking lot. $$, includes one-year membership in the preservation society.

Hillsboro Lighthouse

Pompano Beach: Fisher's Holiday

Known as a retiree haven, quiet Pompano Beach is tucked between the larger cities of West Palm Beach and Fort Lauderdale, and today it has as many young families as retirees. A popular fishing destination, the town is named for the pompano fish. The coral reef also attracts visitors, who appreciate the reasonably priced quaint hotels and older, laid-back atmosphere of the town, which is bordered by a 3.5-mile beach.

LODGING

Cottages by the Ocean

954-956-8999
www.4rentbythebeach.com
3309 S.E. Third St., Pompano Beach
33069

These renovated and fully refreshed 1940s resort cottages come complete with kitchen, king-size bed, and sleeper sofa in the living room. Privately owned, the establishment is located in a quiet neighbor-hood with restaurants and a block

Preserving the Past

I met a brilliant woman who has invested in rental units in Pompano Beach. She began with two condominiums in 2000, and soon she had established enough equity to purchase a small complex of resort cottages, which she fully restored. Four years later she owned five older rental properties, which she rehabbed. Why am I so impressed? All the older properties on the coast are now being sold to developers, who raze the vintage units and build multiunit high-rises, so it's nice to see someone preserve the darling cottages of the sort I remember from my younger days.

Cottages by the Ocean Elaine Fitzgerald

from the beach—the Intracoastal Waterway and golf are close by. Rent by the week or by the month. $$.

Pineapple Place
954-761-8176
www.4rentbythebeach.com
3217 N.E. Seventh Place, Pompano Beach 33062

Rated a Superior Small Lodge in 2003, this like-new 1950s rental offers one- and two-bedroom apartments with all-new everything but the walls. Enjoy the amenities of modern life with the charm and spaciousness of yesteryear. $$–$$$.

Sands Harbor Resort and Marina
954-942-9100, fax 954-785-5657
www.sandsharbor.com
125 N. Riverside Dr., Pompano Beach 33062

In business for more than 50 years, Sands Harbor was one of the first businesses to settle Pompano Beach, building a yacht basin to serve visitors and residents from Palm Beach to Miami. On the Intracoastal Waterway near the Hillsboro Inlet, the Sands is convenient to local yacht brokers, dive shops, glass-bottom boat rentals, and snorkel tours. A favorite of fishers and boaters, the resort hosts two annual fishing tournaments, the Pompano Beach Fishing Rodeo in May and the Pompano Beach Saltwater Slam in June. Accommodations in the tall, balconied waterfront building range from hotel rooms to penthouse apartments. $$–$$$$.

DINING

Darrel & Oliver's Café Maxx
954-782-0606
2601 E. Atlantic Blvd., Pompano Beach 33062

This deceptively modest dining establishment near the Intracoastal Waterway has earned its reputation for serving excellent

Darrel & Oliver's Café Maxx

fare. Nationally known as a purveyor of fine foods, Café Maxx has been highlighted by restaurant critics around the world. The dark dining room is brightened with fresh flowers, and there are fresh meats and baked goods on display. The atmosphere only hints at the caliber of the food to come. Specialties include Hudson Valley foie gras, coconut flan, and apple torte. The cozy comfort of this corner restaurant belies the elegance of the dishes, though the prices betray the ambience. $$–$$$$.

Fisherman's Wharf
954-941-5522
222 N. Pompano Beach Blvd., Pompano Beach 33062

This restaurant, which serves seafood and burgers, is located on one of the East Coast's longest fishing piers. $.

Froggie's French Country Restaurant
954-941-0906
900 E. Atlantic Blvd., Pompano Beach 33060

The feel and flavors of Provence have settled in this tiny south Florida strip mall, thanks to the atmosphere, style, and cuisine of a French country inn. Spiced with antique lace, good red wine, and fragrant herbs, it's a little pocket of delight. Try the roasted rack of lamb or roasted duck with lemon

sauce—which you can order à la carte or as part of a full dinner (which includes a choice of appetizers such as pâté or a goat cheese and tomato tart). Perhaps the fresh frog's legs with garlic and seafood bouillabaisse is a tribute to Froggie's Florida home. $$.

Joe's Riverside Grill
954-941-2499
125 N. Riverside Dr., Pompano Beach 33062

This award-winning, four-star restaurant specializes in deliciously prepared fresh seafood, with stone crabs a house favorite, but aged beef also highlights the menu. Try the blackened tuna steak, rum-peppercorn–marinated tuna, or jerked grouper for some of the best seafood around. Whatever you choose, you're sure to enjoy the waterfront location on the Intracoastal Waterway. $–$$.

Romantico
954-946-9100
1903 E. Atlantic Blvd., Pompano Beach 33060

Romantico serves a small but exquisite Italian menu that includes memorable pasta dishes, salmon with lemon sauce, and seafood and lobster specials. $$

Romantico

ATTRACTIONS, PARKS, AND RECREATION

Lighthouse Dive

954-788-0208
www.lighthousedive.com
101 N. Riverside Dr., Pompano Beach 33062

Lighthouse Dive offers diving instruction as well as snorkel and dive charters. Open 8:30–5 daily. $$$–$$$$.

Pompano Boat Rental

954-943-7260
www.atlanticboatrentals.com
101 N. Riverside Dr., Pompano Beach 33062

A visit to Florida would be incomplete without spending some time on the water, whether swimming, snorkeling, fishing, or just relaxing. Small 20- to 25-foot speedboats come with instruction for half- and whole-day rentals for those who wish to explore the ocean reefs or the inland waterways, parks, and beaches of the area. Fishing and dive charters are available, as well as dockage for visitors. Open 9–5 daily. $$$$.

CULTURE

Pompano Beach Amphitheatre

954-946-2404
1806 N.E. Sixth St., Pompano Beach

This venue, open to the fresh outdoors (and raindrops), is shaped like a giant cup: up the stairs and over the rim, and you're in, looking down at the stage on one side. It's small enough that every seat is a good one, and the open air lends a peaceful ambience (even when I had a crowd of raucous bikers behind me at a Willie Nelson show). Tickets $$–$$$$.

SHOPPING

Festival Flea Market

954-979-4555
www.festival.com
2900 W. Sample Rd., Pompano Beach 33073

Flea-market lovers will love this one, which has endless booths of clothing, jewelry, gadgets, and games, plus a farmer's market. Open 9:30–5 Monday through Friday and 9:30–6 on weekends. Free admission.

Lauderdale-by-the-Sea: Surfer's Sands

Popular with families and surfers, this retro village maintains its premodern charm. A great place for a self-contained vacation, Lauderdale-by-the-Sea has shops, restaurants, and hotels (many of the small, charming vintage variety) that are all within easy walking distance of each other yet just a cab ride away from Fort Lauderdale's busier beaches and nightlife.

LODGING

Courtyard Villas on the Ocean

954-776-1174, fax 954-491-0768
4312 El Mar Dr., Lauderdale-by-the-Sea
33308

This quaint, private inn offers oceanfront rentals at reasonable rates. $$–$$$$.

High Noon Resort

954-776-1121; fax 954-776-1124
4424 El Mar Dr., Lauderdale-by-the-Sea
33308

A fabulous old beachfront hotel with rooms and suites that are perfect for those seeking a peaceful beach getaway. Advance planners may wish to inquire about renting the beach house on the property. $$–$$$$.

DINING

Aruba Beach Café

954-776-0011
1 Commercial Blvd., Lauderdale-by-the-Sea 33308

This beachfront café has a Caribbean atmosphere and serves West Indian favorites. Try the jerked chicken. Sunday breakfast buffet. $$.

Athena by the Sea

954-771-2900
4400 Ocean Dr., Lauderdale-by-the-Sea
33308

The Greek fare served here can't be beat for taste and cost, and Athena's is convenient to area hotels. It's also open for breakfast. $$.

Blue Moon Fish Co.

954-267-9888
www.bluemoonfishco.com
4405 W. Tradewinds Ave., Lauderdale-by-the-Sea 33308

A popular spot for romantic dining on the Intracoastal Waterway, Blue Moon is well

Bells on the Beach

The beach house at the High Noon Resort provides a fabulous place for a wedding. My husband, Jim, and I rented the three-bedroom oceanfront house for our wedding, which was held on the backyard patio overlooking the beach. The ceremony began at dusk, and the moon rose over us as we shared our vows. Our guests were seated on the lawn, but a crowd of strangers gathered in the sand below to watch, too. Afterward, the lawn was the perfect setting for an outdoor party under the stars. We and our kids stayed the night at the house and woke up to the sunrise over the ocean. This beach house is a rare treasure on the oceanfront, where so many small properties have been plowed under to make way for multiunit buildings that can be more profitable.

known for its delicious fine cuisine, prepared by chef Daniel Cournoyer. The backdrop of glistening water beautifully complements the elegant atmosphere. What could be better than watching the boats go by on a sunny day while supping on grilled scallops with chipotle-tomatillo ratatouille and blackened mahimahi? Sunday brunch. $$$.

Sea Watch

954-781-2200
6002 N. Ocean Blvd., Lauderdale-by-the-Sea 33308

This elegant oceanfront restaurant has, by virtue of its staying power over the decades, become an old standby for family celebrations. It's a wonderful way to let loved ones know they're special. The restaurant still serves the traditional seafood dinners that have contributed to its lasting power and fame, such as oysters Rockefeller and crab cakes, but newer additions to the menu, such as seafood paella and grilled dolphin marinated in a peppery soy sauce, help it keep pace with other area restaurants. $$–$$$.

Wilton Manors: Preserved Past with a Modern Attitude

This fun, funky town, with an openly gay and completely accepted mayor, was designed in the 1960s by Jim Pederson of Boca's Africa USA fame. The charming terrazzo-floored, single-storied brick homes are being lovingly revitalized and enjoyed instead of razed and replaced by high-rise condominiums, as is happening in so many communities. There are great restaurants here, as well as vintage and art shops.

DINING

By Word of Mouth
954-564-3663
3200 N.E. 12th Ave., Wilton Manors 33334

As if it's still a secret, this little pressed-linen dinner spot hides alongside the railroad tracks, boasting of nothing other than the fact that advertising is avoided: patrons discover this place by word of mouth. The fragrance of fresh-baked cakes and pies greets diners at the door, and those who make their way through a delectable dinner soon discover why advertising isn't necessary here. Although the place has a little more style than a buffet, diners still select dishes from those on display, and the selection is likely to change from one visit to the next. One thing is certain, and it's probably the basis for that spreading rumor: Everything is prepared with exquisite flavor. Some samples: chicken tarts with tarragon and walnuts; asparagus with curry; brandied cherry Brie with walnuts; pork tenderloin with Dijon and rosemary glaze; duckling "lacquered" with peach apricot barbecue. You get the drift. $$–$$$.

Old Florida Seafood House
954-566-1044
1414 N.E. 26th St., Wilton Manors 33305

This venerable landmark offers reasonably priced seafood in numerous variations. Quaint as its name sounds, this is a large restaurant in an aged shopping center, and it serves the area's freshest seafood in a clean, friendly, honest, down-home atmosphere with a nautical theme. Diners can dig clams by the dozen, or have their shrimp baked or broiled, scampi, tempura, gratinée, de Jonghe, or Florentine. In other words, there is something for everyone, no matter your favorite flavor or style of food. Pastas, meat, and poultry round out the extensive menu. $$.

By Word of Mouth is Wilton Manors's not-so-best-kept secret.

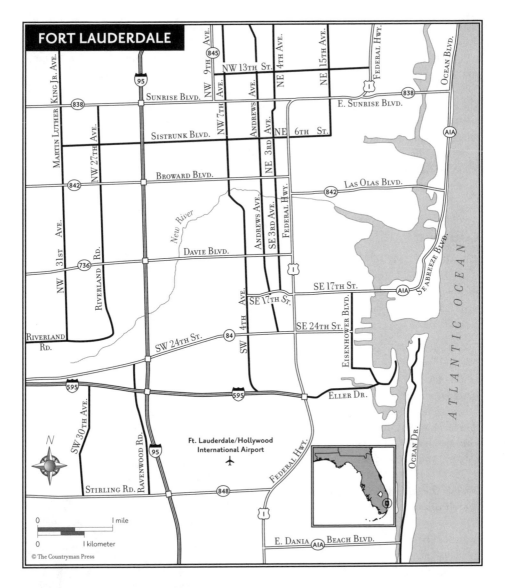

Fort Lauderdale: Angel Food Cake

Fort Lauderdale began on the New River. Stranahan House, which served as an early trading post, post office, and bank, was one of the first structures, and it's one of few remaining from the city's earliest days. But it's interesting to learn how the city established itself from the river connection. The river provided trade with the Indians and transportation to and from town. It was, in effect, the Main Street of the times for Fort Lauderdale, which eventually became known as the Venice of America because of its intricate network of more than 300 miles of waterways, creating prime real estate in a labyrinth across the city.

There are many places to visit that herald those early days: the Stranahan House; the New River Inn, now the Old Fort Lauderdale Village and Museum, home of the Fort Lauderdale Historical Society; the King Cromartie House, next door to the museum; and the Bonnet House, near Hugh Taylor Birch State Park, where an artist and his wife lived during those golden years.

Fort Lauderdale has tremendous museums, including the Fort Lauderdale Museum of Art, which served as the nation's first stop for a recent exhibit of Princess Diana's wardrobe and mementos, and the most visited museum in the nation, the Museum of Discovery and Science, which has an IMAX theater. There is the grand Broward Center for the Performing Arts, as well as an array of restaurants and shops that span the world in flavors, tastes, and price ranges.

Fort Lauderdale is an even more wonderful destination for spring break than it was when Marilyn Monroe helped the world discover it—but it's a splendid place for winter and even summer, too.

Lodging

The Atlantic
954-567-8020
www.starwood.com/luxury
601 N. Fort Lauderdale Beach Blvd., Fort Lauderdale 33304

Newly opened in 2004, the Atlantic is a premier luxury offering on Fort Lauderdale's beach. With sleek styling and spacious rooms decorated with colorful accents and complementary earth tones and black marble baths, the hotel offers the latest amenities, including poolside cabanas and a spa. $$$$.

Avalon Waterfront Inns, Beach Resort Waterfront Inn
954-564-4341
www.waterfrontinns.com
521 Fort Lauderdale Beach Blvd. (FL A1A), Fort Lauderdale 33304

This family-owned enterprise is holding strong against the wave of corporate invasion of Fort Lauderdale Beach. The Grimmé family has earned several awards for their attentiveness to customer service and personal approach to business, all of which add up to better experiences for guests. Rather than raze vintage 1950s inns, the Grimmé approach is to bring them into the future as boutique hotels. The Beach Resort has 59 fully renovated and redecorated

rooms with all the modern amenities, such as Internet access, massage services, and conference facilities (for an intimate group of 12). Across the street from the beach (no hotels mar the beachfront on this stretch of A1A), the hotel also offers a pool. $$–$$$$.

Baymont Inn and Suites
954-485-7900, 1-877-BAYMONT
www.baymontinns.com
3800 W. Commercial Blvd., Fort Lauderdale 33309

Intimate dining with a view at the sleek, sophisticated Atlantic hotel The Atlantic

This is a great choice for a reliably clean room if you have a car and prefer highway access to the beachfront. The Baymont has consistently offered rooms and prices that are superior to those of the other roadside hotels. $$.

Best Western Pelican Beach Resort
954-568-9431
www.pelicanbeach.com
2000 N. Atlantic Blvd., Fort Lauderdale 33305

Family owned since 1989, the Pelican recently underwent a massive renovation project to create an all-new resort. Freshly redecorated to recall the charm of old Florida, rooms feature French-paned doors, wrought-iron beds, and colorful, plush linens and upholstery. Most have balconies with ocean views and include coffeepots and Internet access. With a rare beachfront location, the resort also features two pools and a tube ride for the kids. $$$.

Doubletree Guest Suites
954-565-3800, fax 954-561-0387
www.doubletreegalleria.com
2670 E. Sunrise Blvd., Fort Lauderdale 33304

This lovely hotel, on the Intracoastal Waterway, is within walking distance of the beach and the Galleria Shopping Mall. The rooms are nice, clean, and well cared for. $$–$$$$.

Doubletree Oceanfront Hotel
954-424-8733, fax 954-467-7489
www.doubletreeoceanfront.com
440 Seabreeze Blvd., Fort Lauderdale 33316

It's hard to beat the ocean views at this hotel in the heart of Fort Lauderdale's "Strip," where vacationers sun on the beach by day and hike from restaurant to pub by night. If that's what you're here for, this (and a few others up and down the street) is the place. $$–$$$.

Embassy Suites
954-527-2700, fax 954-760-7202
www.embassysuitesftl.com
1100 S.E. 17th St., Fort Lauderdale 33316

Off the beaten path (i.e., the beach), this hotel is convenient to the Broward County Convention Center and the Intracoastal Waterway. Its nice yet comfortable atmosphere and interior courtyard and hallways make it a good choice for group events. $$–$$$$.

Hyatt Regency Pier Sixty-Six
954-525-6666, fax 954-728-3541
www.pier66.com
2301 S.E. 17th St. Causeway, Fort Lauderdale 33316

One of Fort Lauderdale's most enduring landmarks, the Hyatt maintains the aura of glamour and sophistication the rooftop restaurant has always brought to the hotel. Elegant, well-cared-for rooms. $$$–$$$$.

Ireland's Inn Beach Resort
954-564-2331
www.irelands.com
2220 N. Atlantic Blvd., Fort Lauderdale 33305

This family-owned beachfront hotel features freshly updated rooms, Jacuzzi tubs, and sitting rooms for privacy when traveling with children. It's comfortable with a hint of luxury. Café and restaurant on the water. $$$–$$$$.

Marriott's Harbor Beach Resort
954-525-4000, 1-800-222-6543, fax 954-766-6152
www.marriottharborbeach.com
3030 N. Holiday Dr., Fort Lauderdale 33316

A longtime Fort Lauderdale hotel, this one has a corner on the beach—literally. It's located at the end of the public beach, with a wide section it calls its own, providing plenty of fun in the sun for guests. The hotel is large and popular with meeting planners, and its spa is highly regarded. $$$–$$$$.

Radisson Bahia Mar Beach Resort

954-525-5194, fax 954-523-5424
www.bahiamar.net
801 Seabreeze Blvd., Fort Lauderdale 33316

Access is everything—and this hotel has access to the marina, so if you've brought your boat or plan to spend some serious time fishing, boating, or diving, then this could be the best place for you. $$–$$$$.

Riverside Hotel

954-467-0671, fax 954-462-2148
www.riversidehotel.com
620 E. Las Olas Blvd., Fort Lauderdale 33301

Broward County's leaders have been meeting to discuss plans and celebrate conquests at this lovely waterfront hotel since 1936, which was practically the beginning of time for today's Fort Lauderdale. The hotel has been expanded to include the all-new 12-story Executive Tower, and all the rooms now include data ports and the latest amenities—while retaining the vintage property's charm and elegance. Bring your boat—the hotel has a riverside dock. $$–$$$$.

Sheraton Yankee Clipper

954-467-1111, fax 954-462-2342
www.sheratonclipper.com
321 N. Atlantic Blvd., Fort Lauderdale 33304

The Yankee Clipper has helped define the Fort Lauderdale beach since I was a kid (a long time). Maintaining its popularity as well as its property, the hotel offers distinctive accommodations for business travelers, with easy access to the convention center, airport, and port, and vacationers enjoy the proximity to the beach, shopping, and the marina. $$–$$$.

Sheraton Yankee Trader Beach Hotel

954-467-111, 1-800-958-5551
www.sheratontrader.com
321 N. Fort Lauderdale Beach Blvd.
(FL A1A), Fort Lauderdale 33304

This classic hotel offers well-maintained rooms and features the delicious Shula's on the Beach steakhouse. Very respectable digs. $$–$$$.

DINING

Alligator Alley

954-771-2220
www.alligatoralleyflorida.com
1321 E. Commercial Blvd., Oakland Park 33334

This is a small, rugged sort of place where music fans can listen to live music without distractions as they enjoy native Floridian food: alligator bites, of course, and award-winning gumbo and bourbon wings. I like to wash it all down with a locally brewed beer called Fresh Beer #11, and there are many other microbrews to choose from. The owner, "Kilmo," aka Carl Pacillo, selects a mix of local and national acts to please the crowd—I love the house band, the Shack-daddys, who play "swamp music," and sometimes my husband, Jim Wurster, plays with his band, the Atomic Cowboys. $.

Atlanta Bread Company

954-522-0880
www.atlantabread.com
301 E. Las Olas Blvd., Fort Lauderdale 33301

The scent of fresh-baked bread may draw you in off the sidewalk for a hearty lunch or snack. The Atlanta Bread Company's menu features soups, salads, and sandwiches, including an Italian vegetarian and mozzarella portobello, all on breads baked fresh daily. A revolving weekly selection of soups tantalizes, with several vegetarian selections

Betty's Soul Food Restaurant

such as veggie chili, roasted garlic lentil, and mushroom with barley and sage. Salads, fruit, gourmet coffees, and pastries round out the menu. $.

Bahia Cabana

954-524-1555
www.bahiacabanaresort.com/restaurant.htm
3001 Harbor Dr., Fort Lauderdale 33316

This popular waterfront bar and restaurant is where boaters and boat lovers mingle over frozen daiquiris and hot wings. $$.

Betty's Soul Food Restaurant

954-583-9121
601 N.W. 22nd Rd., Fort Lauderdale 33311

If you're longing for collard greens and grits, they're here. Slow-cooked ham hocks and oxtails (tails of oxen?) and hog maws and pig's tails are all part of the old South. African American cuisine somehow was bypassed by fast-tracking West Indian flavors over the past couple of decades, but Betty hasn't forgotten the thick, saucy macaroni and cheese or smothered ribs, barbecue chicken, and catfish. She keeps the soul alive for all who like a little reminder once in a while of those deep, rich flavors. And she serves a mean red velvet cake to top it off. $.

Brio Mediterranean Bistro

954-525-3710
720 Las Olas Blvd., Fort Lauderdale 33301

When Brio boasts about serving natural Mediterranean cuisine, they mean it. The restaurant filters its water, uses raw sugar and sea salt, roasts its own coffee beans and turkey, and makes its own soups, dressings, spreads, and sauces. The result is delicious fresh Italian and Greek plates from grilled eggplant with yogurt, mint, and pine nut sauce to Penne con Funghi, pasta with porcini and peas in asiago cream. $.

The Capital Grille

954-446-2000
www.thecapitalgrille.com
The Galleria Mall, 2430 E. Sunrise Blvd., Fort Lauderdale 33304

Huge hunks of tender steak have made the Capital Grille famous here, in Miami's financial district, and across the nation, perhaps because of the house aging process that guarantees the deepest flavor. The dark, rich, men's-club atmosphere lends itself to business meetings and romantic dinners. $$$.

Carlos and Pepe's

954-467-7192
1302 S.E. 17th St., Fort Lauderdale 33316

Ease your worries as you sip limey margaritas in the darkness of this atmospheric, wood and low-lights place with soft music playing in the background. Or take one of a few tables outside in a corral facing the parking lot—either place provides a view of any of several TV screens strategically positioned for patrons. Carlos and Pepe's serves the usual Mexican fare with an extra touch, such as six different choices of nachos and seven kinds of quesadillas, including a red-hot chipotle chicken variety. There's also a famous tuna dip, crab enchiladas, wild tostadas, and fried ice cream. $$.

Catfish Dewey's

954-566-5333

4003 N. Andrews Ave., Oakland Park 33309

A local favorite since 1984, Catfish Dewey's is the place for inexpensive seafood, especially if you like it fried and crispy. As its name implies, this restaurant specializes in catfish (all you can eat nightly), but they fry everything else, too, from shrimp and frog's legs to pickles and mushrooms. In keeping with the tradition, hush puppies, collard greens, and coleslaw are served on the side. But if you're watching your calories and cholesterol, you can have your mahimahi, grouper, or salmon baked, grilled, broiled, or blackened instead of dredged in the traditional cornmeal. Or go with the peel 'n' eat shrimp all-you-can-eat deal on Monday and Tuesday. $$.

Charley's Crab

954-561-4800

3000 N.E. 32nd Ave., Fort Lauderdale 33308

Dock your boat and enjoy the view of the Intracoastal Waterway at this welcoming, cut-above-the-rest restaurant. Elegant and peaceful, Charley's is a bit hard to find, as it is positioned off the main drags of Fort Lauderdale and among the waterfront residential homes and apartments. Perhaps the best way to get there is by yacht. Once you do find it, you can enjoy imaginative seafood dishes such as Typhoon Thai's

cashew shrimp, shrimp encrusted with Brazil nut and vanilla bean, cedar-plank salmon with mustard-tarragon glaze, and Florida stone crabs (October through May). $$.

Chef's Palette Café and Grille

954-760-7957

1650 S.E. 17th St., Fort Lauderdale 33316

Feeling like a guinea pig? Have no fear. Chef's Palette is the laboratory restaurant of the culinary division of the Art Institute of Fort Lauderdale. Students prepare and present meals, serving the public gourmet cuisine for a song. Reservations recommended. Closed Sunday and Monday. $$.

Creolina's

954-524-2003

209 S.W. Second Ave., Old Town Fort Lauderdale 33301

Chef and owner Mark Sulzinski keeps his Culinary Institute of America diploma posted in the ladies' room, and while I don't know what that's about, his training shines through without the document. He crafts a mean gumbo, serves it up with rice topped with green onions, and calls it an appetizer—add a salad (served with a delicious ginger house dressing) and it's the perfect meal. Heartier appetites may prefer the crawfish étouffée, all washed down with a couple of bottles of Blackened Voodoo, a rich, dark Dixie beer. $$.

Old Town Fort Lauderdale (aka Himmarshee Village)

Once the main drag and marketplace of downtown Fort Lauderdale, Old Town continues to be popular as a dinner-date destination. The area alongside the New River at southwest Second Avenue and Second Street teems with activity on the weekends and provides a serene dining experience during the week. The peaceful Riverwalk curves along the community, providing a pleasant after-dinner walk, and the area is anchored today by the Broward Center for the Performing Arts and the Museum of Discovery and Science, both fulfilling destinations matched with lunch or dinner. A few nightclubs add a fast pulse to weekend nights, and this is the site of the SunTrust Jazz Brunch that runs from 11 AM to 2 PM the first Sunday of each month.

15th Street Fisheries' World-Famous Tuna Filet Mignon

2 cups thin Chinese Soya
1 tbsp. chopped fresh ginger
1 tbsp. chopped garlic
1 tbsp. coarse ground pepper
1/2 cup rice vinegar
1/2 cup sherry
1 cup chopped scallions
1/2 cup sugar

From center-cut, yellow fin tuna loins, have your local fresh fish market cut 9- to 10-ounce filet mignon–shaped steaks (about 2 1/2 inches thick).

Combine all ingredients above to create the marinade. Set aside 2 tablespoons per tuna steak. Marinate the steaks for one minute or less in the remaining marinade.

Marinade used as a post-cooking topping should be set aside before the raw meat is soaked in the marinade to avoid all possibility of food poisoning.

Broil or grill steaks to medium rare.

Plate the steaks and top with 2 tablespoons of the marinade.

Downtowner Saloon

954-463-9800
10 S. New River Dr. E., Old Town Fort Lauderdale 33301

This casual restaurant and bar, on the waterfront under the New River Bridge and tucked behind the county jail, offers sandwiches, seafood, and steak. $.

15th Street Fisheries

954-763-2777
www.15streetfisheries.com
1900 S.E. 15th St., Fort Lauderdale 33316

This seafood house has earned its reputation as one of the finest dockside fish

purveyors, and its offerings have moved it into the upper echelon of restaurant choices. There's casual dining downstairs, and upstairs is a bit more upscale and requires reservations. Both offer waterfront dining overlooking the Intracoastal Waterway as an added treat and a dock for those with boats. The grilled tuna is legendary (see recipe), and ingredients can be ordered online. The upstairs dining room is closed Sunday. $$$.

The Floridian

954-463-4041
1410 E. Las Olas Blvd., Fort Lauderdale 33301

This friendly, bustling place on trendy Las Olas is a great place to catch a late-night snack or early-early breakfast. Open 24/7. $.

Food Lovers Café

954-566-9606
1576 E. Oakland Park Blvd., Oakland Park 33334

Here you'll find delicious country French fare served in a casual atmosphere. Even the salad basket is a treat, with whole fresh leaves of Romaine, fresh vegetables, and memorable, tangy, homemade vinaigrette. Other favorites include salmon Florentine in puff pastry and Steak Diane. Dinner only; closed Monday. $$.

French Quarter

954-463-8000
215 S.E. Eighth Ave., Fort Lauderdale 33301

Let yourself be pampered at this delightful French eatery. Just a block off the beaten path, this is one to find and enjoy for its attention to detail and for its refusal to rush you through a pleasant dining experience. Enter the restaurant and enjoy the cozy, gardenlike atmosphere of lush plants, old brick arches, and sunlit ceilings. The menu, which includes French and continental cuisine with a Cajun–New Orleans twist, brings you oysters Rockefeller, crab cakes, Brie, or pâté to start; French onion soup, gumbo, or vichyssoise; and entrées of quail, beef Wellington, or medallions of veal *au citron*. This place is warm, friendly, dark, and delicious. $$.

Greek Islands Taverna

954-565-5505
3300 N. Ocean Blvd., Fort Lauderdale 33308

While the delicious Greek fare served at this busy spot is popular, the Taverna's not the place for heady romance: it's your table is ready, ma'am; eat; and out. Start with *saganaki* (fried cheese)—don't skip the salad—and consider an entrée of roast leg of lamb or charbroiled swordfish. Save room for the baklava. Rich! $$.

Hi-Life Café

954-563-1395
www.hilifecafe.com
Plaza 3000, 3000 N. Federal Hwy., Fort Lauderdale 33306

This cozy, comfortable café and bar, owned by Chuck Smith, boasts a rich wine list with a number of "great value" selections for the modest budget, paired with delicious yet moderately priced entrée selections. Chef Carlos Fernandez creates unique dishes with a French foundation but are inspired by whimsy and tropical flavors. Reservations are recommended. Closed Monday. $$.

Johnny V

954-761-7290
625 E. Las Olas Blvd., Fort Lauderdale 33301

Enjoy tapas and cocktails in the lounge or move into the dining room for Caribbean–New American cuisine from chef Johnny Vinczencz, formerly of De La Tierra at Sundys in Delray Beach. Try the jerked lamb loin or wild mushroom pancakes

Le Café de Paris

with sundried tomato butter. This is a standout. $$$.

Le Café de Paris

954-467-2900
715 E. Las Olas Blvd., Fort Lauderdale 33301

Taking a break on trendy Las Olas can be a high-profile experience or a relaxed afternoon at a sunny sidewalk café—I like the latter, especially when solo. One never knows when a charming admirer with sophisticated tastes might happen by, but this is surely the place to find him or her. Try pâté, French onion soup, and salad with a nice dry red wine. Scotch salmon, steak tartare, Brie *en croute*, or escargots bourguignon, followed by mussels *marinière* (mussels cooked in garlic, onion, and lemon) or curried shrimp with chutney, will make you feel exquisitely special. Try the fresh berries with crème or liqueur to finish with flair and extend the sweet moments just gazing at passersby. $$–$$$$.

Mai-Kai

954-563-3272
www.maikai.com
3599 N. Federal Hwy., Fort Lauderdale 33308

Once you enter this Fort Lauderdale landmark, you'll think you've been transported to the Polynesian islands. Flavorful Cantonese seafood and traditional roasts are served along with tropical drinks. Hula dancers and warriors perform twice nightly on a torchlit stage while delighted children and adults, wearing complimentary flower leis, watch from their tables. $$–$$$.

Mark's Las Olas

954-463-1000
1032 E. Las Olas Blvd., Fort Lauderdale 33301

Upscale, tasty, and famous, Mark's is a must-try. This trendy, modern establishment created and stylized by locally famous chef Mark Militello presents a picture of cool chic with its swirls of mosaic tiles dancing across the floor and stacked columns supporting the ceiling. The lights bathe the space with spots of warmth, setting a sleek backdrop for mahogany tables covered by crisp linen cloths. Artistic cuisines are based on fresh ingredients, sometimes organic, with exotic Caribbean and tropical flavors. $$$$.

Max's Grille

954-779-1800
www.maxsgrille.net
300 S.W. First Ave., Old Town Fort Lauderdale 33301

Here you'll find fine cuisine offered at rock-bottom (and hopefully trend-setting) prices. In an apparent effort to invigorate traffic to the Las Olas riverfront, which has unfortunately been filled with modern chunks of consumer-driven concrete, the restaurant has slashed prices. You can steal a Caribbean jerked grouper sandwich here for less than $10, at lunch and dinner. Also try the filet mignon and Atlantic salmon, which are priced the same. Try to go wrong. $.

Cabana dining at Nabab

Mezzanotte

954-761-8787
www.mezzanotteofbroward.com
300 S.W. First Ave., Old Town Fort Lauderdale 33301

I'm not typically fond of festival marketplaces such as the Las Olas riverfront, where Mezzanotte is located, but in this case I'll make an exception. The sleek restaurant has a cool, clean, high-tech interior that exudes an aura of prestige. Or choose an outdoor table and enjoy watching the New River flow by, along with the crowds of happy tourists. The first-rate Italian cuisine includes *bistecca pulcinella* (pepper steak), Scampi Mama Mia (shrimp with arugula, garlic, and mushrooms), and linguine *vongole* (pasta with clams). $$.

Nabab Indian Cuisine

954-567-3617
3025 N. Ocean Blvd., Fort Lauderdale 33308

Enjoy a casual dinner indoors or outside in a private, curtained cabana. This small restaurant provides reliably delicious Indian naan, vindaloo, tandoori chicken, mango pickles, and lassi. The lunch buffet is a bargain. $$.

Pier Top Lounge

954-525-6666
2301 S.E. 17th St. Causeway, Fort
Lauderdale 33316 (In the penthouse of
the Pier Sixty-Six Resort and Marina)

This revolving rooftop restaurant has the
best panoramic views of Fort Lauderdale
available without catching a plane. You can
fully appreciate the views from the terrace,
or just enjoy them indoors at your table,
which is strategically placed by the windows
so you can enjoy the full panorama over the
course of your meal. This is a wonderful
place for drinks and appetizers, such as
shrimp cocktail, artichoke dip, and a
cheese plate. $$–$$$.

River House

954-525-7661
301 S.W. Third Ave., Old Town Fort
Lauderdale 33312

Located in a historic home on Fort
Lauderdale's New River in Old Town, River
House's outdoor patio provides a scenic and
pleasant dining destination, and the indoor
dining and bar are equally charming. The
food matches the atmosphere, with fresh

The view is lovely at Shula's on the Beach.
Shula's on the Beach

flavors spiking traditional favorites such as
horseradish-crusted salmon and anise-
ginger calamari served in generous por-
tions. Happy hour (all days except Saturday;
complimentary sushi); Sunday brunch.
Closed Monday. $$$.

Rustic Inn Crabhouse

954-584-1637
4331 Ravenswood Rd., Fort Lauderdale 33312

This Fort Lauderdale landmark has been
dumping piles of crabs on newspaper-
covered waterfront tables since 1955.
Served with a bib and wooden mallet, the
fresh food is delicious, and the prices are in
keeping with the décor. Over the years, the
place has served Arthur Godfrey, Armand
Assante, Jimmy Buffett, and Johnny Depp,
all one-time locals. $$.

Sage

954-565-2299
2378 N. Federal Hwy., Fort Lauderdale
33305

Delicious country French cuisine is served
in a sophisticated yet comfortable atmosphere. Meals begin with an olive tapenade
that's irresistible, but don't spoil your
appetite—the real fun is yet to come. Try the
mustard-crusted *poulet* (chicken) or a crêpe
for dinner or dessert. Nice selection of
wines. $$.

Shula's on the Beach

954-355-4000
www.shulasbeach.com
321 N. Atlantic Blvd. (FL A1A), Fort
Lauderdale 33304

Come here for the lovely setting, lovely
view, and the classic menu of aged beef and
fresh seafood, presented by chef Chris
Gilmore and former Dolphin's coach Don
Shula, whose successful restaurants now
span the nation. While the aged Angus beef
is the star here, the house salad—crumbled

blue cheese and sugared-walnut vinaigrette over a wedge of iceberg lettuce—is also unforgettable. $$$$.

Sublime World Vegetarian Cuisine

954-615-1431
www.sublimeveg.com
1431 N. Federal Hwy., Fort Lauderdale
33304

Animal-rights activist and dishy bikini babe Pamela Anderson came to town to herald the opening of this upscale vegetarian palace in 2003, and the restaurant seems to have warranted the attention. With its cool stone interior and waterfall wall, Sublime's atmosphere helps diners feel as good as the guilt-free fare. Like many Sublime dishes,

the sundried tomato carpaccio and arugula with black olive tapenade and garlic chips is unique as well as delicious. The raw avocado and organic beet soup is also lovely. Who could miss meat with entrées such as eggplant Parmesan, veggie lasagna, and grilled portobello with Swiss chard, rutabaga, mango, and ginger? $$.

Sushi Rock

954-462-5541
1515 E. Las Olas Blvd., Fort Lauderdale
33301

The epitome of cool hides behind this unassuming though colorful facade. Dark, fun, and chic, the restaurant has a small sushi bar as well as tables. This little bar not far from the sea has a big-city feeling and some of the best Japanese cuisine around. $.

Thai on the Beach

954-565-0015
www.thaionthebeach.com
901 N. Fort Lauderdale Beach Blvd./FL
A1A, Fort Lauderdale 33304

Sushi Rock

Thai on the Beach

This is a wonderful spot for lunch or a cozy, exotic dinner with a view of the ocean. Thai specialties include the mouthwatering Thai Beach Salad spiced with chiles and lime juice and comforting pad Thai with rice noodles, peanuts, and tamarind juice. $$$.

Timpano Italian Chophouse
954-462-9119
450 E. Las Olas Blvd., Fort Lauderdale 33301

Although it appears unassuming from the street, a step through the wood and glass double doors reveals a dark, elegant restaurant and bar. With rich, dark woods, candle-like chandeliers, and lots of leafy greens, the place exudes sophistication, a perfect draw for barristers and judicial referees from the Broward County Courthouse around the corner. Rich flavors fill the menu as well, with blue cheese salads or tomato, mozzarella, and basil caprese; steaks, chops, and veal dishes cooked with garlic, sage, capers, mushrooms, and butter; grilled seafood with linguine; and Tuscan-style chicken with asparagus on the side. $$.

Tom Jenkins Bar-B-Q
954-522-5046
1236 S. Federal Hwy., Fort Lauderdale 33316

Jenkins's own down-home hot and spicy barbecue sauce comes slathered on chicken, ribs, beef, or pork straight off the fiery, constantly rotating rotisserie just off the small, picnic table–filled dining area. Collard greens, hush puppies, and sweet potato pie round out the meal. Takeout is available, or buy the sauce by the bottle and (try to) make your own. Closed Sunday and Monday. $.

Tropical Acres Restaurant
954-989-2500
www.eatattropicalacres.com
2500 Griffin Rd., Fort Lauderdale 33312

Owned by the Studiale family since 1949, this classic steak and seafood restaurant is very popular with seniors and longtime area residents, some of whom eat here daily instead of cooking. $$.

Victoria Park Restaurant
954-764-6868
900 N.E. 20th Ave., Fort Lauderdale 33304

Although its French chef founder has moved on, tiny Victoria Park continues to deliver the tasty, innovative fare for which it is known far and wide. With perhaps only about a dozen tables, this elegant little café, decorated in a colorful Caribbean-style theme, is a perfect special-occasion spot. The food is a blend of French and Caribbean. The Jamaican grilled pork is famous: tender slices of barely cooked viand surround a pile of garlic mashed potatoes, all drenched with just enough spicy yet rich gravy. Pair it with your server's

Victoria Park Restaurant

wine recommendation and follow with the flourless chocolate cake, a pudding-textured, mocha-flavored dream. Breakfast is served on weekends. Reservations are recommended for dinner (served Monday through Saturday). $$.

When in Rome
954-563-1349
3311 N. Ocean Blvd., Fort Lauderdale 33308

Friends of mine who are frequent travelers to Italy introduced me to this thin, crusty pizza, which they deem most authentic. Other delicious Roman entrées include veal Marsala, salmon Sciliana (in a white wine sauce), and gnocchi alla vodka. Closed Sunday. $$.

Windows at Ireland's
954-564-2331
Ireland's Inn Beach Resort, 2220 N. Atlantic Blvd., Fort Lauderdale 33305

Enjoy fine dining in a lovely glass-walled dining room overlooking the ocean with a fireplace for cool, breezy nights. Traditional fare includes Southern fried chicken served with mashed potatoes, gravy, peas, and biscuits; filet mignon; liver and onions; roast pork; and shrimp scampi, all deliciously prepared. $$–$$$.

ATTRACTIONS, PARKS, AND RECREATION

Bonnet House Museum and Gardens
954-563-5393
www.bonnethouse.org
900 N. Birch Rd., Fort Lauderdale 33304

This fascinating home was built in 1920, on a large 35-acre oceanfront lot, by Hugh Taylor Birch for his daughter, Helen. The home was a wedding gift upon her marriage to Frederic Bartlett, an artist. After Helen's death, Frederic married Evelyn, also artistic. The home reflects the creative whimsy of the Bartletts and is unique and beautiful. The grounds are thickly wooded, and a colony of wild monkeys lives in the trees. Seasonal schedule; call for details. $.

Harbor Tour's CARRIE B. Sightseeing Tour
954-768-9920
Departs from Riverwalk at Los Olas Blvd. and S.E. Fifth Ave., Fort Lauderdale

The one-and-a-half-hour cruise of the New River and Intracoastal Waterway eases past the homes of sunglasses kings and bakery queens, including many famous and familiar names from industry, commerce, and the entertainment world. Runs daily at 11, 1, and 3. $$.

Hugh Taylor Birch State Recreation Area
954-564-4521
3109 E. Sunrise Blvd., Fort Lauderdale 33304

This peaceful park across FL A1A from the beach was created by one of Florida's early pioneers, who came from Chicago in 1893 and settled in this near-wilderness, buying the oceanfront property for about a dollar an acre. In 1940, at the age of 90, Birch built his last home here. To protect his tropical wilderness from the surrounding development, Birch had the foresight to leave the 180-acre property to the state to preserve as a park. Today a family of gray foxes and hundreds of raccoons call the place home. The opportunity to stroll under the old oak and widespread banyan trees is a great pleasure to enjoy. The park features nature trails, fishing on the Intracoastal, camping, swimming, and an underground pass to the beach. Open 8–sunset daily. $.

International Swimming Hall of Fame Aquatic Complex
954-468-1580
501 Seabreeze Blvd., Fort Lauderdale 33316

This organization has a museum that commemorates feats of excellence in swimming and also hosts championship swim events, but its mission is to help ensure that every child learns to swim. Open 9–7 Monday through Friday and 9–5 Saturday and Sunday. $.

The JUNGLE QUEEN
954-462-5596
www.junglequeen.com
Bahia Mar Yachting Center, 801 Seabreeze Blvd. (FL A1A), Fort Lauderdale 33316

The *Jungle Queen* has become a legend, touring the New River for the past 60 years by day and offering a dinner cruise by night. It's a fun, quaint way to see the city from the water. Tours at 10 and 2 ($$); dinner cruise at 7 ($$$).

King Cromartie House
954-463-4431
229 S.W. Second Ave., Fort Lauderdale 33301

Built in 1907, the girlhood home of Frank Stranahan's wife, Ivy Cromartie, has been preserved to offer a glimpse of pioneer life. The home is reminiscent of a grandparent's bungalow, furnished with period antique furniture and decorated with lace doilies and china dolls. Open 2–3 PM Tuesday through Sunday. $.

Las Olas Riverfront Cruises
954-267-3699
Departs from Riverwalk at Las Olas Blvd. and S.E. Fifth Ave., Fort Lauderdale

These tours cruise the New River and inland waterways that weave throughout the city. It's sweet to imagine living in some of the grand homes with mega-yachts, or even the few older cottages that still show up in tree-filled patches during the one-and-a-half-hour cruise. Runs every two hours, 10:30–8:30. $$.

Museum of Discovery & Science
954-467-6637
www.mods.org
401 S.W. Second St., Fort Lauderdale 33312

Here young scientists can explore space and learn about atoms and sound waves, and budding engineers can study construction principles and values at the "home" that displays hidden pipes, insulation, and foundation. Hours of fun can be rewarded with a relaxing break at the IMAX theater, where films run continuously. Open 10–5 Monday through Saturday and noon–6 Sunday. Admission includes museum exhibits and one IMAX film. $$.

Old Dillard Museum

754-322-8828
1009 N.W. 49th St., Fort Lauderdale 33309

Built in 1924, Fort Lauderdale's first school for African Americans is now a museum that displays local African American culture and artifacts. Open 11–4 Monday through Friday. Free; donations welcome.

Old Fort Lauderdale Village and Museum

1905 New River Inn, 237 S.W. Second Ave., Fort Lauderdale 33301

Originally an inn for Fort Lauderdale's turn-of-the-20th-century visitors, the renovated building makes a great museum. Located in the Old Fort Lauderdale area, the village is composed of a cluster of historical buildings at the site where Flagler's railway crossed the New River. Open 11–5 Tuesday through Friday and noon–5 Saturday and Sunday. $.

SeaEscape Cruises

954-453-2230
3045 N. Federal Hwy., Landmark Bldg. No. 7, Fort Lauderdale 33306

Take an evening's ride out to sea, have dinner, play the casino or watch a show, and be back at port just after midnight. You can even get married on a SeaEscape cruise—I did! Arrange for a little privacy on board by booking a cabin for your evening cruise (call for rates).

Sea Experience Glassbottom & Snorkel Adventures

954-467-6000
801 Seabreeze Blvd., Fort Lauderdale 33316

Swimmers and those who prefer to stay dry will enjoy spending a few hours exploring the coral reef in the waters just off Fort Lauderdale beach in this glass-bottom snorkeling boat. All equipment is provided, drinks are available on board, and there is a freshwater shower for rinsing afterward.

The Stranahan House

954-524-4736
www.stranahanhouse.com
335 S.E. Sixth Ave., Fort Lauderdale 33301

Florida's first house was built by pioneer Frank Stranahan as a trading post in 1901, and it served as a bank and post office as Stranahan took on the roles of the town's postmaster and banker. The house became a home in 1906 after his marriage to another pioneer, Ivy Cromartie. Ivy became a young widow and owner of the home when Stranahan committed suicide in the New River after his bank failed in the Depression. She lived there until her death in 1971, and the home, protected by its listing on the National Register of Historic Places, has been restored to its glory days, around 1913. Touring the place, it's fun to imagine life in the durable Dade County pinewood home with its wraparound porches in the hot Florida wilderness and swamps. The ghosts of its earliest residents are reputed to waft about, so beware. The ghosts of the future loom overhead, however: high-rises cast shadows on this little house. Open 10–3 Wednesday through Saturday and 1–3 Sunday. $.

Cruising the Waterways of Fort Lauderdale: The Venice of America

Sunny, restive Fort Lauderdale has long been a popular destination for the rich and famous—but where do they hide? Residential neighborhoods near the downtown area around Las Olas Boulevard are certainly prestigious, yet they're still fairly modest, and it's rare to see the walled fortresses you might expect for movie stars and corporate moguls. The secret to finding the crème de la crème is our river of gold: a cruise of the Intracoastal Waterway provides a back-door glimpse into the lives of some of south Florida's well heeled and financially fortunate.

There are a handful of sightseeing cruises to choose from. The Las Olas riverfront hosts a luxury 55-foot catamaran, the JUNGLE QUEEN has offered tours aboard a double-decker riverboat for more than 50 years, and Harbor Tours has both the CARRIE B. riverboat (but not in the summertime) and a sophisticated air-conditioned yacht.

On my cruise, the captain makes the dubious-sounding claim that Jean Huizenga, mother of one of the nation's wealthiest men, waves from the couch inside her living room two or three times each day. Unbelievably, there she is, flapping away through the tinted window of her beautiful home. Mrs. Huizenga's son Wayne and his wife, Marti, have a rambling home jutting into the river on a point in Las Olas Isles, the area that gives Fort Lauderdale its nickname the Venice of America, thanks to the numerous islands created when the causeway was dredged.

Wayne came to Fort Lauderdale in the 1950s, took a job with a sanitation company, and became king of the trash industry, retiring from waste management as a multibillionaire and then moving on to develop a home-video empire, Blockbuster Entertainment, which he later sold. Today Huizenga and his wife are very active in local charitable events.

In addition to his mother, whose home is on the Intracoastal Waterway, Wayne's neighbors include his son's and daughter's families and a brother-in-law. Nearby is Bahia Mar, where impressive internationally flagged yachts and a pretty wooden sailing sloop are tied up at the dock—at a cost of $2 per foot, per day.

As we pass these local landmarks, we cross under the 17th Street Causeway bridge, and the shoreline takes on a whole different look. We've entered the realm of Port Everglades, where a tremendous amount of industrial commerce flows in and out of the country. Huge tankers and barges carry products that will find their way across the nation. Oil-storage towers and warehouses cover the landscape until we reach the ocean and turn around to make our way back along the Intracoastal to the New River.

There are homes that are owned—or were once owned—by the CEOs of Sunglass Hut, Renaissance Cruise Lines, and the FORT LAUDERDALE SUN-SENTINEL newspaper; the Firestone family; Presley Anheiser of Anheiser-Busch fame; the owners of Pet Supermarket; and the Maroone family, which owns 30 car dealerships in south Florida.

Some owners prefer to remain anonymous, including a physician whose Mediterranean-style villa with wrought-iron veranda boasts a $3 million bronze statue in the yard, and the owners of a 16-bedroom, 11-bath manse with its own gymnasium and spa. Some of the newer homes are owned by builders who bought the properties, razed the quaint older homes, and constructed multimillion-dollar fortresses, called spec houses, which look a little incongruous among the warm and inviting, lushly landscaped, gracious domains of a gentler time.

It's fun to imagine the Gatsbyesque lives that must be lived in this very real but fairy tale–like hidden part of Fort Lauderdale by peering into their backyards from this breezy perch. Too bad the cruise lasts just an hour and a half.

Water Taxi

954-467-6677

www.watertaxi.com/fortlauderdale/fllhome.asp

651 Seabreeze Blvd., Fort Lauderdale 33316

A fun way to explore the city, water taxis run continuously, making several stops along the Intracoastal Waterway and New River from Charley's Crab to the River House. Ask your hotel about discount passes. Kids ride for half price on Sunday. $.

Windridge Yacht Charters

954-525-7724

www.windridgeyachts.com

2950 N.E. 32nd Ave., Fort Lauderdale 33316

Windridge offers party yachts for private conventions, as well as corporate, wedding, and fun cruises. $$$$.

CULTURE

African American Research Library and Cultural Center

964-625-2800

www.broward.org/library-aarlcc.htm

2650 Sistrunk Blvd., Fort Lauderdale 33311

The beautiful new Sistrunk library provides a full range of general library services to the immediate community. It serves as a research library and cultural center for scholars, students, and the general public and contains more than 75,000 books, documents, artifacts, and related materials that focus on the experiences of African Americans. The auditorium and exhibit areas provide a forum to exchange ideas and cultural values and to promote an understanding and appreciation of the contributions of persons of African descent. Open 10–9 Monday through Thursday, 10–6 Friday and Saturday, and 1–5 Sunday. Free.

Broward Center for the Performing Arts

954-468-3337

www.browardcenter.org

201 S.W. Fifth Ave., Fort Lauderdale 33312

This huge, state-of-the-art facility with intimate and grand stages features Broadway shows and national performances. It's convenient to downtown and Old Town shops and restaurants. Tickets $$–$$$$.

Parker Playhouse

954-764-1441

707 N.E. Eighth St., Fort Lauderdale 33304

Located at Holiday Park, this is a nice, smaller, older venue for stage performances. Tickets $$$–$$$$.

War Memorial Auditorium
954-761-5380
www.ci.ftlaud.fl.us/warmemorial
800 N.E. Eighth St., Fort Lauderdale 33304

Located at Holiday Park, this is a nice venue for trade shows and events. Tickets $–$$$.

SHOPPING

Broward Mall
954-473-8100
www.browardmall.com
8000 W. Broward Blvd., Plantation 33388

Shop the Gap, Victoria's Secret, Burdines-Macy's, and Sears at this centrally located shopping mall. Open 10–9 Monday through Saturday and 11–6 Sunday.

The Galleria at Fort Lauderdale
954-564-1036
2414 E. Sunrise Blvd., Fort Lauderdale 33304

Home to the finest department chains, the Galleria is a shopping destination for those seeking pricey gifts from trusted names. Shops include Saks Fifth Avenue, Neiman Marcus, Burdines-Macy's, and Dillard's. Open 10–9 Monday through Saturday and noon–6 Sunday.

Hittel the Bookseller
954-563-1752
www.equa.com
3020 N. Federal Hwy., Fort Lauderdale 33306

This musty little two-story shop is piled floor to ceiling and wall to wall with more than one hundred thousand books, specializing in rare and out-of-print titles. Bibliophiles can get happily lost for hours. Open 10–6 Monday through Saturday and noon–6 Sunday.

Las Olas Boulevard Shops
S.E. Eighth Ave., along Las Olas Blvd., Fort Lauderdale

Las Olas Boulevard has been the hottest commerce center in Fort Lauderdale for the city's entire history. Home to the first post office and residence, Stranahan House, and transformed from an Indian trading post, Las Olas still draws crowds today with its fashionable shops, trendy art galleries, and wide variety of sidewalk cafés and elegant restaurants. With its tree-lined esplanade, the boulevard is a pleasant place to stroll day and night, and there are always interesting activities, from art fairs to antique auto shows. From Seldom Seen, a gift shop filled with functional art in all price ranges, to Chico's, a Fort Myers–based national chain of women's fashion shops that specializes in sleek, becoming, and comfortable designs for women who've passed the teen model look, Las Olas has something for everyone carrying a well-padded pocketbook.

Nautical Furnishings, Inc.

954-771-1100
60 N.W. 60th St., Fort Lauderdale
33309

Claiming to have the "world's largest
assortment of unusual and authentic
nautical items," this shop sells nautical
furnishings and props to restaurants
and other businesses, theme parks, and
the movie industry. This purveyor of all
things nautical will envelop you in an
intimate atmosphere of wood, brass,
and artifacts from the golden age of
seafaring. Open 8:30–5 Monday
through Friday or by appointment.

Victoria's Attic has an eclectic collection of antiques.

The Swap Shop

954-791-SWAP
www.floridaswapshop.com
3291 W. Sunrise Blvd., Fort Lauderdale 33311

The world's largest open-air flea market, the Swap Shop has a house circus, farmer's market, and drive-in theater in addition to 800 vendors on 88 acres. This community landmark is a bargain-lover's heaven. Open 8–6 Monday through Friday and 8–7:30 Saturday and Sunday.

Victoria's Attic

954-463-6774
Gateway Plaza, 1928 E. Sunrise Blvd., Fort Lauderdale 33304

Proprietor David Fernan has an eclectic collection of consignment furniture from Victorian to midcentury modern, and he'll try to find whatever you're looking for if it's not already among the goods packed wall to wall in his shop. A narrow path winds through the showroom so you can see it all, but his overflow has found another home, Victoria's Attic ETC, across the Gateway Shopping Center (which has several interesting shops, restaurants, and an offbeat movie theater) at 1998 East Sunrise Boulevard.

Whole Foods Market

954-565-7423
2388 N. Federal Hwy., Fort Lauderdale 33305

The Whole Foods chain continues to grow as more and more consumers become aware of potential hazards and allergy problems associated with the foods we eat. Whole Foods offers a full line of organic produce, hormone- and antibiotic-free meats, and prepared and packaged goods made only with the healthiest, purest ingredients. The staff is friendly and well informed and can help shoppers make well-educated selections. Whole Foods also carries vitamins, cosmetics, cleaning products, and pet supplies. Open daily 8 AM–10 PM.

Dania Beach: Ancient Antiques

Broward's first city, Dania Beach was incorporated in 1904 and named for the Danish farmers who settled the community and made it famous for tomatoes, although first it was called Modelo, for Henry Flagler's Model Land Company, which initiated the agricultural community. Dania Beach is now known for its historic antiques shopping district. Its dusty main drag, Federal Highway, is lined with antiques shops that seem to have been there forever, as well as an antiques mall of 30 dealers (most open daily). This town is just a few miles south of the Fort Lauderdale/Hollywood International Airport, making it a good spot to spend a layover between flights.

The public Dania Beach has a fishing pier and is popular with snorkelers and divers, who can swim offshore to the reef. The John U. Lloyd State Recreation area offers a shady beach and picnic areas. A sleepy town tucked between Fort Lauderdale and Hollywood, Dania Beach is a great hideout for a quiet day on the shore.

LODGING

Sheraton Fort Lauderdale Airport

954-929-3500, fax 954-920-4979
1825 Griffin Rd., Dania Beach 33004

Convenient to the airport, the Sheraton is also right next door to the fascinating DCOTA (Design Center of the Americas), where the latest and most unusual items for home and business are displayed in hundreds of designer showrooms. It's a clean, friendly hotel with meeting space and restaurants. $$–$$$$.

Dania Beach pier

Islamorada Fish Company

Wyndham Fort Lauderdale Airport

954-920-3300
www.wyndham.com
1870 Griffin Rd., Dania Beach 33004

At the Wyndham there are finely appointed rooms for business travelers, as well as a few amenities the family might enjoy, including a pool, Web TV, and Nintendo games. Convenient to the airport, DCOTA, and the Dania antiques district. $$$–$$$$.

DINING

Islamorada Fish Company

954-927-7737
200 Gulf Stream Way, Dania Beach 33004

Surrounded by a tropical lagoon with a veranda, the restaurant serves fresh seafood specials daily, or you can buy the fresh catch at the restaurant's fish market to prepare yourself. The restaurant is located in a huge water-sports and angling buying complex. $$–$$$.

Jaxson's Ice Cream Parlor

954-923-4445
128 S. Federal Hwy., Dania Beach 33004

Opened in 1956, Jaxson's is a bit of an institution in south Florida. With more than 50 flavors of homemade ice cream and sorbet and piles of candies and chocolates, the place is a kid's dream and a parent's nightmare. But just about everyone finds a way to make a pig of him- or herself here sooner or later. $.

Jimmie's Garden Café
954-921-0688
148 N. Federal Hwy., Dania Beach 33004

This is a wonderful spot for a light lunch, nighttime snack, or delectable dessert of home-made chocolates and confections. $.

Royal India
954-964-0071
3801 Griffin Rd., Dania Beach 33301

One of the region's most popular and enduring Indian restaurants, Royal India has delicious *chana sasala* (chickpeas cooked with onion and tomato), kashmiri chicken (prepared with herbs, fruit, and nuts), and shrimp *sag* with spinach and curry. Daily lunch buffet. $.

ATTRACTIONS, PARKS, AND RECREATION

Boomers and Dania Beach Hurricane Roller Coaster
954-921-1411
www.boomersparks.com
1700 N.W. First St., Dania Beach 33004

Here you'll find batting cages, bumper cars, miniature golf, and a rickety-looking but much-prized wooden roller coaster that brings shrieks and smiles hour after hour.

The Hurricane roller coaster at Dania Beach

International Game Fish Association Fishing Hall of Fame Museum

Open 10 AM–midnight Sunday through Thursday and 10 AM–2 AM Friday and Saturday. Buy tickets for individual attractions or get an all-day pass. $–$$.

International Game Fish Association (IGFA) Fishing Hall of Fame Museum

954-922-4212
300 Gulf Stream Way, Dania Beach 33004

A huge mecca for fishing and boating enthusiasts, the IGFA has information here about fish species, habitats, and anglers' conquests that will amaze even the most jaded fisherman. Hemingway's boat sits in the pond outside the museum, and an outdoor walk through a manufactured wetland provides an interesting glimpse of Florida's natural terrain. Open 10–6 daily except Thanksgiving and Christmas. $.

John U. Lloyd Beach State Recreation Area

954-924-3859
www.floridastateparks.org
6503 N. Ocean Dr., Dania Beach 33004

This peaceful, natural beachfront park provides a unique shaded beach devoid of shops and commercial activities, which makes it very, very special in south Florida. Perfect for picnicking and swimming, the 244-acre park offers access to the Intracoastal Waterway as well as the Atlantic Ocean, so bring your boat or canoe, surfboard, and snorkeling gear to explore the offshore reef. Nova Southeastern University maintains an oceanographic center here where students and scientists study marine issues, including sea turtles, coral, and water quality. Open 8–sunset daily. $.

SHOPPING

Antique Center Mall of Dania

954-922-5467
3 N. Federal Hwy., Dania Beach 33004

Among many antiques shops on Main
Street, this shop houses 30 antiques
dealers in one place. Closed Monday.

Bass Pro Shops Outdoor World

954-929-7710
200 Gulf Stream Way, Dania Beach
33004

Design Center of the Americas

A fishing and boating enthusiasts'
heaven, this huge warehouse is filled with every imaginable water-sports product, including everything from fishing poles and snorkeling gear to camping gear and boats. Open
9 AM–10 PM Monday through Saturday and 10 AM–7 PM Sunday.

Design Center of the Americas (DCOTA)

954-920-7997
www.dcota.com
1855 Griffin Rd., Dania Beach 33004

The largest designer showcase campus in the world, DCOTA has 775,000 square feet with 150
showrooms on three levels where designers exhibit their wares to the trade. The public is
admitted only when accompanied by a designer or on special sale days. Designers, on hand
for on-the-spot consultation, can also accompany you into the showroom and aid you in
selecting the perfect items for your décor. Open 9–5 Monday through Friday and 10–4 every
second Saturday.

Gordon's of London

954-927-0210
www.gordonsoflondon.com
5456 N. Federal Hwy., Dania Beach 33004

Gordon and his wife, Carole, import fine antique furnishings from Europe and sell them to
individuals, designers, and shops. Large pieces, heavy woods, and ornate styling characterize
their showrooms. Vintage Vuitton steamer trunks, linens and
lace, china, daggers, coins, and artwork are also scattered about.
Open 10–4:30 Monday through Saturday and noon–4 Sunday.

Jimmie's Chocolates & Confections

954-922-0441
148 N. Federal Hwy., Dania Beach 33004

Homemade chocolates and confections and fabulous much-loved gifts are sold here. Candy,
candy, candy! Open 11–6 daily. $.

*Jimmie's
Chocolates &
Confections*

Hollywood: Vintage Charm

Hollywood was founded by Joseph Young in 1920. Its main thoroughfare, Hollywood Boulevard, once stretched from the ocean to the Everglades, although now the Everglades have been pushed many miles farther west by development. Young's stately home still sits among many beautiful homes from the era on the palm-lined boulevard, one of the loveliest drives in south Florida. Moviegoers will recognize the bucolic beauty from the movie *The Hours,* which featured Julianne Moore cruising the streets as she struggled with mental illness.

Hollywood's downtown is a charming district of shops and restaurants. Though the city tries to recast the community as a tourist destination on par with Las Olas, it remains a pleasant haunt accessible to the less worldly and affluent. Hollywood is a working-class city with great appeal for tourists looking for affordable vacations in the sunshine that feature good food and fun without the glitter and gloss of South Beach and Las Olas.

Hollywood Beach has a unique "Broadwalk" (not boardwalk), a wide, pedestrian-only road that runs along the beach between the shoreline and the shops. The result is a friendly environment for beachgoers, and it makes for a particularly nice family vacation spot.

LODGING

The Westin Diplomat Resort and Spa
954-602-6000, 1-888-627-9057
www.westin.com/diplomat
3555 S. Ocean Dr., Hollywood 33019

The largest hotel in the county, with one thousand rooms, this is a bit of an anomaly on Hollywood's beach. The flashy high-rise came into being with lots of promises to bring revenue and glamour to the city. Some headaches were included, however, such as a problem with beach erosion that makes the towering building look as if it could tumble into the surf at any moment (don't worry, it won't). But the end result is an undeniably beautiful hotel, with rooms fit for royalty. $$$$.

DINING

Giorgio's Grill
954-929-7030
606 N. Ocean Dr., Hollywood 33019

You can make a night of it at this upscale Greek restaurant along the Intracoastal Waterway. At this evening hot spot, diners emerge from their cars like screen royals at the Academy Awards. Once you're

Hollywood's "Broadwalk"

The Westin Diplomat Resort and Spa   Jim Wurster

inside the flashy, Mediterranean Giorgio's, the feel is definitely elite supper club for the middle-ritzy. Those patrons not welcomed by valet might arrive by yacht, several of which are often displayed at the dock along the restaurant's wide windows. The restaurant serves a rich menu of Greek fare, including ouzo, as well as blue-ribbon favorites such as lobster tail, filet mignon, and seafood linguine. Giorgio's is a popular dinner spot for the holidays, too, when the menu features traditional turkey and lamb, as well as champagne. $$$.

Istanbul Turkish Restaurant

954-921-1263
707 N. Broadwalk, Hollywood Beach 33019

This is a fine place to stop for a tasty Mediterranean snack of hummus and Turkish salad, lamb kebabs, or baklava—each a bit different from the similar Greek or Lebanese dishes. It's a tiny shop with a few tables, opening onto the sidewalk of the Broadwalk and facing the ocean. Delicious. $.

Le Tub

954-921-9425
1100 N. Ocean Dr., Hollywood 33019

Just the kind of waterfront watering hole Hemingway would have loved, this cash-only pub hidden in a lush little jungle is famous with writers and artists who like to muse and moan over beers in an atmosphere that mixes poor-boy elements with cozy, comforting style. A woodstove warms the place with flames and aroma, and several booths are outdoors on the dock so dreamers can watch the boats go by or spy manatees in the Intracoastal Waterway. Others love the place for its collection of toilets—a duet of them serves as a favorite photo op for poseurs—and tubs, some serving as planters for tropical treasures. The fare—sirloin burgers, chili, gumbo, and fries—isn't spectacular. Open until 4 AM daily. $.

Martha's on the Intracoastal

954-923-5444
6024 N. Ocean Dr., Hollywood 33019

This is the perfect spot for a special occasion. A waterfront dinner spot for family elders and upscale traditionalists, Martha's offers a nice selection of seafood and steaks

Istanbul Turkish Restaurant

served in an elegant—if large—upstairs dining room with a view of the Intracoastal Waterway. It is especially popular for its Sunday brunch and is a long-standing holiday tradition for many locals. Menu options include roast leg of lamb, prime rib, Long Island duckling, lobster tails, and salmon. $$.

Now Art Café

954-929-9922
1820 S. Young Circle, Hollywood 33020

With a selection of teas, pastries, wines, and cheese, the café also serves up live jazz Wednesday through Saturday nights, hosts local art exhibits, and is open to ideas from citizens with a cause to champion. $$.

O'Hara's Jazz Café

954-925-2555
1903 Hollywood Blvd., Hollywood 33020

This blues and jazz club has indoor, patio, and sidewalk dining for lunch and dinner and music that lasts into the night. Traditional fare such as Brie and fruit, fried cheese sticks, and wings is served. $$–$$$.

Organic Juice Bar

Harrison St. at the Broadwalk, Hollywood
Fresh fruit and vegetable juices are mixed and served on an outdoor beachfront terrace. Open in the evenings only Monday through Thursday and all day Sunday. $–$$.

Sugar Reef Tropical Grill

954-922-1119
600 N. Surf Rd., Hollywood 33019 (on the Broadwalk)

Evolved from a tiny beachfront restaurant to a larger, brightly decorated restaurant thanks to the reputation gained by its delicious French, Caribbean, and Asian food, Sugar Reef offers some of the finest fare on this piece of the ocean. Owned by the same couple that founded Victoria Park, Robin

O'Hara's Jazz Café

Seger and chef Patrick Farnault, the restaurant offers the same delicious Jamaican jerked pork tenderloin as well as unique dishes such as the Sugar Reef Pho, a Vietnamese-style noodle soup with shrimp, chicken, and ginger. $$.

Sushi Blues Café and Blue Monk Lounge

954-929-9560
www.sushiblues.com
2009 Harrison St., Hollywood 33020

My favorite sushi bar, Sushi Blues is owned and operated by saxophonist Kenny Millions and his family. Millions roams the premises, waiting for his chance to take his seat on the small stage, sometimes with special guests (including his daughter on bass), and begin serenading diners with his acclaimed blues and jazz. Nibble edamame; grilled mozzarella, tomato, and basil sandwich; a rainbow roll; or ahi tuna—it's all outstanding. $$.

Taverna Opa

954-929-4010

www.tavernaoparestaurant.com

4010 N. Ocean Dr., Hollywood 33019

Delicious, sensual food is served in small, noisy dining rooms or on the Intracoastal Waterway patio. (There are also Taverna Opa restaurants at 3051 N.E. 32nd Avenue in Fort Lauderdale and at 36–40 Ocean Drive in South Beach.) *Horiatiki,* a Greek country salad, is a delicious combination of fresh tomatoes, cucumbers, onion, kala-mata olives, and a hunk of feta cheese in a rich Greek vinaigrette, and the marinated oak-grilled pork loin competes with the grilled lemon chicken for my favorite entrée. I like to arrive early for a peaceful meal, but if raucous fun and dancing on the tables is more your style, make a night of it. $$.

Try My Thai

954-926-5585

2003 Harrison St., Hollywood 33020

An original, privately owned restaurant whose rise to fame was meteoric, this place wins accolades for both its menu and its comfortable, sophisticated atmosphere. This small spot has a trendy, young urban ambience that fits right in with hip down-town Hollywood. It's dark and crowded, yet the space is cut into a few areas, which eases the sense of tight quarters and offers a little privacy for diners. In addition to traditional Thai favorites such as pad Thai and panang curry, try Sweetheart Lady—snapper with tomatoes, cucumber, pineap-ple, and onion—or golden curry duck. Also try the Magic Scallops, with garlic and sher-ry sauce, or Macho Gator—you guessed it—Thai-spiced Florida alligator. $$.

ATTRACTIONS, PARKS, AND RECREATION

Anne Kolb Nature Center at West Lake Park

954-926-2410

www.floridaconservation.org

751 Sheridan St., Hollywood 33019

Named for a south Florida naturalist who had the foresight to help protect the land from overdevelopment and loss of habitat, the nature center at West Lake Park offers educa-tional programs and exhibits as well as musical performances, yoga, and other community activities. The park itself is uniquely situated among mangrove forests and wetlands along the Intracoastal Waterway and offers a boardwalk tour of the various habitats and an obser-vation tower. Canoe and kayak rentals and tours are available (my favorite is the monthly full-moon tour), as are fishing and picnicking. Open 9–5 daily. $–$$.

Eco Golf Club

954-922-8755

1451 Taft St., Hollywood 33020

You can walk or ride the course at this nine-hole golf course. Open 6 AM–dusk daily. $$. (prices vary by tee time and time of year).

Hollywood Beach Golf and Country Club

954-927-1751

1600 Johnson St., Hollywood 33020

Walk or ride this 18-hole course, or practice at the driving range. Open 7–5 daily. $$–$$$. (prices vary by tee time and time of year).

Hollywood North Beach Park
954-926-2444
www.broward.org/parks
3501 N. Ocean Dr. (FL A1A at Sheridan St.), Hollywood 33019

This nice oceanfront park has picnic facilities and trees but no shops or restaurants. Open 8–6 daily. Free (parking, $).

Native Village, Seminole Indian Reservation
954-961-4519
www.seminoletribe.com
3551 N. FL 7, Hollywood 33319

This Seminole showcase of Native American life features a live alligator and reptile show and tours. Open 9–4 Monday through Saturday and 11–4 Sunday. $.

Sea Legs Marina
954-923-2109
5400 N. Ocean Dr., Hollywood 33019

Here you'll find charter boats, day fishing, Jet Skis, night fishing, and party boats. Open 8–7 daily. $$$.

SE Oceanic
954-922-8134, 1-877-277-3481
www.divefortlauderdale.com
5400 N. Ocean Dr., Hollywood 33019

Dive and snorkeling charters are available here, as are equipment and instruction. Open 7:30 AM–7:30 PM daily. $$$–$$$$.

CULTURE

Art and Culture Center of Hollywood
954-921-3274
www.artandculturecenter.org
1650 Harrison St., Hollywood 33020

Housed in a charming, historic, Spanish Mediterranean–style mansion built in 1924, the Art and Culture Center offers gallery space, a library, workshops, lectures, classes, and performances. It's a full-service yet intimate and engaging arts center. Open 10–5 Tuesday through Saturday (open until 8 on Thursday) and 1–4 Sunday. $$–$$$$.

SHOPPING

Doris' Italian Market

954-921-9647

www.dorismarket.com

2424 Hollywood Blvd., Hollywood 33020

Here you'll find gourmet Italian ingredients, meat, and fish in a village-style
market. (There are other locations in Plantation, Sunrise, Coral Springs, Boca Raton,
and Pembroke Pines.) Open 9–6 daily.

Organics by Josh

Organics by Josh

Harrison St. at the Broadwalk,
Hollywood

This fabulous organic market, on an outdoor terrace facing the beach, offers a wide range of
fresh organic fruits and vegetables gathered from local and global sources. Open 10–6 Sunday.

Suburban Delights: A Roundup of Inland Cities' Special Features

While a lot of what's special in Broward County is situated along the eastern shoreline, a
few gems have emerged as development has stretched into the Everglades. If you'll be
extending your range (via vehicle, FYI), here are a few of my favorites.

DINING

Brasserie Max

954-424-8000

Fashion Mall, 321 N. University Dr., Plantation 33324

Brasserie, the perfect place for a break from a shopping extravaganza at the Fashion Mall,
has a lot more style than the ubiquitous food court. Assess your shopping spoils over a
huge dish of the latest pastas, or perhaps try the seafood and vegetable mixes, or the
nice soups and salads. A glass of wine or a cocktail can help take the edge off the grind
of searching for that perfect something. $$.

Chef Steve's Carried Away Cuisine

954-385-5600

www.chefsteves.com

2221 N. Commerce Pkwy., Weston 33326

Nationally known food journalist and chef Steve Petusevsky happens to keep a deli sort of
shop close to home so his Weston neighbors can eat gourmet every day. As author of *The
Whole Foods Market Cookbook*, national director of creative food development for the chain,

and graduate of and instructor at the Culinary Institute of America, Chef Steve's offerings are guaranteed to be good for you as well as delicious—his claim to fame. Pick up a picnic if you find yourself in the far western reaches of Broward County. $–$$.

Chinatown
954-473-8770
8934 FL 84, Davie 33324

Chinese and Japanese specials, including a fresh sushi bar, are offered at this delicious neighborhood restaurant, located in a deceiving strip mall. I love the sashimi; the Yummy Roll (a wild concoction of crab, shrimp, masago, and avocado with crunchy tempura flakes); the avocado salad, with an unusual blend of seasonings and sauce; the Kamikaze Salad, with seafood and cucumber in a spicy mustard sauce; the fresh, clear soups; and the fried banana dessert. Owner Sue Chan works around the clock (with an occasional catnap in the back) to serve and satisfy her customers. $.

The Grapevine
954-475-1357
Plantation Community Plaza, 256 S. University Dr., Plantation 33324

This family-owned gourmet shop is a food lover's paradise. With deliciously prepared items for lunch or dinner or to take home for later, the Grapevine also offers fine wines to accompany the meal as well as the rare ingredients that make the dishes so special. $$.

Indochine Vietnamese Restaurant
954-452-8502
8916 FL 84, Davie 33324

Located in a strip mall a few miles west of downtown off I-595 at Pine Island Road, Indochine's Vietnamese specialties include fresh, barely cooked vegetables in a variety of light, tangy, and sweet sauces—none overpowering, all delicious. My favorites include Royal Soup, a curry and chicken broth blend with chicken and shrimp (single or family-size portions are available, or ask to "upgrade" the dinner soup for a nominal fee); shrimp curry; vegetable Bird's Nest, a pile of crisp steamed vegetables in a sweet garlic sauce in a nest of thin, crispy, quick-fried egg noodles; Pork Caramel, slices of tender pork simmered in a caramel garlic sauce and served with rice; and garlic frog's legs. $.

Pizza Gaetano
954-434-7945
4751 S. University Dr., Davie 33328

Pizza Gaetano is still run by Antonette and Gaetano, who opened the restaurant in 1979. He tosses the pizzas while she concocts tangy fresh marinara and white-wine sauces and the Italian dinners served with salad and garlic rolls. It's not a fancy establishment, but the fare is excellent and the service friendly. Closed Sunday. $.

Rosey Baby Crawfish & Cajun House
954-749-5627
4587 N. University Dr., Lauderhill 33351

This little strip-mall pub offers unusual fare—crawfish fresh from New Orleans—and music to match. Locals love it, and it's a nice suburban relief from the glitzy, touristy places. Late-night live music and food. $.

Wolfgang Puck Café

954-846-8668

2610 Sawgrass Mills Circle (the Oasis at Sawgrass Mills Mall), Sunrise 33323

Famous for his California restaurant-of-the-stars, Spago, Wolfgang Puck has gone on to create a winning chain of restaurants and a "fast" version with a few of the same delicious specialties for takeout. Puck's motto, "Live, love, eat," can be lived out in the easygoing, colorful atmosphere of his properties and in the scrumptiousness of every dish. My favorites are the butternut squash soup and the pumpkin ravioli with brown butter glaze and pine nuts. Puck's pizzas are legendary. Sit back and pretend you're a star. Enjoy lunch or dinner at the patio restaurant in Oasis, the open-air section of the mall, or get takeout from Puck's fast-food shop inside the mall. $$.

ATTRACTIONS, PARKS, AND RECREATION

Flamingo Gardens

954-473-2955

www.flamingogardens.org

3750 S. Flamingo Rd., Davie 33330

Flamingo Gardens has evolved into a nonprofit nature center dedicated to preserving a slice of Florida's natural environment. Once a private home set on 2,000 acres, the gardens now comprise 60 acres of various natural habitats and ecosystems featuring native flora and fauna, including alligators, tortoises, flamingos, and strutting peacocks. An aviary houses predatory birds, including eagles, hawks, and several types of owls. Tram tours and walking paths guide visitors through the menagerie and under the canopy of champion trees and fragrant flowers, all marked with identification. A snack bar, nursery, and gift shop complete the offerings. Watch for specially priced special-event days. Open 9:30–5:30 daily (except Monday, June through September). $$.

Markham Park and Range

954-389-2000

www.broward.org/parks

16001 W. FL 84, Sunrise 33326

On the edge of the Everglades, this park provides a nice view of the River of Grass (the nickname for the Everglades coined by Marjory Stoneman Douglas, who authored the book of the same name). Hike through the woods paths in the southwest corner of the park to reach a land bridge over the canal, and then climb the dyke for a fabulous view of the Everglades. Although there have been one or two reports of rare Florida panthers in the park, they were likely stray cats from the 'Glades. Since the creatures have a huge roaming range, they are certainly not residents of this expansive, edge-of-development park. The park is home, however, to deer, fox, raccoons, alligators, and other wildlife. Humans enjoy the model-airplane field; target-shooting range; boat ramps into the New River Canal, which accesses the Everglades; swimming pools; and night-sky observatory. A dog park is in the works. Open 8–sunset daily. Free weekdays; $ per person weekends.

Sawgrass Recreation Area
954-389-0202
www.evergladestours.com
US 27, 2 miles north of FL 84, Everglades 33329

Tour the Indian village and take a breathtaking airboat ride across the River of Grass, the Everglades. Oh, and be sure to stop and sample alligator bites before you leave—if one doesn't bite you! Gift shop, boat rentals, and camping. Open 9–5 daily. $$.

Vista View Park
954-370-3750
www.broward.org/parks
4001 S.W. 142nd Ave., Davie 33330

Vista View provides a rare vantage point above sea level in flat-for-miles south Florida, and one would be astute to wonder how and why there is suddenly a hill to climb. Officially opened in 2003, this "park" sits on 160 acres of the now-closed Davie Landfill. Bring your horse, fish in the lakes (catch and release only), or just spend the day playing with the kids. Don't mind the little exhaust pipes that poke out of the ground here and there, and pay no attention to the bits of broken plastic and Styrofoam you might notice mixed with the dirt on the ground. Nature will deal with all that—there's no problem here. Or so they say. (I'm not so optimistic.) Open 8–6 daily. Free.

Shopping

Fashion Mall
954-370-1884
321 N. University Dr., Plantation 33324

Quiet and sophisticated—my favorite mall. Open 10–9 Monday through Saturday and noon–6 Sunday.

Sawgrass Mills Mall
954-846-2350
12801 W. Sunrise Blvd., Sunrise 33323

Still billed as the world's largest discount outlet mall, Sawgrass Mills keeps expanding to keep up the reputation. The complex of stores provides one of the most popular shopping opportunities in the universe, apparently. Travelers are said to arrive from South America with empty suitcases to fill with the bargains they find here at outlet stores from chains like the Burlington Coat Factory and Saks Fifth Avenue (where shoes can still cost as much as $1,000!). It's easy to believe when you see the carts piled high with goods moving throughout the mall, which is so long that many senior citizens use it as an exercise trail. Kids like the mall too, thanks to Wannado City, a place where they can don the uniform of up to 250 different careers and pretend to be anything from a teacher to a doctor, fire-fighter, or police officer. Speaking of officers, keep your eyes peeled for officers on duty. Like many malls, this one's a hot spot for purse snatchings and car thefts. Open 10–9 Monday through Saturday and 11–8 Sunday.

WEEKLY AND ANNUAL EVENTS

Saturday
Pompano Beach Green Market Time
Flagler Ave. and NE First St., Pompano Beach

Local vendors offer fresh fruits, vegetables, plants, and more. Proceeds benefit the Pompano Beach Historical Society. Open 8–2 October through May.

Sunday
SunTrust Sunday Jazz Brunch
954-828-5985
www.fortlauderdale.gov
Downtown Fort Lauderdale and the Riverwalk

Held the first Sunday of every month from 11 to 2, this is a nice opportunity for a peaceful and pleasant stroll along the waterfront, with three or four jazz bands set up along the way, in the gazebo, in the amphitheater, and on the greens. In between the stages are booths offering signature dishes and drinks from several area restaurants, although some prefer to bring a picnic and blanket or chairs to enjoy the easygoing festivities. Free admission; fee for food booths.

January
Florida Renaissance Festival Quiet Waters Park
954-776-1642
www.ren-fest.com
401 Powerline Rd., Deerfield Beach 33442

Each year the Florida Renaissance Festival comes to Broward County for five consecutive weekends of medieval history come to life. Ladies and lords, fairies, magicians, jesters, and jousters gather in full medieval regalia to play out the past for the entertainment of thousands of fascinated fans. Join a game of human chess, dine on food fit for a king, and learn the ropes of master falconers in the birds of prey exhibit. Twelve stages provide continuous entertainment. You can also learn how to make period crafts and buy the hand-iwork of artisans. $$.

April
Air and Sea Show
http://nationalsalute.com

An estimated 4 million people crowd onto Fort Lauderdale's beaches to watch this two-day military air show. Free.

April Pompano Beach Seafood Festival

954-570-7785
www.pompanobeachseafoodfestival.com
Atlantic Blvd. and FL A1A, Pompano Beach

Relax beachside for a few hours or a few days to the sounds of classic rock (performed by national vintage bands and cover shows, including local retro-rockers the Low Tides). Also enjoy games, crafts, and more seafood than you can imagine from several area restaurants. This is a nice spring festival—don't forget your beach gear and chairs. $.

Ocean Fest Dive & Adventure Sports Expo

954-462-6000
www.oceanfest.com
Lauderdale-by-the-Sea

This festival offers scuba and snorkel instruction, more than two hundred dive-related exhibits, an underwater treasure hunt, an underwater music festival, shore diving, and prizes. $–$$.

May

Cajun Zydeco Crawfish Festival

954-828-5934
Fort Lauderdale Stadium

This annual festival features music and food from New Orleans. Eat, dance, listen, and enjoy! $$–$$$.

June

Mango Festival

954-480-4433
www.deerfield-beach.com
Westside Park, Deerfield Beach

This fun festival celebrates the beautiful ripe mango and the multicultural population that enjoys the delicious fruit throughout the tropics. Enjoy mango jellies and shakes while listening to rhythm and blues, gospel, hip-hop, and poetry and perusing arts and crafts. The weekend festival kicks off with a Saturday-morning parade. $.

National Week of the Ocean Festival

954-462-5573
www.national-week-of-the-ocean.org

Not just a single event, National Week of the Ocean is a banner under which many ocean-related activities are joined to help raise awareness of the seas. During this week a school fair is held to showcase student projects, community beach and waterway cleanups are held, and special events are held at area attractions and retailers, including a marine fair at the IGFA Hall of Fame Museum (www.igfa.org; 300 Gulf Stream Way, Dania Beach 33004). Price varies by event.

Oceanwatch Reef Sweep and Beach Cleanup
954-467-1366
www.oceanwatch.org

Hundreds of divers and beach walkers pitch in to clean up Broward and Palm Beach County beaches and reefs. The total take since 1989 is more than 24 tons of trash. Call for the beach and dive location where you can join the fun. Free.

August
Hollywood Beach Clam Bake
954-924-2980
Hollywood Broadwalk

This all-American celebration, which takes place in August and September, includes sand castle displays and a contest as well as a treasure hunt on the Broadwalk. Free admission.

September
Savor Greater Fort Lauderdale
954-921-6176
www.savorfl.com
Fort Lauderdale

Enjoy prix fixe bargains at primo restaurants around town all month long. $$–$$$.

October
Fort Lauderdale International Film Festival (FLIFF)
954-760-9898
www.fliff.com
Cinema Paradiso, 503 S.E. Sixth St., Fort Lauderdale 33301

Film screenings of more than one hundred movies are shown at FLIFF's home, Cinema Paradiso, and in theaters from Boca Raton to Miami. $–$$.

November
Hollywood Jazz Festival
954-424-4440, 1-877-877-7677
www.southfloridajazz.org
Hollywood Central Performing Arts Center, 1770 Monroe St., Hollywood 33020

This weekend festival features national jazz performers. The South Florida JAZZ is dedicated to promoting the American art of jazz by providing educational programs, opportunities for local musicians to share their talents and venue for national performers. $$.

December
Annual Holiday Boat Parade
954-941-2940
www.pompanobeachchamber.com/boat_parade.html

Touted as the nation's oldest boat parade. Spectators watch from the shores of the Intracoastal Waterway as decorated yachts and smaller boats make their way from Lake Santa Barbara in Pompano Beach north to Deerfield Beach. Prizes for decorations. Free.

Ocean Dance
954-921-3274
www.artandculturecenter.org
Hollywood Beach

Ballet on the beach—it's worth enjoying for the wafting classical music under the night sky even if you can't get a seat in view of the stage. Free admission.

Winterfest Boat Parade
954-767-0686
www.winterfestparade.com
Fort Lauderdale

Touted as the "world's most watched parade," Winterfest is tied to a month of parties and events, all centered around the colorful boat parade that lasts about an hour and a half. Traffic to the waterfront can be heavy, and it can be tough to get a seat to enjoy the show, but it's one of the most enjoyable events in town for participants and spectators alike. Reservations at waterfront restaurants are booked weeks in advance for premium-priced seats by those who enjoy the view while dining. Grandstand seats are also available at Hugh Taylor Birch State Park along the Intracoastal Waterway. $$.

EMERGENCY NUMBERS

In an emergency, dial 911.
Poison information: 1-800-222-1222
Police, nonemergency: 954-967-4357
Fire, nonemergency: 954-967-4248
Hurricane information hotline: 954-831-4000

HOSPITALS

Broward General Medical Center
954-355-4400
1600 S. Andrews Ave., Fort Lauderdale 33316

Hollywood Medical Center
954-966-4500
3600 Washington St., Hollywood 33021

Imperial Point Medical Center
954-776-8500
6401 N. Federal Hwy., Fort Lauderdale 33308

Memorial Regional Hospital
954-987-2000
3501 Johnson St., Hollywood 33021

North Broward Medical Center
954-941-8300
201 E Sample Rd., Pompano Beach 33064

Plantation General Hospital
954-587-5010
401 N.W. 42nd Ave., Plantation 33317

Westside Regional Medical Center
954-473-6600
8201 W. Broward Blvd., Plantation 33324

NEWSPAPERS

Broward Herald
954-538-7227
www.miami.com

Daily Business Review
954-468-2600
www.dailybusinessreview.com

Fort Lauderdale Sun-Sentinel
954-356-4160
www.sun-sentinel.com

South Florida Business Journal
954-359-2100
www.southflorida.bizjournals.com

TRANSPORTATION

Amtrak
800-872-7245

Fort Lauderdale/Hollywood International Airport
Info line: 954-359-6100
www.broward.org/airport
320 Terminal Dr., Fort Lauderdale 33315

Greyhound Lines Station
954-764-6551, 1-800-231-2222
515 N.E. Third St., Fort Lauderdale 33301

Tri-Rail Stations
1-800-TRI-RAIL
www.tri-rail.com

Cypress Creek station (6151 N. Andrews Way, Fort Lauderdale 33309)
Deerfield Beach station (1300 W. Hillsboro Blvd., Deerfield Beach 33442)
Fort Lauderdale/Hollywood International Airport at Dania Beach (500 Gulf Stream Way, Dania Beach 33004)
Fort Lauderdale station (200 S.W. 21st Terr., Fort Lauderdale 33312)
Hollywood station (3001 Hollywood Blvd., Hollywood 33021)
Pompano Beach station (3491 N.W. Eighth Ave., Pompano Beach 33064)
Sheridan Street station (2900 Sheridan St., Fort Lauderdale 33070)

TAXIS AND LIMOUSINES

Bel-Air Limousine Service
954-925-5555

Bradley Executive Limousine
954-370-0505

Broward County Transit
954-357-8400

Dolphin Limousine Service
954-989-5466

The Tri-County AIRPORT EXPRESS
954-561-8888
Reserve shuttle service to the airport.

TOURISM CONTACTS

Greater Fort Lauderdale
954-357-5700
www.broward.org/arts

Greater Fort Lauderdale Convention & Visitors Bureau
1-800-22-SUNNY
www.sunny.org
100 E. Broward Blvd., Suite 200, Fort Lauderdale 33301

The Hollywood Office of Tourism and Tourism Information Center
1-800-231-5562
www.visithollywood.org
330 N. Federal Hwy., Hollywood 33020

VISIT FLORIDA
850-488-5607
www.flausa.com
661 E. Jefferson St., Suite 300, Tallahassee 32301

Miami-Dade County

Glittery Cookie Crust

We've visited the crème de la crème icing in Palm Beach and the angel cake in Fort Lauderdale, and now we've reached Miami, the Magic City, land of glitter and glitz, glamour and mystique. Miami is the crust of the cake, the foundation of south Florida. Here you'll find everything imaginable and more. It's called the Magic City thanks to its practically instant development at the turn of the 19th century, and Miami's magic continues to evolve.

Thanks to pioneers Mary Brickell and Julia Tuttle, Miami is said to be the only city in the nation settled by women. These women invited Henry Flagler to consider bringing his railway to their town after a freeze rendered his resort mecca of Palm Beach too cold for fun. They drove their point home with a gift of fresh citrus blossoms, untainted by the recent freeze that had devastated crops in central Florida and Palm Beach. The train soon was under way, although some early Miami settlers, including Commodore Ralph Munroe of Cocoanut Grove (as it was spelled at the time), were not so excited to see the signs of progress. Munroe understandably preferred to keep his paradise to himself, but progress came to town just the same, and more quickly than Munroe could stop it.

Today Miami is known as the Gateway to the Americas because it serves as an entry point for cargo and immigrants from Cuba and Central and South America. The Latin influence is more than noticeable in Miami—the population is now more than half Hispanic. More than 125 languages are spoken in homes across Miami-Dade County. This is the land of opportunity, and countless thousands of people have risked their lives and disrupted their families for the chance to come here and achieve the American Dream.

This amazing diversity brings many riches to the city. Visitors can sample a huge variety of authentic cuisines, as well as culinary offerings from nationally acclaimed, cutting-edge chefs, many of whom either started here or found their way to this international hot spot. Foodies will love visiting the Homestead farmland during the December–June growing season for fresh strawberries, tomatoes, and a wide variety of tropical fruits.

Shopping opportunities are exceptional here, too, thanks to the fact that our port welcomes goods from worldwide trade markets. Look to South Beach and Lincoln Road for the offbeat, to Bayside for international gifts, to Coral Gables for sophisticated goods, and to Coconut Grove for quirky fun.

Miami's beaches have garnered some acclaim of late. *USA Today* rated Miami as the number-one city for "best clothing-optional beach" in 2004. Haulover, North Miami's beach, has distinctly separate beach areas for nudists, gays, and families.

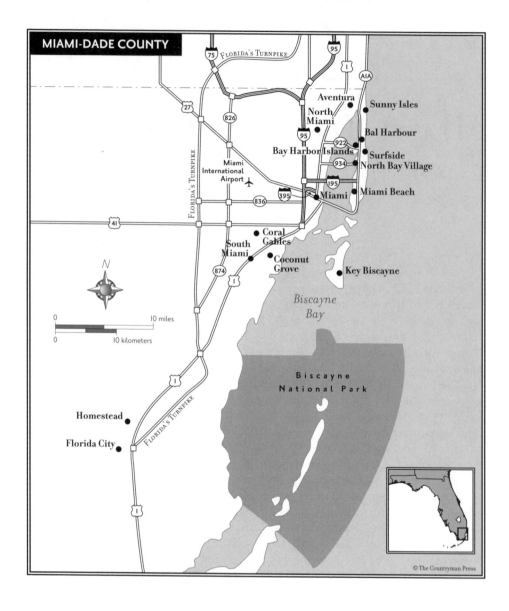

USA Today also ranked South Beach as the number-one beach for best nightlife, and *National Geographic Magazine* listed Miami beaches among its top ten favorites. *Hispanic Magazine* rated Miami as the number-one city for Hispanic living, and *Natural Health* rated Miami the number-one healthiest city.

In 2003 Miami hosted 10.5 million visitors, with an impact of $15.4 billion on the local economy. Travelers are kings and queens in this town. While the traveling life can often be a little tedious, you can bet that you won't find the same old shops and the same old restaurants in Miami—there's nothing humdrum here. Miami has some of the best-known names in retail and cuisine, and the most wonderful corners of this beautiful town can't be found anywhere else in the universe.

Aventura: High Roller's Haven

An upscale residential and shopping community on the northeast tip of Miami, this is a land of high-rises, high-style stores, and high prices.

DINING

The Bamboo Club Asian Bistro

305-466-7100
www.thebambooclub.com
19501 Biscayne Blvd., Aventura 33180

This is the perfect place for a pre-, mid-, or postshopping snack at the Aventura Mall. Try the delicious lettuce wraps, spicy soup, or Korean steak. Many different Asian cuisines are successfully represented on the menu at this small chain. $$.

Chef Allen's Restaurant

305-935-2900
www.chefallens.com
19088 N.E. 29th Ave., Aventura 33180

At this highly rated restaurant, chef Allen Susser turned Florida's luscious mangos into the haute cuisine complement of the decade. With his peers, Susser pioneered New World cuisine, which combines influences of Caribbean and Latin cultures to create a subtropical, south Florida flavor featuring mangos and citrus. The menu here fuses the ingredients and flavors of many cuisines and cultures, such as the Mediterranean, including Provence, Sicily, and Basque Country; the Americas and the Caribbean; and Asia, including Thailand, Vietnam, Japan, and India. Susser has a great summer deal for diners: he offers dinner for two in trade for a wheelbarrowful (200 pounds) of fresh mangos. Although it's not likely you'll find one in your hotel courtyard, these tall trees grace many south Florida lawns, and their ripe pink and purple fruit sags from branches throughout the summer. Open daily for dinner only; jackets suggested. $$–$$$.

Red Thai Room

305-792-0232
Promenade Shops, 20301 Biscayne Blvd., Aventura 33180

Although the menu boasts a huge variety of imported beers, many were unavailable, so I finally chose wine. The restaurant is cozy and red, just as its name indicates. The spicy shrimp salad wasn't as flavorful as it might have been, but the curried duck didn't disappoint. Closed Monday. $–$$.

SHOPPING

Aventura Mall

305-935-1110
www.shopaventuramall.com
19501 Biscayne Blvd., Aventura 33180

From Abercrombie and Fitch to Bloomingdale's, Caché, and Chico's, there are more than two hundred shops and department stores to keep spenders happy for untold hours. Open 10–9:30 Monday through Saturday and noon–8 Sunday.

North Miami: Neighborly and Nice

North Miami is a nice place to get away from the glitz of the Gold Coast for a few hours and spend an evening as a local. The strip of Northeast 123rd Street (exit I-95 at 125th Street and head east; it curves into 123rd) is mellow and a little easier on the pocketbook than most shorefront activities. On Friday nights special events are frequently offered at both the Museum of Contemporary Art (MOCA) and the Luna Star Café. Begin the evening with comfortable yet distinguished and delectable continental fare at Biscayne Wine Merchants—all are within an easy stroll of one another.

DINING

Biscayne Wine Merchants
305-899-1997
738 N.E. 125 St., N. Miami 33161

This wine seller and restaurant offers a wonderful respite in a cultured yet casual and relaxing atmosphere. Rich French country and continental dishes are drenched in delectable sauces and include flaky pastries and tender meats. It's sophisticated comfort food in an urban environment. The outstanding selection of 700 wines and 150 beers is a great plus. Lunch and dinner specials promise something delicious as well as affordable. The menu includes goat, trout, bouillabaisse, rack of lamb, veal Parmesan, and New York strip, plus sandwiches, salads, and desserts. The restaurant prides itself on preparing rich foods without butter—instead using olive oil and herbs, and using a wok for healthful cooking. Closed Sunday. $$.

Little Saigon
305-295-4411
16752 N. Miami Ave., N. Miami Beach 33162

There's nothing fancy about this authentic Vietnamese diner, which has a dozen or so tables served by waitresses who prefer to take orders by number rather than navigate language barriers. The expansive menu provides color photos of many of the dishes, which are generous and simply delicious. My favorites include number 13, Goi Du Du (green papaya salad); number 61, Bun Ga Nuong (dark chicken with vermicelli noodles); number 70, Bun Tom Xao Xa Ot (shrimp lemongrass with vermicelli); number 157, Canh Chua Chay (hot and sour vegetable soup); and number 163, Cai Ngot Zao Toi (mustard greens with garlic). Add Vietnamese iced coffee or red bean paste with coconut milk for a sweet, refreshing finish. You can sample quite a few offerings here for a modest price. The restaurant is located just east of the Golden Glades interchange—where I-95 and Florida's Turnpike meet FL 826 at 163rd Street—and a block north on Miami Avenue. It's in a very nondescript building next to a convenience store. $.

Museum of Contemporary Art (MOCA) Greater Miami Convention and Visitors Bureau

Luna Star Café and Gallery
305-892-8522
775 N.E. 125th St., N. Miami 33161

A showcase for local talent and traveling minstrels, this tiny storefront is a favorite among the Florida folk-music community. There's a wide selection of imported beers, and the kitchen offers a few snacks. Most weekend evenings include a montage of local talent, storytelling, and often a traveling musical act. $.

ATTRACTIONS, PARKS, AND RECREATION

Museum of Contemporary Art (MOCA)
305-893-6211
www.mocanomi.org
770 N.E. 125th St., N. Miami 33161

This 23,000-square-foot space celebrates contemporary art such as that of Roy Lichtenstein, star of the comic-book look, and others of the avant-garde but not gone genres. Frequent events include films, lectures, and concerts on the large outdoor patio that opens onto the street. The great gift shop sells nifty gifts reflective of contemporary art—there's something for everyone. Open 11–5 Tuesday through Saturday and noon–5 Sunday. $.

Oleta River State Recreation Area
305-919-1846
3400 N.E. 163rd St., N. Miami Beach 33160

This bayside paradise offers respite from the asphalt city in the form of towering trees, camping, canoeing, and swimming. At more than 1,000 acres, this is the largest urban park in Florida. Visitors may have the pleasure of seeing porpoises, manatees, and a wide variety of birds. Mountain bikers meet here to race along the well-developed pathways set aside for them, while picnickers enjoy the breezy ambience. Cabins are considered primitive but sport air conditioners, front porches with swings, and fire rings and overlook the water. There are canoe trails and rentals, a swimming beach, a fishing pier, and picnic areas. Park services have been privatized, so call America Reserves for reservations: 1-800-326-3521. Park admission $; bike and boat rentals $$; cabins $.

Bay Harbor Islands: Secluded Enclave

Passing from mainland Miami over to the beachfront is definitely a move from one world to another. If you should happen to cross on the Broad Causeway, 125th Street, you'll pass through yet another world on your way: the Bay Harbor Islands. The village of Bay Harbor is a quaint and cozy community that was conceived and built by visionary Shepard Broad on a pair of mangrove-covered sandbars. Incorporated in 1947, the self-contained community manages to keep its 1950s atmosphere in spite of slightly rising apartment buildings on its eastern shorelines, a concession to the increased expenses of running a tiny city. In the shadow of the most coveted destination in the world, the Bay Harbor Islands comprise less than 1 square mile and have 5,100 residents, many of whom grew up here and are now raising their own families in the same neighborhood. Mr. Broad served as mayor for 26 years and lived in the community until his death at age 95 in 2001. Primarily residential, the area has a few fine restaurants lining the causeway before it arrives in Bal Harbour on Miami Beach at 96th Street.

DINING

Caffe Da Vinci
305-861-8166
www.caffedavinci.com
1009 Kane Concourse/96th St., Bay Harbor Islands 33154

With the current best-seller *The Da Vinci Code* propped on the host's desk and reproductions of the *Mona Lisa* and other Leonardo Da Vinci masterpieces gracing the walls, this multi-award-winning restaurant makes no bones about its heritage: executive chef Ricardo Tognozzi's culinary skill was honed in his hometown south of Rome. A long list of regular celebrity customers as well as locals and tourists enjoy the fabulous fresh homemade pasta and sauces along with inventive salads, including Insalata del Maestro, a salad of baby greens, fennel, Granny Smith apples, and Gorgonzola cheese with a honey-mustard vinaigrette; Ravioli Stolichnaya, cheese ravioli in a pink vodka sauce; and Agnolotti al Filetto, ricotta- and spinach-stuffed ravioli with fresh tomato and basil sauce. The house specialty is seaweed *spaghetini* (a flourless and eggless pasta with just 3 carbohydrates and 10 calories) tossed with a tomato-basil sauce and topped with baby shrimp and shiitake mushrooms. When I visited, my server was unusually accommodating, offering to split entrées for my friend and I when we couldn't decide. $$–$$$.

The London Tavern and Islands Café
305-868-4141, fax 305-867-9094
Bay Harbor Inn, 9660 E. Bay Harbor Dr., Bay Harbor Islands 33154

The rich wooden bar and dark, ornately carved furnishings of a London tavern were imported from an old English hotel, lending a warm, familiar atmosphere to this tiny, eight-table pub. The bar has a Cheers sort of neighborhood feeling. Billie Holiday wails from the stereo, and white-coated students busy themselves delivering trays of fruit and fresh herb garnishes to the bar and the Islands Café. The Bay Harbor Inn is owned and operated by the famed culinary arts school Johnson and Wales University, which guarantees that dining here will be a provocative experience. New American cuisine is served inside, or enjoy a poolside appetizer and cocktail. The inn offers live jazz on weekends and a famous Sunday brunch that features salads, bagels and lox, blintzes, and seafood and chicken entrées with vegetable sides. The Thursday-night seafood menu includes smoked salmon, shrimp and scallop scampi, bacon-wrapped scallops with guava barbecue sauce, black jack tenderloin, and raspberry sorbet or chocolate decadence cake. You can't go wrong. Breakfast daily; dinner served Tuesday through Thursday (no lunch). $$–$$$.

Bal Harbour and Surfside: Exclusive Paradise

Bal Harbour (Haulover Inlet to 96th Street) is perhaps the ritziest of the Miami Beach communities, calling itself the Gold Coast (although the rest of the state considers the moniker Gold Coast to encompass the entire tricounty area of Palm Beach to Miami). The area is home to the most exclusive department stores—Neiman Marcus and Saks Fifth Avenue—and features fashion boutiques of the best names in the industry, such as Louis Vuitton, Chanel, Giorgio Armani, Prada, and Pratesi, while Cartier, Bvlgari, and Tiffany's polish the look at Bal Harbour Shops.

Haulover Beach to the north of Bal Harbour is known as the city's official nude beach (though many bathers go topless at Miami Beach, too), and Haulover also has a popular gay beach area.

The coast is lined with condominium high-rises, home to those who love to shop and dine at only the best. Naturally, there is a nice collection of delicious restaurants, most within walking distance of the condominiums, which is convenient for the retirees who call the area home. Sunny Isles (Aventura to Haulover Inlet) is currently a city under renovation as father-and-son team Michael and Gil Dezer single-handedly (well, with the help of Donald Trump) raze the vintage Rat Pack hotels (we'll admit they're looking rather old and shabby) and replace them with tall, shiny, view-obstructing condo hotels such as the Trump Sonesta Beach Resort.

Surfside (96th Street to 87th Terrace) is a small beachside city with a bit more modesty, though it's still incorporated as part of the Gold Coast. The community is well known for its clean, peaceful beach and community center, which is open to the public for a fee. North Bay Village boasts a few trendy restaurants and a nice community feel, though I did encounter a skirmish between local kids after a late dinner one night. The kids had no interest in me, fortunately.

LODGING

Trump Sonesta Beach Resort

305-692-5600, fax 305-692-5601
www.sonesta.com/sunnyisles
18001 Collins Ave., Sunny Isles Beach 33160

This all-new complex has 390 rooms, some with hot tubs on the balconies, all exquisitely appointed and spacious. The beachfront pool complex has waterfalls, a spa, air-conditioned cabanas, water sports, a fitness center, and kids' activities. Salon; restaurants. $$$$.

DINING

Timo
305-936-1008
17624 Collins Ave., Sunny Isles Beach 33160

Try northern Italian fare courtesy of chef Tim Andriola, formerly executive chef at Mark's South Beach, named *Gourmet*'s number-one Miami favorite during his reign. Enjoy pizzas from the wood-burning oven, fresh pastas, or full entrées of seafood, veal, or chicken complemented with Parmesan and polenta. $$.

ATTRACTIONS, PARKS, AND RECREATION

Haulover Golf Course
305-940-6719
www.miamidade.gov/parks/golf.asp
10800 Collins Ave., Bal Harbour 33154

Haulover Golf Course offers a quick game of golf at an unbeatable price, right on Biscayne Bay. Try the nine-hole, par-3 course. Open 7:30–6 daily. $.

Miami Beach and South Beach: Glamour and Babes

Miami Beach has long been a coveted destination for its sun-drenched beaches and sultry social scene. Soaking up daiquiris by night and rays by day forms the basis of a near-perfect vacation for some. But since you're here, maybe you'd like to spend a little time learning about the things that set Miami apart from the rest of the world.

The South Beach air is fresh and light in the mornings, and you may see film and photo crews out staging scenes and getting their shots, as well as grading trucks lumbering along the beach, churning and smoothing the sand for a new day of bronzing and castle building. Mornings at South Beach, nicknamed SoBe, are a world apart from the nighttime scene, but the beauty remains, and it's a great time to take a morning tour of the beach architecture, which is called art deco, although it's really more closely related to the German Bauhaus design movement—spare, efficient, and sleek.

The facade on Miami's toniest stretch is ever evolving. Many ocean-gazing retirees were moved out of the stylish buildings in the 1980s to make room for a flashy future, attracting the likes of Madonna and Sly Stallone, who bought homes nearby and frequented the bar scene, as well as investors Cameron Diaz and Michael Caine, whose bars became part of the nightlife. Madonna and Sly have moved on now, but the beach still draws tourists searching for celebrities, and a few can almost always be found. (Ugly secret: Some clubs actually pay dishy celebs to grace their salons.) A younger set has moved in, adding hip-hop and rap to the hottest musical scene in town. Today's beach is the domain of the very young, hip, and buff, and SoBe continues to be a welcome haven for creative gays, whose imagination and hard work helped transform the aging deco beach into the vibrant, world-class destination that it is today. Although South Beach seems cut out for the young and trendy whose day begins at midnight, it makes a great family vacation destination, too.

South Beach's art deco facade Greater Miami Convention and Visitors Bureau

Lodging

The Alexander Hotel

305-865-6500, fax 305-341-6553
www.alexanderhotel.com
5225 Collins Ave., Miami Beach 33140

This oceanfront hotel is an impressive renovation on Miami Beach's Millionaire Row between Bal Harbour and South Beach. Its Caribbean décor of deep, rich woods and colorful fabrics lends elegance to the popular hotel. Features include conference facilities, a spa, oceanfront pools and dock, and the premier restaurant for beef, Shula's Steakhouse. One- and two-bedroom suites. $$$.

Avalon Hotel

305-538-0133, 1-800-933-3306,
fax 305-534-0258
www.avalonhotel.com
700 Ocean Dr., Miami Beach 33139

Decorated with Danish-style furnishings and plush linens, the 104 recently redone rooms at the Avalon also have data ports and refrigerators. Complimentary breakfast buffet. $$–$$$.

The Blue Moon

305-673-2262, 1-800-724-1623
www.bluemoonhotel.com
944 Collins Ave., Miami Beach 33139

Renovated from a pair of art deco and Mediterranean hotels, this 75-room vintage property boasts smallish but stylish rooms featuring all the amenities. There's also a sensuous lounge, a nice respite from the SoBe swirl. $$$–$$$$.

Casa Grande

305-672-7003, 1-866-420-CASA,
fax 305-673-3669
www.casagrandehotel.com
834 Ocean Dr., Miami Beach 33139

Dark and mysterious, cool and comfortable, the Casa Grande is unique on the beach. With Indonesian styles, mahogany and teak woods, and heavy furnishings, the feel is of an elegant African safari: romance meets adventure. The all-suite hotel has full kitchens and concierge service plus private beach. $$$–$$$$+.

Clevelander Hotel
305-531-3485, 1-800-815-6829
www.clevelander.com
1020 Ocean Dr., Miami Beach 33139

This is a hot spot for the hip. Ear plugs and dark window shades are among the amenities offered at the Clevelander, which is party central on South Beach. The rooms are small, simple, bright, and cool, but what else do you need? Even if you're not staying here, chances are you'll enjoy a few drinks at one of the five bars, such as the alluring poolside bar that opens onto Ocean Drive at 10th—where "the buzz" starts, they say. $$–$$$.

Comfort Inn and Suites South Beach
305-531-3406
1238 Collins Ave., Miami Beach 33139

This beautifully renovated 1929 boutique hotel features 28 rooms and suites with crisp damask linens and cool lines. Retro terrazzo lobby and bar, conference room, continental breakfast, and multilingual staff. A fitness center is close by. $$–$$$$.

The Creek
305-538-1951, 1-866-445-4800, fax 305-531-3217
www.thecreeksouthbeach.com
2360 Collins Ave., Miami Beach 33139

In town for fun but on a budget? The Creek is a hip retro motel that serves those who have more to think about than luxury. Deck rooms reminiscent of *The Jetsons* open onto the pool/bar area, where the action's at, and other rooms feature dorm-style bunk beds: hostel-type atmosphere for the college set. $–$$$$.

Crescent Suites Hotel
305-531-5197, 1-800-634-3119
www.crescentsuites.com
1420 Ocean Dr., Miami Beach 33139

This all-suites Hilton Vacation Club property is clean and super convenient, with rooms with kitchenettes and separate bedrooms—a plus for families. The décor is SoBe chic. $$$–$$$$.

The Delano
305-672-2000, 1-800-555-5001
1685 Collins Ave., Miami Beach 33139

Created by Ian Schrager of Studio 54 fame in New York, this is not your average hotel. Oozing cool, sleek chic, it's simple and breezy, with polished wood floors and gauzy curtains suspended from high ceilings. At the legendary pool, designed by Philippe Starck, the water actually flows over the edges. Surrounded by private bungalows and dining cabanas, the pool actually makes the beach in the background seem a lesser destination. Rooms are white on white and, like the rest, sleek yet bare. This is a place for the haves: the rich and famous are at home here. U.S. Secretary of Defense Donald Rumsfeld was recently spotted here. $$$–$$$$+.

Eden Roc Renaissance Resort and Spa
305-531-0000
www.edenrocresort.com
4525 Collins Ave., Miami Beach 33140

Designed by famed architect Morris Lapidus in 1956, the Eden Roc was updated in 1999 to refresh yet preserve Lapidus's unique and luxurious styling, which includes beautiful natural materials such as black marble and mahogany. The broad lobby welcomes guests with a vast view of the ocean. I attended a wine tasting at the Eden Roc with my friend Kathleen one afternoon only to get drenched as we ran from the car to the hotel. We found our way to the famous Spa of Eden, where we were welcomed with hair dryers and towels. The atmosphere is so glamorous that we kept imagining stars such as Elizabeth Taylor, Ann Margret, and Frank Sinatra visiting the hotel in the past. More recent guests include gorgeous George Clooney and the beautiful Whitney Houston. $$$–$$$$.

Fontainebleau Hilton

305-538-2000
www.hilton.com
4441 Collins Ave., Miami Beach 33140

One of Miami Beach's older and memorable properties, the Morris Lapidus–designed Fontainebleau retains its charm and glamour while jet-setting into the future with the latest in room styling and amenities. A renovation project is under way. The large complex includes pools, the beach, and fitness and business accoutrements to meet the needs of everyone in the family. $$$–$$$$.

The Hotel

305-531-2222, 1-877-843-4683
www.thehotelofsouthbeach.com
801 Collins Ave., Miami Beach 33139

Even though it's a block off Ocean Drive, you can still catch a view of the ocean from the rooftop pool of this exclusive Todd Oldham–designed boutique hotel. J.Lo and Lenny Kravitz are said to have stayed here before buying their own Miami Beach digs. The Hotel features a full gym, a lounge bar, and the nationally famous Wish restaurant. The whimsical rooms are decorated in earthy hues with tie-dyed accents. $$$–$$$$.

Hotel Impala

305-673-2021, 1-800-646-7252,
fax 305-673-5984
www.hotelimpalamiamibeach.com
1228 Collins Ave., Miami Beach 33139

Mick Jagger, Julia Roberts, Sean "P. Diddy" Combs, and Danny Glover are among the luminaries who have availed themselves of this Mediterranean-style treat, which has just 17 carefully appointed rooms and an award-winning restaurant, Spiga. $$–$$$$.

The Loews Miami Beach Hotel

305-604-1601, fax 305-604-3999
www.loewshotels.com
1601 Collins Ave., Miami Beach 33139

Tall, imposing, and relatively new compared to the historic properties around it, the Loews has its own cachet. From its beautiful grand entrance to its sculpted beachfront pool, this hotel was created with your pleasure in mind. Fitness club, kids' camp, data ports, and six restaurants and lounges. $$$$.

The Marlin

305-604-5063, 1-800-OUTPOST
www.marlinhotel.com
1200 Collins Ave., Miami Beach 33139

Created by music-industry honcho and hotelier Chris Blackwell, the Marlin caters to the music crowd. If you like the hip-hop and techno that prevail on the beach today, you'll love the sleek, sci-fi stainless look and pulsing activity that never ends at this locale. It's home to South Beach Studios, where rock 'n' roll reigns. $$$–$$$$.

The National Hotel

305-532-2311, 1-800-327-8370
www.nationalhotel.com
1677 Collins Ave., Miami Beach 33139

If you like to swim laps, you'll love the challenge of the 205-foot-long pool at this hotel. Built in 1939 at the start of the Beach's art deco days, the National continues to serve as an icon of sustainability in a fast-paced environment. Fully renovated in 1996, the family-owned hotel is one of the largest in the historic district, with 150 rooms and a trilevel penthouse, conference facilities, restaurant, pool lounge, and martini bar. It's a favorite among those who like historic tradition as well as upscale amenities in a chic setting. City view and oceanfront rooms. $$$–$$$$.

The Palms

305-534-0505, 1-800-550-0505
www.thepalmshotel.com
3025 Collins Ave., Miami Beach 33140

A large, business-oriented hotel located just north of the nightlife, the Palms has the beach, a pool, and elegant dining in addition to conference and meeting facilities. The rooms are sleek and spare, decorated for function as well as form. $$–$$$$.

The Raleigh

305-534-6300, 1-800-432-4317
www.raleighhotel.com
1775 Collins Ave., Miami Beach 33139

With its beautiful, elegantly outlined pool made famous by Esther Williams's water ballet, the Raleigh has retained its original art deco charm and historic beauty throughout the decades, and it continues to generate rave reviews from *Condé Nast Traveler* and *Travel + Leisure*. Decorated in a casual island style, the rooms are cool and charming. In addition to the restaurant, bar, lounge, and pool, the hotel features a ballroom and conference facilities. The 104 rooms and penthouse feature Egyptian cotton, 400-thread-count sheets as well as gourmet mini bars. $$$–$$$$.

The Ritz-Carlton, South Beach

786-276-4000
www.ritzcarlton.com
1 Lincoln Rd., Miami Beach 33139

How about your own beachside bed? Cabanas at the Ritz-Carlton are curtained plush beds perfect for daytime sunbathing, massage, and private evenings *à deux* (or *trois?*). Renovated from the 1953 DiLido Hotel and designed by legendary architect Morris Lapidus, this Ritz is definitely ritzy. Diners may enjoy fine cuisine outdoors on the beach at the DiLido Beach Club or "restyled American" cuisine—comfort food with a twist—at Americana. Just about all other cuisines, including Asian, Mediterranean, African Euro, and Caribbean, are offered at the hotel's other restaurants and lounges. The Parisian spa exemplifies the elegance of this hotel, unmatched on South Beach. There are 376 rooms, including an exclusive VIP club level and penthouse. $$$$.

Royal Palm Crowne Plaza Resort Miami Beach

305-604-5700, fax 305-604-2059
www.royalpalmcp.crowneplaza.com
1545 Collins Ave., Miami Beach 33139

This traditional high-rise, with art deco touches and 1950s–'60s MiMo (Miami Modern) flair, has modern amenities. It's a short walk to the SoBe nightlife and celebrity-studded beach. Restaurant, pool, lounge. $$$–$$$$.

The Shore Club

305-695-3100, 1-877-640-9500
www.shoreclub.com
1901 Collins Ave., Miami Beach 33139

Another exclusive property created by Ian Schrager, the Shore Club has Asian- and Moroccan-inspired gardens, a sleek rooftop pool and spa, a penthouse, and shops. Its sultry Red Room lounge features glowing red walls and a polished red floor, and the world-renowned SkyBar is a late-night destination of the hip and famous. $$$$.

The Tides Hotel

305-604-5070
www.thetideshotel.com
1220 Ocean Dr., Miami Beach 33139

Renovated from an enduring landmark into a destination hotel considered to be one of the most beautiful on Ocean Drive, the Tides's wide-stair entry sets a dramatic stage for the most exciting events. Built in 1936, this property has seen its share of celebrities, including Lauren Hutton, Katie Couric, Ben Affleck, and J.Lo. (My parents, who are celebs in my book, honeymooned here in 1946.) Today, instead of its original 115 rooms, the hotel has 46 rooms and suites, each coolly appointed with crisp cottons, polished wood, CD players with CDs, and a telescope to keep a close eye on what's arguably the most famous beach in the country. The Tides is also well known for its signature restaurant, 1220 at the Tides. $$$$+.

The Tudor Hotel

305-534-2934, 1-800-843-2934,
fax 305-531-1874
www.tudorsouthbeach.com
1111 Collins Ave., Miami Beach 33139

This basic hotel in the heart of South Beach is not as chic as some, but it's not as expensive, either. The rooms have tile floors and dark décor, and the penthouse suites have nice rooftop terraces. $$–$$$$.

Waldorf Towers Hotel

305-531-7684, fax 305-672-6836
www.waldorftowers.com
860 Ocean Dr., Miami Beach 33139

This small, cool hotel in the heart of the SoBe action has a terrace restaurant from which diners can keep an eye on passersby—the thing to do on Ocean Drive. Famous guests have included Ivana Trump and Florida governor Jeb Bush. In-house restaurant Primetime offers breakfast, brunch, and dinner. Rooms have city or ocean view. $$–$$$$.

DINING

Barton G

305-672-8881
1427 West Ave., Miami Beach 33139

Over-the-top big with more than anyone could want, Barton G is considered the hottest new ticket in town. Owned by Barton G. Weiss, an event planner whose services for top companies evolved to include delectable cuisine, this restaurant was planned like a grand party. Eat inside or in the lush garden, dining on traditional American fare colored with 21st-century style: rainbow trout with herbs and grilled zucchini, grilled liver with onion confit, barbecue beef ribs, and macaroni and cheese. Closed Monday. $–$$$.

Carnevale

305-672-3333
907 Lincoln Rd., Miami Beach 33139

The fresh Venetian fare served here is getting attention from the locals. Quattro Formaggi (four cheese) pizza could be just the thing for a casual night at the pedestrian mall, or step inside the small, unassuming dining room for Pagila and Fieno Shrimp Absolut (wine and green spinach spaghetti in an alla vodka pink sauce), scampi, or veal Marsala. Happy hour. $–$$.

Escopazzo

305-674-9450
www.escopazzo.com
1311 Washington Ave., Miami Beach 33139

Husband-and-wife team Giancarla and Pino Bodoni use fresh and imported ingredients to create exceptional Italian fare from their homeland. Flavors such as pumpkin and amaretto enhance ravioli; homemade pastas blend with truffles, cream, and cheese. Famous diners include Patti LaBelle, Cameron Diaz, Harrison Ford, Michelle Pfeiffer, David Geffen, and the late Gianni Versace. Closed Monday. $$–$$$.

A Fish Called Avalon

305-532-1727
700 Ocean Dr., Miami Beach 33139

The fare here is excellent: Bang Bang Shrimp with orange mint sauce, tuna tartare with gazpacho vinaigrette, mushroom salad, jerked grouper, or Guinness barbecue shrimp. $$–$$$$.

The Forge

305-538-8533, fax 305-538-7733
www.theforge.com
432 41st St., Miami Beach 33140

Known for its steaks, the Forge has been serving grilled beef here for decades, long before its South Beach competitors were on the scene. Created from an imposing building that was originally home to a blacksmithing business (a forge) in the 1920s and then a steakhouse in the 1930s, the current invocation, decorated with dark woods and huge crystal chandeliers, was created by Alvin Malnik in the late 1960s and continues under the direction of his son, Sharif Malnik, who added Jimmyz at the Forge, an all-night club famous for its Wednesday-night soirees. Madonna, Al Pacino, Michael Douglas, and Oliver Stone are among the luminaries seen here. Enjoy a little Beluga caviar with dinner. Reservations recommended. $$$–$$$$.

Joe's Stone Crab Restaurant

305-673-0365, 1-800-780-2722
www.joesstonecrab.com
11 Washington Ave., Miami Beach 33139

Joe's has been serving seafood since its inception in 1913, when Hungarians Joe and Jennie Weiss came to Miami Beach from New York to improve his asthma condition. They served breakfast, lunch, and dinner on the front porch of their home, spilling into their dining room on busy days, without any local competition for the first eight years. When a scientist brought a bag of stone crabs to Joe's in 1921 and asked them to find a way to cook the crustacean—previously considered to be inedible—history was made. The restaurant still serves the delicacies cold with the same potatoes and slaw that Jennie and Joe offered to famous customers such as Al Capone, J. Edgar Hoover, the Duke and Duchess of Windsor, Gloria Swanson, and Joe Kennedy. The menu also includes a gourmet selection of seafood, beef, and chicken, with premium prices for the crabs, surf and turf, and Alaskan king crab legs. Dinner for two can be purchased online and shipped all over the country, although stone crabs are available only in season, October 15 through May 15. Reservations are not accepted, and the long lines are as legendary as the cuisine and clientele. Open October–May. $$$–$$$$.

Kafka's Cyber Kafé

305-673-9669
www.kafkaskafe.com
1464 Washington Ave., Miami Beach 33139

In addition to sandwiches and coffee, here you'll find Internet access, fax, phones, magazines and newspapers, and used books. Open late. $.

La Piaggia Beach Club

305-674-0647
1000 S. Pointe Dr., Miami Beach 33139

The southern point of South Beach offers a few gems, including La Piaggia, which features French cuisine. Come dressed to the nines or clad in a bikini for a cool time around the pool—it all works. It's a refreshing addition to the nouveau American that prevails on the beach. Open to nonmembers by reservation only. Closed Monday through Wednesday. $$–$$$$.

Metro Kitchen + Bar at the Hotel Astor
305-531-8081
www.hotelastor.com
956 Washington Ave., Miami Beach 33139

Dark woods, crisp linens, stainless, and stone—all bathed in bright light—set the stage for no-nonsense yet whimsical and creative cuisine. A fusion of French, Italian, and Asian cuisines reflects the Caribbean and Latin cultures of south Florida, resulting in dishes such as jerked mahimahi, guava and mascarpone spring rolls, and foie gras with lychees. A quiet respite from the SoBe hustle, the Metro lounge serves its signature martinis nightly and at its hot Tuesday-night parties. $$–$$$.

News Café
305-538-6397
www.newscafe.com
800 Ocean Dr., Miami Beach 33139

This 24/7 newsstand/café serves breakfast, lunch, and dinner in a conspicuous location right on the main drag of Ocean Drive. It's popular with visiting workers (such as models, photographers, and film crews) for a quick, inexpensive bite as well as with those hoping to be discovered Lana Turner–style at the soda counter. Indoor/outdoor seating. $–$$.

Nexxt
305-532-6643
700 Lincoln Rd., Miami Beach 33139

Enjoy soups and salads, eggs, steaks with Mediterranean influences, and gorgeous pastries indoors, fast-café style, or outside under umbrellas on the mall (fans keep diners cool while they remain immersed in the scene). Sunday brunch. $–$$.

Ouzo's Greek Taverna and Bar
305-864-9848, fax 305-864-9893
www.ouzosmiamibeach.com
940 E. 71st St., Miami Beach 33141

Small but cozy. At Ouzo's diners enjoy a wide range of delicious *meza* (appetizers), including *saganaki* (flaming kaseri cheese), hummus, and baba ghanoush, with grilled lamb, moussaka, or lemon chicken. Begin or end the meal with ouzo, the anise liqueur of Greece. Open late; belly dancing Thursday through Saturday; prix fixe feast Monday and Tuesday. $$–$$$.

Talula
305-672-0778
210 23rd St., Miami Beach 33139

One of Miami Beach's most acclaimed new restaurants, Talula is the brainchild of a couple of award-winning chefs, Frank Randazzo and his wife, Andrea Curto-Randazzo, who have both achieved great national fame. Together they've created an intimate atmosphere with warm woods, brick, and copper, as well as a garden terrace for those who enjoy south Florida's temperate clime. Billed as New American cuisine, the menu offers many worldly variations on the theme, such as conch seviche and Australian lamb. Barbecue quail gets rave reviews as a starter, and comfort foods such as acorn squash and collard greens provide home-style flavors. Closed Monday. $$–$$$.

Tantra
305-672-4765
1445 Pennsylvania Ave., Miami Beach 33139

Sensuous and suggestive, Tantra's décor is designed to be aphrodisiac. Fragrance wafts from hookah pipes scattered about, and the low lights, grass floors, pillows, and reclining lounges beckon. Moroccan cuisine with rich flavors and spicy aromas melts the last of the holdouts. It's extremely pricey, but if you have someone hot to dine with, the ambience is worth it. Open late. $$$–$$$$.

1220 at the Tides

305-604-5070
www.thetideshotel.com
The Tides Hotel, 1220 Ocean Dr., Miami Beach 33139

This highly acclaimed restaurant is just a small side bar to the hotel lobby, all open with just a dozen or so seats, spilling out onto the imposing and grand front steps of the hotel for perfect streetside viewing. Chef Paul Blouin presents classic French dishes, including escargot, shrimp Florentine, lobster bisque, and Chateaubriand, and his nod to the sea and popular fusion cuisine includes seared tuna with tamarind- coconut sauce. Sunday brunch. $$–$$$.

Wish

305-531-2222
www.wishrestaurant.com
The Hotel, 801 Collins Ave., Miami Beach 33139

Wish is one of the best restaurants in the world according to *Condé Nast Traveler*. It's chef, Michael Bloise, is a graduate of Miami's Johnson and Wales University, and he presents amazing fare. Try avocado vichyssoise and other delectable soups, the signature salad of mango and cashews in a sherry vinaigrette, grilled wraps, and vegetable pastas. (Some are offered in half portions.) Sip perfect margaritas and strawberry daiquiris on the lushly planted outdoor patio as you wait for the sun to fall and the nightlife to begin on one of the most famous party strips in the world. Or, if you're a guest of the hotel, take it to the rooftop pool for a view of the surf or a rubdown under the sun before siesta. $–$$.

Outdoor dining on the patio at Wish Wish Restaurant

Yuca

305-532-9822
501 Lincoln Rd., Miami Beach 33139

Escape from the summer heat at Yuca (that's Young Urban Cuban Americans, not the root veggie) with a signature Cuban mojito—a foamy green concoction of lime juice, mint leaves, and light rum dashed with a little sour mix and sugar. The highly acclaimed nuevo Latin fare includes seviche (fresh fish marinated in lime and citrus juices with hot peppers and onion), frijoles negro (black beans simmered in spices with garlic and onion), and chorizo and manchego cheese Cuban sandwiches. Among those said to have especially enjoyed the Cuban flavors here are Robert DeNiro, Marisa Tomei, Bette Midler, Ted Koppel, and Oprah Winfrey. Sit back and enjoy watching the parade of muscled bladers and occasional celebrities for a while. $$–$$$.

NIGHTLIFE

Strolling the streets of South Beach after dinner one evening, I chanced upon an amazing metamorphosis: As dinner crowds faded into the night, a surge of youth seemed to come upon the city. South Beach nightlife is the hottest late-night scene in south Florida for the over-21 crowd. The club parties don't begin until after dinner, and many clubs offer happy hours from 10 or 11 PM until midnight, when the fun gets started and lasts until the clubs close at 5 AM. There is a club for everyone, but if celebrity-watching is high on your list of priorities, look for the velvet ropes and long lines that signal exclusivity and expect to pay cover charges of $20 and way up from there.

Crobar

305-531-5027

1445 Washington Ave., Miami Beach 33139

The high-tech DJ and dance scene here is for those who are here to be discovered or do some discovering of their own. This is the ultimate nightclub, with unrelenting beat, pulsing lights and music, and piles of bodies on the dance floor, on the catwalk, in the curtained cubbyholes, and in the upstairs VIP room.

Jazid

305-673-9372

1342 Washington Ave., Miami Beach 33139

There's jazz downstairs and a new room upstairs decorated in stainless steel, cool blue, and sci-fi chic that features electronica and techno pop.

Mansion

305-532-1525

1235 Washington Ave., Miami Beach 33139

The newest nightclub on the scene, Mansion is making a good showing, thanks to owners Eric and Francis Milon, whose track record was proven by forerunners Opium Garden, next door, and the exclusive private club Privé. It hardly seems fair that a pair of pretty French boys (Eric is a former model for Giorgio Armani and *GQ*) should have all the luck, but their Midas touch, partnered with music scene insider Roman Jones, son of guitarist Mick Jones of Foreigner, is the last word. Mansion is in a huge old building that served as a casino in the 1930s. On Friday hip-hop rules, with Euro dance next door at Opium, and on Saturday the scene switches clubs, with Euro at Mansion and hip-hop at Opium, to keep the crowds flowing between them. Open until dawn.

Nikki Beach Club

305-538-1231

1 Ocean Dr., Miami Beach 33139

Everyone knows Nikki Beach, perhaps because it's always been here, or maybe because it's the only place to go for those awake during the daylight hours. SoBe insiders hang here for what they call "nightlife during the daytime" on Sunday. Go ahead, lie on the sand while sipping piña coladas. The night scene here is hot, too.

Opium Garden

305-531-5535

136 Collins Ave., Miami Beach 33139

Another Milon brothers and Roman Jones project, Opium Garden has withstood the fickle phasic nature of South Beach chic—it's been here since 2000 and is still going strong. The Thai-inspired outdoor courtyard rocks all night long. If the famous SoBe nightlife is what you're here for, this is the place.

Pearl

305-673-1575
1 Ocean Dr., Miami Beach 33139

Upstairs from the Nikki Beach Club, Pearl dominates the traditional beach-party scene with its SoBe art deco—*Jetsons* look and glowing ambience. Sean Penn, Sting, and Naomi Campbell have been seen sidling up to the bar here. DJ party on Thursday nights.

SkyBar Miami Beach

305-695-3100
1901 Collins Ave., Miami Beach 33139

SkyBar is the pool/beach bar of the legendary Ian Schrager's Shore Club—a place for late-night relaxing, dancing, drinking, and rendezvousing in private cabanas and cubbies scattered about the grounds. Come sip and sizzle with the best of them. Thursday and Saturday are the big nights here.

ATTRACTIONS, PARKS, AND RECREATION

Bass Museum of Art

305-673-7530
www.bassmuseum.org
2121 Park Ave., Miami Beach 33139

Established in 1963 through the donation of the art collection of Johanna and John Bass, the museum is a treasure trove of medieval and Renaissance art from Europe and Latin America as well as traveling exhibits from around the world. With a goal of bringing art and culture to the community, the museum is housed in what was originally the Miami Beach Public Library & Art Center, which was designed in 1930 by Russell Pancoast, a grandson of Miami Beach pioneer John A. Collins. The building is on the National Register of Historic Places. The museum collection includes architectural archives documenting the development of Miami Beach. Open 10–5 Tuesday through Saturday (until 9 on Thursday) and 1–5 Sunday. $; free admission 6–9 the second Thursday evening of each month.

Miami Beach Botanical Garden

305-673-7256
2000 Convention Center Dr., Miami Beach 33139

Nestled between the busy streets of Miami Beach lies a green oasis that's a perfect spot for a quick break from the day. A half hour spent strolling the small, shady patch of growth or contemplating life from the bench overlooking a pond filled with water lilies in the Japanese garden can restore your enthusiasm. A bamboo garden and stone pagoda complete the peaceful ambience. A circular fountain lined with dark red miniature roses graces the entryway, and the garden's boardroom and the glass-roofed conservatory flank a terrace with tall

An outdoor sculpture at the Bass Museum of Art
Greater Miami Convention and Visitors Bureau

hedges. A tall palm frond stretches through the second-story ceiling of the glass shelter, which protects the garden's collection of more than three hundred orchids. The gardens are cool and colorful, with native butterfly catchers and fragrant subtropicals forming a hedge against the city streets, but the roar of traffic can still be heard over the cackling green parrots roosting in the trees. A gift shop sells gardening implements and accessories, artwork, and unusual books. Special art and music events are frequently held here; call for details. Open 9–5 Tuesday through Sunday. Free.

Miami Beach Golf Club

305-532-3350
www.miamibeachgolfclub.com
2301 Alton Rd., Miami Beach 33140

Totally renovated from its earliest days in 1923, this course has been patronized by Miami Beach pioneers and served as a training ground for soldiers during World War II. It continues to be a beautiful course in a great location. Open daily 6:30 AM–8 PM. Price includes cart and range balls. $$$$.

South Beach Art Deco Tour, Miami Design Preservation League

305-672-2014
www.mdpl.org
Art Deco Welcome Center, 1001 Ocean Dr., Miami Beach 33139

If your interests in the area extend beyond bars and beautiful people to include the unique candy-colored architecture, perhaps you'd like the 90-minute guided Art Deco Tour provided by the Miami Design Preservation League. Or pick up an audiotape for $10 in English, Spanish, German, or French 10–4 daily at the Welcome Center. Wear comfortable shoes and cool (casual chic) attire. The Miami Design Preservation League also offers private tours by appointment: a boat tour of Miami Beach, an Underworld Tour of gangster hangouts and Prohibition highlights, and a World War II tour that recaptures the days in 1941–45 when five hundred thousand U.S. soldiers trained on Miami Beach. Tours: 6:30 Thursday; 10:30 Wednesday and Friday through Sunday. $$.

The Wolfsonian-Florida International University

305-531-1001
www.wolfsonian.org
1001 Washington Ave., Miami Beach 33139

The Wolfsonian collection contains art and artifacts collected from North America and Europe from 1885 until World War II, including the country's largest collection of political propaganda from the United States, Germany, and Italy. The collection also includes "persuasive" materials from other countries, including Great Britain, Holland, Russia, Hungary, the former Czechoslovakia, and Spain. The collectiom examines how propaganda materials influence decision making—a particularly interesting study for today's climate. In addition, the museum documents the impact of design on lifestyle and culture. The museum also holds an array of furniture, glass, industrial objects, books, paper, and textiles, and the largest known collection of artifacts from world fairs, dating back to 1851. Open 11–6 Monday, Tuesday, Friday, and Saturday; 11–9 Thursday; and noon–5 Sunday. Shorter summer hours. $.

Yoga on the Beach

Miami Beach behind the Alexander Hotel; park free after 6 PM at 53rd St. and Collins Ave., Miami Beach

Enjoy community yoga on the beach 6:30–7:30 on weeknights. $.

CULTURE

Colony Theater

305-674-1026
1040 Lincoln Rd., Miami Beach 33139

This vintage theater, built for films in the 1930s, today offers live productions of local dance companies, plays, and opera with the occasional film. Tickets $–$$$.

Gold Coast Theater Company

305-538-5500
P.O. Box 402964, Miami Beach 33140

If it's called Gold Coast, it must be good! Specializing in mime, this company is a favorite with children. Established in 1982, it performs more than two hundred shows per year for as many as one hundred thousand patrons, at schools throughout the county, at the Miami Children's Museum, and at other events.

Holocaust Memorial Greater Miami Convention and Visitors Bureau

Holocaust Memorial

305-538-1663
www.123miami.net/holocaust-memorial.htm
1933 Meridian Ave., Miami Beach 33139

A giant bronze hand reaching toward the heavens, this solemn memorial features 50 photographs and lists of names of victims of Nazi concentration camps. A peaceful pond and walkway at the base of the 42-foot-tall sculpture by Kenneth Treister provides a restful setting for reflection. Open 9–9 daily. Free.

Jackie Gleason Theater

305-673-7300
www.gleasontheater.com
1700 Washington Ave., Miami Beach 33139

This fantastically beautiful theater, older and smaller than the mega houses built today, provides a perfect, intimate environment to enjoy a show. $$–$$$$.

Cool Cafés and Commerce

Lincoln Road (10 blocks between Washington and Lenox Avenues) is one of Miami Beach's most enchanting shopping and dining districts. Instead of being torn down and rebuilt, as so many places have been in south Florida, it was refurbished. Two rows of galleries; book, gift, and clothing shops; offices; and small eateries are joined by a wide pedestrian walkway that makes for some very interesting people watching. In-line skaters blast by diners at outdoor cafés, and couples with their pretty pets, young families, hipsters, and happy retirees help create a diverse crowd of sophisticates. On Sunday from 9–6 the mall is home to a farmer's market, where you can find a bouquet of orchids to grace your hotel suite. From October to May there is a twice-monthly antiques and collectibles market on Sunday also. Coming from a non-shopper: make time to check it out.

Greater Miami Convention and Visitors Bureau

SHOPPING

Epicure

305-672-1861

1656 Alton Rd., Miami Beach 33139

This market of the stars serves the needs of the most discriminating residents and visitors to the beach. Here you'll find fall manner of fresh seafood, meats, breads, produce, deli items, flowers, fine wines—the best of everything. It's a small shop with friendly service. Open daily 10–8.

Epicure

Espanola Way

Between 14th and 15th Streets and between Drexel and Washington Avenues

This historic Spanish village was built as an entertainment district in 1925. A festival market is sponsored by the Market Company every Friday 7–midnight, Saturday 10–midnight, and Sunday 11–9. The fair features a charming open-air market along the historic pedestrian-only street with jewelry, candles, pottery, clothing, artwork, and hand-crafted items plus fresh flowers. Musical entertainment is offered in the evenings.

The Market Company
305-531-0038
www.themarketcompany.org
428 Espanola Way, Miami Beach 33139

The company that brings the fresh farmer's markets to the city's malls also has its own small gallery of all things Florida, including artwork, gifts, and tropical fruit sauces. Open 9–5 Monday, 10–9 Tuesday through Thursday, 9 AM–midnight Friday and Saturday, and 10–10 Sunday.

Miami: The Magic City

DOWNTOWN

The times, they are a-changing in downtown Miami. The city is evolving to accommodate phenomenal growth. With cranes spearing the sky at every turn, there are currently 16,000 condominium units under construction in Miami-Dade County. They are selling quickly, but an estimated half are going to investors whose intention is profit—they hope to sell the units again before they're even built. Who will live in these units, particularly those whose cost has been driven up into the hundreds of thousands and millions of dollars? Does the nation's poorest city really have that kind of buying base? Every spectator and even the

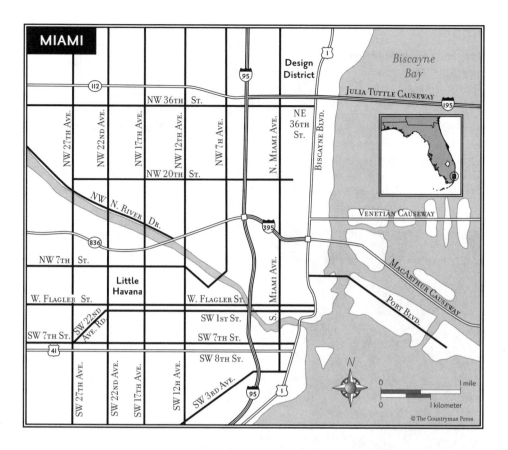

speculators look at the issue with the caveat that no one knows how it will end. Miami and south Florida have proven to be very lucrative markets for creative financiers. But it's never been a rocket's path—it's a roller coaster. Economic disasters, hurricanes—there's always something that dulls the shine of the gold, but no one's ever given up. Progress comes back more vigorously than ever before. Visionaries see the danger looming on the horizon and urge us to take heed and make the right moves now to forge a path into the future that will take Florida to a place we can all enjoy—not to wait until an economic or environmental disaster blows our world out of proportion. If we take care now to preserve the amazing natural treasure that Florida is, perhaps we can continue to live here harmoniously for generations to come.

It is entirely possible that this massive building phase will benefit not only the developers and savvy investors but also the entire city, bringing a fresh, urban livability to downtown that's been lacking. And why not? Miami is one of the most beautiful cities in the nation, so it should be enjoyed 24/7, not just during business hours or from afar by night. We'll see. The Magic City in transition is certainly something to keep a bead on.

LODGING

Four Seasons Hotel Miami

305-358-3535
www.fourseasons.com
1435 Brickell Ave., Miami 33131

The city's tallest building is home to one of the most sleek and sophisticated hotels in town. Elegance is the standard here, from the amenities and rooms to the spa and signature restaurant, Acqua, serving Latin American seviche and Italian specialties. $$$$.

Four Seasons Hotel Miami Four Seasons Hotel Miami

Intercontinental Hotel

305-577-1000
www.ichotelsgroup.com
100 Chopin Plaza, Miami 33131

Featuring two restaurants, an outdoor pool, and a fitness center, the Intercontinental Hotel serves Miami's business crowd and elite visitors who prefer a little distance from the celebrity scene, but not too much. It's right downtown on Biscayne Bay, adjacent to Bayside Marketplace. $$$.

The Mandarin Oriental

305-913-8288
www.mandarinoriental.com
500 Brickell Key Dr., Miami 33131

Widely regarded as Miami's finest hotel, the Mandarin Oriental is the city's only AAA five-diamond hotel and was rated among the top one hundred hotels in the world by *Condé Nast Traveler* in 2004. The only hotel situated on the primarily residential Brickell Key, adjacent to the city financial district, the Mandarin provides privacy and exclusivity to celebrities and sophisticated travelers who desire—and can afford—the best in accommodations. The hotel's sparkling guest list includes the King and Queen of Spain, Mick Jagger, Whitney Houston, Jada Pinkett, and Will Smith. In the Asian themes of the hotel's corporate foundation, bamboo and orchids, sliding rice-paper doors, cool marble, and linens all combine to create an air of privilege and perfection. The hotel is also home to one of the nation's top spas, where guests and visitors may luxuriate in a variety of massage and relaxation techniques from around the world, including Thailand, India, China, Europe, and Bali. Yoga, Pilates, Tai Chi, and meditation classes are conducted regularly. A popular and unique service called "Time Rituals" allows guests to simply book spa space and professionals by the hour for custom-designed service packages. Spa services $$$$+, classes $$–$$$$+, hotel accommodations $$$$+.

The sleek, Asian-themed lobby of the Mandarin Oriental hotel

Miami River Inn

Miami River Inn

305-325-0045, 1-800-468-3589
www.miamiriverinn.com
118 S.W. South River Dr., Miami 33130

The Miami River Inn, a collection of four historic buildings circa 1906–10, is Miami's longest continually run rooming house/hotel, where rooms once rented for $14 a night. The fully restored inn is unique in an environment of big money and fast-talking politicians. Furnished with antiques collected by owner Sallye Jude, the inn's quaint rooms are in buildings surrounding a peaceful pool and garden area, a lush retreat set against a rather harsh urban backdrop. $–$$$.

Sheraton Hotel

305-373-6000
www.starwoodhotels.com
495 Brickell Ave., Miami 33131

Overlooking Biscayne Bay and the Miami Circle (which is now obscured by a protective covering of soil but marked by indicators), the Sheraton Biscayne Bay offers convenience to downtown as well as the pleasure of water views. With cool, colorful Miami styling, the hotel's amenities include a lobby bar, pool, patio garden, and fitness center. $$$–$$$$.

DINING

Azul

305-913-8288
Mandarin Oriental Hotel, 500 Brickell Key Dr., Miami 33131

With the most distinguished rating of any restaurant in Miami—the AAA five-diamond

Miami Circle

Miami River tours begin with Miami Circle (401 Brickell Avenue)—the enigmatic and still unresolved ring of stone unearthed at the mouth of the Miami River where the town's earliest settlers, the Tequesta Indians, lived for perhaps as long as ten thousand years, followed by Miami pioneers Mary and William Brickell. The circle was discovered in 1998 during excavation in preparation for a new condominium structure, halting the project while archaeologists and authorities attempted to discern its origin, carbon-dated at A.D. 100. Local, state, and federal funds were used to buy the property—at a whopping $23 million—but the 38-foot circle remains a mystery, today shielded by a 6-foot chain-link fence while awaiting its destiny. Will city officials create a monument or a park? What if the circle isn't of Indian origin at all but is instead a natural stone formation, as some scientists believe? For now the site has simply been covered with soil to await future scientific inquiry. A semipermanent prayer corner—decorated with articles, artifacts, and feathers and beads woven into the fence—has been created at the site by Native American Catherine Hummingbird Ramirez, who claims to be a Caribbean princess of Native American descent. It serves to remind visitors and spectators that this could be the site of an ancient temple.

award—Azul is a force to be enjoyed. With an open-air kitchen and cool champagne bar, the restaurant is guaranteed to soothe and relax diners with its peaceful, feng shui–inspired décor, which includes a waterfall wall and a raindroplike curtain of dripping water lining the kitchen. Make time. Closed Sunday. $$–$$$$.

Big Fish
305-373-1770
55 S.W. Miami Ave., Miami 33130

This funky, comfortable, mostly seafood restaurant puts you right on the edge of the Miami River, with an interesting and unique view of the city. The blend of crisp white linens on a decades-old dock seems a bit incongruous, but the elegance is a charming feature, as is the outdoor bar wrapped around a huge banyan tree. $$–$$$.

Bijan's on the River
305-381-7778
64 S.E. Fourth St., Miami 33131

Here you can get seafood specialties at business-lunch prices, but the really cool thing about this place is the fact that it's located in Fort Dallas Park in a historic building that was part of the estate of Miami pioneer Julia Tuttle, who lived on the river in the early 1930s. $–$$.

Garcia's Seafood Grille and Fish Market
305-375-0765
398 N.W. North River Dr., Miami 33128

A family concern for more than 30 years on this working riverfront, the restaurant has its own fishing enterprise, which guarantees the freshest possible catch—ask your server what's fresh. The snapper in champagne sauce was memorable. $–$$.

Gordon Biersch Brewery Restaurant
786-425-1130
www.gordonbiersch.com
1201 Brickell Ave., Miami 33131

Gordon Biersch, a chain steakhouse that offers fresh-brewed beer and a hearty menu of beef and seafood in fresh-flavored modern incarnations, is located in Miami's financial district. You'll pass tiny protected hundred-year-old homes, which are contrasted against the steel and glass skyscrapers of the money keepers. Bankers and financiers naturally frequent this locale. $$–$$$.

Joe's Seafood Market and Restaurant
305-381-9329
400 N.W. North River Dr., Miami 33128

Joe's serves seafood in a casual atmosphere that's popular with the working crowd that serves the river. It's just a few blocks west of downtown on the Miami River. $–$$$$.

Provence Grill
305-373-1940
1001 S. Miami Ave., Miami 33130

This is my favorite place to go for dinner before attending musical events at nearby Tobacco Road. The authentic French cuisine is delicious, and the patio dining is pleasant. Try the palate-pleasing home-made pâté with vegetable sides and poached salmon in white wine sauce. $$.

Tobacco Road
305-374-1198
626 S. Miami Ave., Miami 33131

Claiming to the be the oldest bar in town, Tobacco Road is said to have been built on the site of an Indian trading post on the Miami River. Today it serves up the best in local music until dawn on weekends, enriched by a mean Greek salad and steak dinner specials after midnight. Popular with the after-work crowd as well as music lovers and late-nighters, the Road has two indoor bars and a comfortable patio. $.

A historic building at Lummus Park

ATTRACTIONS, PARKS, AND RECREATION

Dragonfly Expeditions
305-774-9019, 1-888-992-6337
www.dragonflyexpeditions.com
1825 Ponce de Leon Blvd., #369, Coral Gables 33134

Dragonfly Expeditions conducts hundreds of tours across Florida and beyond in cooperation with the Dade Heritage Trust. The trusted and knowledgeable guides can introduce
you to the Everglades by swamp walk, the Florida Keys by seaplane, and Palm Beach by
bicycle—or to any of many other interesting destinations. $$–$$$$.

Fort Dallas
64 S.E. Fourth St., Miami 33131

This City of Miami park was once a fort used in the Seminole Indian War. One building on
the site is left over from the riverfront estate of Miami pioneer Julia Tuttle. It's a small
patch of riverfront overshadowed by downtown skyscrapers. Free admission.

Gold Coast VIP Services
305-653-0591
1302 N.W. 188th Terr., Miami 33169

You're in Miami, so of course you should take advantage of the amazing sea. Why not rent
your own yacht for an evening, afternoon, or weekend cruise? Crew included. $$$$+.

Historical Museum of Southern Florida
305-375-1492
www.historical-museum.org
101 W. Flagler St., Miami 33130

A Cruise with Dragonfly Expeditions

Dragonfly Expeditions runs a few hundred tours each year, covering points of interest all over Florida and beyond. We joined partner Charles Kropke on a tour of the Miami River, which began at the point where the river meets Biscayne Bay, site of Miami's earliest settlements. The Tequesta Indians, who lived here about two thousand years ago, are said to have coined the name of the city; Miami is a Tequesta word for "sweet water," their description for the fresh river water that then flowed from the Everglades, free of industrial pollution and wild with rapids and waterfalls that have since been blasted away by development. Another story says the name came from the word MAYAIMI, which means "very large lake" and probably refers to Lake Okeechobee, accessible by canoe trail through the Everglades from the Miami River.

Once Flagler's railroad reached Palm Beach and he successfully established the community as a choice island winter retreat for the nation's wealthy, he had no interest in extending his railroad farther south, according to Kropke. Then came the freezing winter of 1895, when the citrus crops and tourism satisfaction of central Florida both took a grave hit, as happens on occasion. Julia Tuttle and Mary Brickell, pioneers in Miami who dreamed of creating a new southern metropolis, sent a basket of south Florida citrus blossoms, untouched by the freeze, to Flagler via his scout, James Ingraham. He responded immediately, and, Kropke says, the following week Tuttle gave Flagler some prime real estate at the mouth of the Miami River.

Flagler's railroad reached Miami in 1896, and the town was incorporated that year with 344 residents. Flagler built the Royal Palm Hotel in 1912, and soon he and his railroad brought the wealthy to Miami, helping to establish the town. Fabulous homes were built on the city's south side, creating a millionaires' row now known as Brickell Avenue, the heart of Miami's financial district, although the original homes are long gone. A great real-estate boom continued for five years, and then fortunes began to plummet. Kropke says it all came to an end with the hurricane of 1926, which killed between 325 and 800 people, with another 800 never found.

An intrepid researcher and well-informed authority on Miami, tour guide Kropke took me from the Miami Circle to the Miami River Inn, and then he suggested we make an impromptu visit to a riverfront shipyard. Founded in Jacksonville in 1885 and moved to Miami in 1923, Merrill-Stevens Dry Dock Company (305-324-5211; www.merrill-stevens.com; 1270 NW 11th St., Miami 33125) is the oldest continually operating corporation in the state, we learned from company president Fred Kirtland, who graciously welcomed our unexpected interruption to his day.

A panoramic photo of Miami's bayfront and river, with Flagler's Royal Palm Hotel still perched on the riverside, taken by Vern Williams in 1925, spreads across Kirtland's office wall. We all admired the

This museum houses permanent exhibits that depict ten thousand years of Florida history and hosts traveling exhibits that relate to the local culture, which has been heavily influenced by Latin American and Caribbean neighbors. Local historian, author, and college professor Dr. Paul George conducts several weekend history tours for the museum, including tours of Stiltsville, a collection of once-private homes in Biscayne Bay recently added to Biscayne National Park; Moon over Miami, an evening boat tour of the Miami River; and architecture hikes and bike rides through Miami's historic neighborhoods. Open 10–5 Monday through Saturday (until 9 the third Thursday of each month) and noon–5 Sunday. $; admission by donation on Sunday.

scene, depicting the past we'd been discussing all day during our tour of the river. Our conversation took a surprising turn when we discovered that Kirtland's personal ancestry is interwoven through the history of south Florida. Kirtland is the great-grandson of Jeptha Vining Harris, a Civil War soldier and surgeon who bought Fort Dallas (the historic property that we saw on the riverfront earlier in the day, which today has a building that was once owned by Julia Tuttle and whose former outbuildings are at Lummus Park) from the U.S. government after the war. Kirtland joked that he rues the day when Harris sold the property and moved to Key West. "So in his infinite wisdom, he sold Fort Dallas to the Biscayne Bay Company, and they later sold it to the Brickells. But for colossal mismanagement, I wouldn't have to be scraping hulls here today."

In Key West, Harris built the Southernmost House, the very distinguished Victorian manse built at the southernmost point of the nation that today is an inn and museum of the same name. Harris's only son married the daughter of Florida's first millionaire, William Curry, a very successful Federalist who moved from Charleston (or Savannah) to Green Turtle Cay in the Bahamas and then to Key West, where he established a shipyard, built schooners, and had a ships' chandlery where he held cargo from shipwrecks until its ownership was determined. "He must have been some character," says his great-grandson, Kirtland. "They tell me he made his money because he kept his assets in pound sterling. The people that did that made a bonanza. He took great pride in the fact he was a millionaire. They tell me he enjoyed hobnobbing with Rockefellers, Morgans, and Astors at gala parties at the Waldorf Astoria. The only difference between us, he'd say, is 'They're spending their interest, I'm spending my principal.'"

Kirtland lived with his mother and grandmother in the Southernmost House until he was a third grader, when his mother sold the house. She'd promised her mother, a Christian Scientist, that she'd never sell the family home to anyone who'd serve alcohol, so she passed up offers from hoteliers and sold the home to a private buyer for much less than she might have earned from a commercial concern.

"As usual, some of the wisest decisions weren't made," said Kirtland. "But for a little mismanagement . . ."

In spite of a few historic stumbles, Kirtland seems to have achieved an admirable level of success as president of Merrill-Stevens, one of the most important businesses in Miami, a working boatyard on the river for more than 80 years. The company ensured its success against competitors by investing in an elevator lift that can lift 12,000-pound yachts out of the water for maintenance and repair. Today the boatyard stores and services multimillion-dollar luxury yachts as well as working vessels that belong to their neighbors on the Miami River.

Lummus Park

305-579-6935
404 N.W. Third St., Miami 33128

This park, fragrant with trees and grassy lawns, is located in the midst of the rough urban landscape. A pair of buildings were moved here from Fort Dallas, where they had been used as slaves' quarters, as barracks for Civil War troops, and then as outbuildings on early Miami pioneer Julia Tuttle's estate. A small building on-site now known as the Wagner Homestead is currently being restored by prominent Coral Gables architect Richard Heisenbottle, president of the Dade Heritage Trust. Open 9–6 daily. Free.

Miami Art Museum (MAM) Greater Miami Convention and Visitors Bureau

Miami Art Museum (MAM)

305-375-3000
www.miamiartmuseum.org
101 W. Flagler St., Miami 33130

MAM brings international art to life through its permanent collection, changing exhibitions, and range of programs. The museum also hosts Jam at MAM, a happy-hour party with hors d'oeuvres, cocktails, and a DJ from 5–8:30 each third Thursday. Open 10–5 Tuesday through Friday and noon–5 Saturday and Sunday. $; admission is free every Sunday and the second Saturday of each month.

Miami Net Tours

305-534-7787
Bayside Marketplace, 401 Biscayne Blvd., Miami 33132

Miami Net Tours will arrange passage on the *Island Queen,* a two-story tourist boat that cruises Biscayne Bay, past the homes of the rich and famous. If peeking into the backyardsof those who've given up privacy in favor of fame trips your trigger, climb aboard for a glimpse of the pools, Jacuzzis, tennis courts, and lawns of the likes of Rosie O'Donnell, Gloria Estefan, and Julio Eglesias. Maybe you'll catch a glimpse of a sunbather or—who knows?—whatever else these "beautiful people" might be doing. Arrive early to snag a good top-floor seat. Snacks and beverages are available. Tours on the hour and lasts one and a half hours. $$.

Culture

American Airlines Arena

786-777-1000
www.aaarena.com
601 Biscayne Blvd., Miami 33132

This is a huge venue for huge events, such as the 2004 MTV Awards ceremony and Gloria Estefan's Farewell Concert. Tickets $$$–$$$$.

Bayfront Park Amphitheater

305-358-7550

www.bayfrontparkmiami.com

301 Biscayne Blvd., Miami 33132

This lovely, medium-size outdoor arena is shielded from the traffic by its cup-shaped, earthen walls. Until you have a reason to come here, you probably won't even see it. It's the perfect place for a concert under the stars, a pleasant year-round possibility in south Florida. Tickets $$–$$$$.

Miami-Dade Cultural Center

305-375-2665

101 W. Flagler St., Miami 33130

This elevated plaza is home to the Miami-Dade Public Library, the Florida Historical Museum, and the Miami Art Museum. Parking is discounted at the cultural center parking garage next door at 50 Northwest Second Avenue. Use the elevated walkway from level 2 of the garage to reach the cultural center and have the parking ticket validated at the museums or the library. Can't find the place? Look to the sky for the ominous vultures circling around a pointed building top—that's the Miami-Dade County courthouse, which mysteriously attracts the buzzards (something fishy or rotten here?). The courthouse, or Govern-ment Center, is just across the street to the north of the cultural center. Cultural center hours: 9–6 Monday through Saturday (until 9 on Thursday) and 1–5 Sunday (during the school year only).

Olympia Theater at Gusman Center for the Performing Arts

305-374-2444

www.gusmancenter.org

174 E. Flagler Ave., Miami 33131

The beautifully restored Olympia Theater lends insight into the glamour enjoyed in Miami during the city's early heydays. Opened in 1926 as a silent-movie house, the theater must have been extremely popular, as it was the first air-conditioned building in the South. Rescued from demolition and renovated to its original splendor by Miami philanthropist Maurice Gusman in 1975, the theater's exquisite architecture and design are stunning. The stage has hosted Elvis Presley and Luciano Pavarotti and continues to be the most sophisti-cated venue in town for traveling entertainers. It's home to Miami's Maximum Dance Company and the Miami International Film Festival. Tickets $$–$$$$.

Wall Flower Gallery

305-579-0069

www.wallflowergallery.com

10 N.E. Third St., Miami 33132

This little gallery of local treasures tucked between downtown and the Design District fea-tures art, music, jewelry, clothing, and an eclectic atmosphere favored by a young crowd of hipsters—not the glam group, but the creatives. Owner Flash is just about always on hand to meet and oversee the activity, including frequent musical performances on the small stage. Crafts such as mosaic tables, sci-fi paintings, hand-painted silk clothing, hammered jew-elry, and sculpted wax candles as well as local music are sold in the Wall Flower Bizarre. $.

SHOPPING

Bayside Marketplace
305-577-3344, fax 305-577-0306
www.baysidemarketplace.com
401 Biscayne Blvd., Miami 33132

> **Downtown Miami Shopping**
> You might find bargain fashions or electronics at the rows of stores lining the city blocks in downtown
> Miami. One outstanding shopping opportunity exists at the Seybold Building at Southeast First
> Avenue and Flagler Street, home to numerous jewelry importers and wholesalers, where fine dia-
> monds and gems can be found at bargain prices.

This colorful collection of more than two hundred shops and eateries features goods and
flavors from around the world, aptly representing Miami's rich diversity. A big favorite is
the locally owned Art by God, where you can buy a dinosaur skeleton, raccoon penis bones,
or a 20-pound amethyst—whichever of nature's gifts you desire. The indoor/outdoor market curves around the waterfront, capitalizing on the marina activity and beauty. Make time
to relax with dinner, a tropical drink, or Miami's beverage of choice—café con leche—by
the bay after shopping. Open daily.

Brickell Village News and World Wide Trading Post
305-374-6397
630 S. Miami Ave., Miami 33130

This very interesting, funky vintage gift shop next door to Miami's oldest pub, Tobacco
Road, offers a cool collection of relics from the 1950s and '60s, plus eclectic goods from
around the globe. Run by the man responsible for musical acts at the bar next door, this
shop opens at noon and keeps late nights Thursday through Saturday for the pub crowd.

Some of the eclectic offerings at Brickell Village News and World Wide Trading Post

NORTH BISCAYNE BOULEVARD
Just north of downtown along the Biscayne Corridor is one of Miami's latest neighborhoods to be climbing up the revitalization scale. It was known as Miami's red-light district for as long as anyone can remember, and streetwalkers can still be seen strutting their stuff in front of trendy restaurants and stores. But today this strip is called the Upper East Side, and the area is

fast emerging as a hip, cool, and casual place to dine and shop. Don't let the seedy but timeworn practice deter you from experiencing some of Miami's best new dining options (like Ola). Enjoying the vibrant colors of Miami sometimes means seeing shades you might not care for.

Local area residents are more concerned about encroaching development—high-rises are springing up across downtown, and in some areas they threaten to dwarf more scenic historic neighborhoods, like Morningside at 57th Street and Biscayne. One of Miami's earliest suburbs, this bayside community is protected but surrounded by neighborhoods in transition. Some homeowners are concerned about developments that are considered out of scale with the existing community. The Morningside Civic Association has banded together with several other area neighborhood organizations and formed a legal team to help preserve the integrity of the neighborhood by forging regulations that will keep the inevitable new condominium buildings from creating huge walls of unending concrete.

DINING

North 110
305-893-4211
11052 Biscayne Blvd., Miami 33161

Lobster gazpacho, porcini-dusted goat cheese, grilled fish with wild mushrooms, rack of lamb with red onion—mango marmalade, grilled angel food cake with tropical fruit compote—the menu here is stylized Americana with a tropical flair. Closed Sunday. $–$$$.

Ola
305-758-9195
5061 Biscayne Blvd., Miami 33137

Chef Douglas Rodriguez, who created the nuevo Latin flavors at Yuca before making his way to Ola, holds onto the tropical Latin flavors he's known for and adds them to a good thing: Ola boasts a seviche bar like no other. The chef's table draws the eye with colorfully lit flowing water that cools the atmosphere while guests tingle over rainbow seviche, rum-vanilla cured smoked marlin salad, ahi tuna seviche, or unforgettable Ecuadorian shrimp seviche. Funky chandeliers and candles set the tone for exotic indulgence. Ask to sit at the seviche bar or overlooking it from the dining room, unless you prefer the chef's favorite spot—overlooking the kitchen. Reservations recommended. $$–$$$.

One Ninety Restaurant
305-576-9779
190 N.E. 46th St., Miami 33137

Chef/owner Alan Hughes presents a tasting menu in a comfortable, urban atmosphere that fits nicely in this old Miami community of Bueno Vista, near Morningside, which was once grand and is now up and coming again. Nestled in a vintage storefront, the concrete floors and dingy windows belie the bohemian, eclectic flair within. After hours One Ninety becomes a hipsters' club that showcases live performances, DJs, and dancing. Spanish tapas, South American seviche, and French and Asian flavors all are represented in the edgy offerings. Sunday brunch (with surprisingly traditional dishes). Closed Monday. $$–$$$.

Paquito's
305-947-5027
16265 Biscayne Blvd., N. Miami
Beach 33160

Called the "Best Mexican" by *Miami
New Times*; I found the place to be
colorful and clean but was disappointed by the cheese enchiladas and
carne asada. The Mexican fajitas and
piña coladas were good, though. If
you're in the mood for Mexican, also
consider Los Très Amigos, west of the
Design District (see page 155). $–$$.

One Ninety Restaurant

Roger's Restaurant & Bar
305-866-7111
1601 79th St. Causeway, North Bay Village 33141

This cool, dark, and cavernous space is relieved by a wall overlooking Biscayne Bay, creating a restful cocoon for enjoying the comfort food offered. Chef David Downes's mini
cheeseburgers, Chinese chicken salad, ribs and fries, fried chicken and coleslaw, pork
chops, steaks, and pasta all converge—like the atmosphere—to serve diners a range of
tastes that's sure to satisfy. $–$$.

SHOPPING

Antique Heaven
305-754-0014
www.antiqueheaven.com
7235 Biscayne Blvd., Miami 33138

This reliable shop is filled with traditional
antiques as well as a mix of eclectic 1950s
and '60s furnishings and accessories. The
casual, cozy, musty atmosphere is more
reminiscent of an old aunt's home than a
shop. Any good snoop is sure to find some
treasures. Open 11–5 Monday through
Saturday and 11–4 Sunday.

Antique Heaven

Bagua
305-573-9292
www.bagua9.com
4600 N.E. Second Ave., Miami 33137

This is a "world fusion" shop of feng shui–inspired gifts: handmade silk bags, locally
blended candles, perfumes of fragrant natural oils, colorful Haitian art, vintage clothes,
and an eclectic collection of beautiful things. Feng Shui Fetes are held weekly on Friday

from 8–midnight and feature music, tea, wine, and hors d'oeuvres. Open noon–6 Monday through Thursday, noon–midnight Saturday, and noon–4 Sunday.

C. Madeleine's

305-945-7770
13702 Biscayne Blvd., N. Miami Beach
33181

Looking for that perfect cocktail dress? Why not a vintage taffeta ballgown? You'll never want to shop in conventional stores again if your budget will allow shopping at C. Madeleine's. This warehouse is filled with carefully selected vintage clothes and accessories from the glamour and house-wife eras. Popular with movie and commer-cial costumers and set designers, the store also offers eclectic cultural collections from around the world, including East Indian, American Indian, and Indonesian, among

C. Madeleine's offers vintage clothing and accessories.
C. Madeleine's

others. Open 11–6 Monday through Saturday (until 7:30 Thursday) and noon–5 Sunday.

Divine Trash

305-751-1973
7244 Biscayne Blvd., Miami 33138

A pair of huge, bright macaws in a jungle scene look down upon a few interesting shops and restaurants from the side of a building at Biscayne and 73rd Street. Tommy Trujillo's pottery garden in the courtyard catches the eye: there are piles of fresh terra-cotta pots of all shapes and sizes, direct from Colombia and priced to sell. Amid the pottery is a sparkling find: Trujillo's own handcrafted tables of iron and polished black marble. Indoors, Divine Trash is a collection of cool chic consignment furniture, clothes, Caribbean artwork, and affordable kitsch. Open noon–6 Tuesday through Saturday.

Jerusalem Market and Deli

305-948-9080, fax 305-948-8661
16275 Biscayne Blvd., N. Miami Beach 33160

This is a great little place to pick up prepared Middle Eastern foods, baklava, or delectable ingredients such as primo feta cheese, kalamata olives, and delicious green almonds (in early summer). Open 9–9 Monday through Saturday and 11–7 Sunday.

Morningside Antiques

305-751-2828
www.frenchheritage.com
6443 Biscayne Blvd., Miami 33138

Several vendors share space in this shop, which provides a wide variety of periods to choose from. Named for the charming neighborhood of towering trees and elegant homes from Miami's land-boom pioneer days, the shop no doubt serves as exchange vendor for those cleaning out attics and those restoring the glory to their Mediterranean-style 1920s bungalows. Open 10–6 Monday through Saturday.

THE DESIGN DISTRICT
The Design District is a fabulous, funky enclave favored by interior designers, furniture and fabric distributors, tile and flooring spe-

Morningside Antiques

cialists, antiques lovers, and artists. Just north of downtown and over the bridge from South Beach, it's been quietly and happily conducting business in the shadows of better-known communities, all the more fun for those in the know.

Looking west from Biscayne Boulevard at 36th Street, you'll see some unusual wall art: a dual mural depicting a pair of boxers, one haloed, the other horned, said to represent good versus evil, alongside a sleeper in repose. This is the welcoming beacon of the Miami Design District. You'll find chic restaurants with edgy food, galleries, and nightspots in this small area around Miami Avenue north of Northeast 36th Street. There are more than 50 galleries and interior design shops, most open to the trade, but with some retail traffic as well.

The Design District is home to a new trend in musical entertainment: live performances of nationally known touring acts are offered in small venues such as I/O, also home of the Saturday-night PopLife—a British electro dance scene. The Art & Design Night gallery walk is held the second Thursday of each month.

DINING

Charcuterie
305-576-7877
3612 N.E. Second Ave., Miami 33137

This small, simple French café tucked under an overpass on the south side of the Design District is much loved by locals in the know. The delicate yet rich French specialties include wild salmon baked *en papillote* (in a pastry-crust pillow), escargots, scallops *en croute* (also baked in a pastry crust), and tri-colored fish tartare. Save room for the crème brûlée. Limited hours; closed Sunday. $–$$.

The District Restaurant Lounge
305-576-7242
www.thedistrictmiami.com
35 N.E. 40th St., Miami 33137

The District recently moved into space occupied forever by Piccadilly Garden. It's a tough act to follow, but it's off to a good start. Specialties include smoked onion, goat cheese, and bean salad; citrus-dusted wild salmon; and roots-style banana leaf–wrapped red snapper. Happy hour; late-night music; Sunday brunch. $$.

Grass

305-573-3355
www.grasslounge.com
28 N.E. 40th St., Miami 33137

One of the hottest tickets outside of South Beach, Grass is a walled enclave in the Design District. Entry is by reservation only, and it must be made well in advance. Diners may linger only two hours in order to make way for the next seating. The dining room is an outdoor terrace with low tables, banquettes, and a bar covered by a large tiki hut. More tables rest under the stars. But in spite of the exclusive velvet-rope routine, the atmosphere inside the kingdom is as comfortable and casual as the décor, which includes pots of grass decorating the tables under the grass hut. Chef Pedro Duarte favors delicate flavors with Asian and Latin distinctions. I loved the golden gazpacho, Mérida mixed seviche (there were several to choose from), and Morayaki chicken with teriyaki and raspberries. $$–$$$.

Los Tres Amigos

305-324-1400
1025 N.W. 20th St., Miami 33127

A bit off the beaten path and out of the way of most tourist attractions, this little hole-in-the-wall Mexican restaurant is not fancy, but it's truly an authentic treasure—bring your Spanish dictionary. It's located just north of the Ryder Trauma Center and Jackson Memorial Hospital at the University of Miami School of Medicine. You'll feel more like you've come to the home of good friends when welcomed by the genuine, friendly hospitality that Mexicans call their own. My husband and I wheeled our patient, son Bud, into the restaurant to help lift his spirits when we visited him at the hospital. The staff helped us cheer him up and sold us a cool Mexican T-shirt for him to pull over his hospital PJs. $.

NIGHTLIFE

I/O Lounge

305-358-8007
www.epoplife.com
30 N.E. 14th St., Miami 33132

I/O is home of the weekly PopLife hipster night, a music showcase of independent artists and sometime DJ extravaganza for Brit techno-pop dance fans. Young crowd. Open 10 PM–5 AM daily. Cover charge $$–$$$.

LITTLE HAVANA

What is it about this humble little 24-block strip in the middle of downtown Miami that sets it apart from the rest of the city and attracts millions of visitors each year? While Miami is the gateway to the nation, Little Havana is the acclimating point for many Spanish-speaking immigrants.

It is a place for welcoming the adventurers as they arrive, and it is a place to recall the beauty of lands and people left behind. It is a place to celebrate all that is lost and all that has been gained. It is Cuba's mainland outpost, a place where political honchos are said to broker international deals over *cafeçito Cubano* (Cuban coffee) and cigars. Although the

Dragonfly Expeditions is located in this Craftsman-style cottage in Little Havana

community was founded as a haven for the waves of Cuban immigrants that began some 40 years ago, today people from South and Central America find comfort in its few blocks. Some never leave the safety of the familiar; they settle here and live in the homelike setting with its advantage of freedom, never venturing any farther.

Those who wish to learn more about Miami's Latin culture are welcomed, too. On Southwest Eighth Street, between Fourth and 27th Avenues, you'll find *coco frios* (fresh coconut juice served in the coconut shell) for sale on the curb from a pickup truck filled with coconuts, with its driver standing by, using a machete to hack off a 3-inch piece of hull for inserting a straw. Empty coconut shells are strewn about the sidewalk.

The air is fragrant with steaming pastries, café con leche, and simmering sauces; a sidewalk performer gently beats a drum; and the atmosphere is generally happy. A Chinese restaurant produces some of the most intriguing scents, and finding it here in Little Havana isn't as odd as it may seem—the restaurant and nearby Chinese gift shop reflect a subculture of an actual Chinese community in Cuba.

The botanica shops found in the area cater to those who practice the religion Santeria, an interesting cross between Catholicism and voodoo. These are the folks who from time to time offer up sacrifices of headless chickens on the steps of the Miami courthouse to avenge justice gone awry, at least in their view. Icons of Jesus, wounded and bleeding, and angels and fairies line the shelves, while baskets filled with amulets are under the counter. Against the wall rest rows of liquid spells and colognes—vials marked MONEY and LOVE, REVENGE and LUCK. How-to books and decks of tarot cards are also available. A psychic waits to serve visitors in a back room.

There are many art galleries along the boulevard, and local residents gather at places like the Domino Park on Eighth Street, where they challenge one another at several outdoor tables protected by pavilions. Enjoy a stroll into this world that is so much a part of Miami culture today.

DINING

Casa Juancho
305-642-2452
www.casajuancho.com
2436 S.W. Eighth St., Miami 33135

Serrano hams hang from the wood ceiling, against a backdrop of brick walls and a terra-cotta tile floor, creating an inviting, warm den of luscious smells and jovial patter. A piano player works a corner of the bar, busy red-and-green-vested waiters full of information float all around, and there's a long dessert table filled with everything from cakes and pies to pastries. Seasoned every few months during the 18-month drying process, the hams are the restaurant's signature offering. Sliced to paper thinness, the meat is a tasty combination of salt and seasonings. Casa Juancho is also famous for its paella, a mixture of rice, vegetables, sausage, chicken, and fish. Live Latin and Flamenco music nightly. $$–$$$.

Hy-Vong
305-446-3674
3458 S.W. Eighth St., Miami 33135

As incongruous as it seems, this authentic Vietnamese restaurant sits right on Callé Ocho, the main drag of Little Havana. Passersby might never guess that in this tiny hole-in-the-wall storefront is the best Vietnamese in town, and thanks to its lack of fluff and puff, it's extremely reasonably priced. The place has its own little history, even if it's not about Cuban boat lifts. Owner Kathy Manning, a math teacher, took in a Vietnamese refugee sponsored by her church in 1975, and five years later the pair created the restaurant together. It's a complete success. Chef Tung Nguyen still cooks in the back, and Kathy is hostess and server. There are only a dozen tables, and they don't take reservations, so there's pretty much always a waiting line outside. But the homemade kim chi (an appetizer of fermented cabbage), lettuce rolls, roast duck with black currant sauce and avocado, grouper in mango sauce, and watercress and ripe tomato salad are always worth the effort. There's an eclectic imported beer list, too. Closed Monday. $–$$.

Versaille's
305-445-7614
3555 S.W. Eighth St., Miami 33135

A neighborhood fixture for 30 years, Versaille's, with its white Formica tables and green vinyl and chrome dinettes contrasted against regal wooden columns and chandeliers dangling from the ceiling, is a favorite stop for visiting presidents and politicos. It's well known for its ardent discussions among earnest cigar lovers. Forsake your diet for a day when you choose to dine here—Cuban food is not known for its slimming qualities. The delicious, comfort-style fare is rich with starches and buttery sauces. Each dish, served by white-shirted waiters with black bowties, includes a pile of rice, either white, yellow, or the dark, smoky-flavored *moros* with black beans. Don't forget to sample the sangria. The thick dessert confections are voluptuous treats offered with warm smiles and *cafeçito Cubano*. $.

SHOPPING

Little Havana to Go

305-857-9720
www.littlehavanatogo.com
1442 S.W. Eighth St., Miami 33135

Carole Ann Taylor's shop offers all manner of
colorful Cuban-style souvenirs, including the
popular cotton shirts, *guayaberas;* colorful
hammocks; replicas of toy soldiers; chessmen;
and other artifacts from Cuba's pre-Castro
days. Open 10–6 Monday through Saturday
and 11–5 Sunday.

Stoneage Antiques

Old Cuba, the Collection

305-643-6269
1561 S.W. Eighth St., Miami 33135

The store features books of Cuban history and
others with beautiful pictures of the off-limits
island, as well as Cuban music, artwork, clothing, and trinkets. These souvenirs of the past
are available for a single purpose—to keep Cuban culture alive and thriving for those who
don't know, and for those who can't forget. Owner Jackie Perez keeps the memories alive
for her parents, and for those like her, who were raised in the United States. Open 10–6
Monday through Saturday.

Stoneage Antiques

305-633-5114
3236 N.W. South River Dr., Miami 33142

This mishmash of stuff spilling across the grounds looks like a junkyard shack, but the
warehouse full of 30 years' worth of collected treasures stacked floor to ceiling is sure to
deliver something of interest to everyone. Whether you're in the market for vintage fishing
gear, an Indian-style dugout canoe, signs from Florida landmarks long gone, maps, head-
lights, lanterns, wringer washers, or coils of ships' rope, you'll find it here. Run by father-
and-son team Gary and Ryan Stone, the store specializes in nautical antiques. Providing
film props is a substantial chunk of their business. Open 9–4:45 Monday through
Saturday.

Key Biscayne: Backdoor Getaway

Key Biscayne is a sleepy little key with a residential village, luxury hotels, and some of the
best beaches in the country thanks to wide expanses of sand and trees not blighted by
buildings. Once the winter home of former president Richard Nixon, Key Biscayne has
managed to remain fairly quiet and noncommercial, although the island has seen some
increase in high-rise development over the past decade.

Jutting off the southeast edge of Miami via Rickenbacker Causeway at the southern tip
of I-95, the island offers superb recreational opportunities for beach lovers, sailboarders,

sailors, and kite-boarders. Said to have been visited by Ponce de Leon in 1513, the island was inhabited by Tequesta Indians four hundred years ago. The U.S. government erected a lighthouse to protect ships from crashing against the offshore reefs in 1825, but Seminole Indians still protected the territory, attacking and burning the structure in 1836. Rebuilt in 1855, the lighthouse has 119 steps to the top of the 95-foot tower.

Today another landmark stands strikingly against the skyline on this southern tip of the state: the nuclear power plant at Turkey Point is just south of Key Biscayne.

DINING

Sundays on the Bay
305-361-6777
Crandon Park Marina, 4520 Crandon Blvd., Key Biscayne 33149

This fun, relaxing lunch and dinner spot features Italian specialties ranging from pizza to snapper livornese (snapper baked with olives, tomatoes, and onions) and more. Tropical drinks are the rule of the day at this waterfront hangout for boaters and boat lovers alike. Enjoy a Pain in the Ass, a colorful candy-cane-striped drink so named for the effort involved in preparing it (drink it quickly before the stripes melt together), while watching incoming boats, occasional dolphins and manatees, and spectacular sunsets. Live music on weekends. $$.

ATTRACTIONS, PARKS, AND RECREATION

Bill Baggs Cape Florida State Recreation Area
305-361-5811
1200 S. Crandon Blvd., Key Biscayne 33149

Extending into Biscayne Bay, the long expanse of soft white sand and shallow, clear blue waters of this island recreation area have won many accolades as the best beach over the years. The Cape Florida Lighthouse here, first built in 1825, is said to be the oldest building in south Florida. Lighthouse tours are held daily at 10 and 1. The park is open daily 8–sunset. $.

Crandon Park
305-361-5421
www.miamidade.gov/parks/parks/crandon_beach.asp
4000 Crandon Blvd., Key Biscayne 33149

Crandon Park has 2 miles of popular pristine beaches; a family amusement center with historic carousel, splash fountain, and roller rink; a historic botanical garden (look out for the exotic iguana population!); a tennis center; a golf course; and a marina. Open daily sunrise–sunset. $.

Mangrove Cycles
305-361-5555
260 Crandon Blvd., Key Biscayne 33149

Turtle Nesting Season

 June is the official start of turtle nesting season on the Gold Coast, when the giant mistresses of the sea lumber ashore under cover of night to deposit their treasured offspring for safekeeping. Florida beaches serve as the largest nesting ground for endangered loggerhead turtles in the Western Hemisphere. While the chance to observe this miracle of nature is rare and exciting, it's important to remember to protect the turtles as they lay their eggs, and again a few months later when the tiny hatchlings make their way from their nests back to the sea.

Should you encounter a turtle in the process of nesting, do not approach her. Be careful not to frighten or disturb her, or she will abandon the nest. The state of Florida and the U.S. Endangered Species Act of 1973 prohibit tampering with sea turtles or their nests. You may, however, wish to join a turtle walk at seaside parks along the coast, which include an educational presentation regarding the sea turtles, followed by a guided walk of the beach in the hope of the chance to quietly watch a turtle climb onto land to dig a nest and drop her eggs. Park staff will either fence off the nests or relocate them to safe areas for incubation. At hatching time, community volunteers can help guide the young turtles back to the sea. They are drawn to the light of the moon reflected off the sea but often are misguided by streetlights and end up on coastal highways instead of where they belong. Ask park or beach personnel about turtle programs all along the coast.

Tips for Safe Sea-Turtle Watching

Miami-Dade Parks Sea Turtle Program director Bill Ahern offers the following tips to remember when you're sea-turtle watching:

- DO remain quiet at all times.
- DO walk along the shoreline, being careful not to frighten emerging turtles.
- DO wear dark clothing (light clothing may distract the mother, and she may not nest).
- DO NOT walk up to a nesting turtle.
- DO NOT use flashlights or flash photography at any time.
- DO NOT attempt to touch a sea turtle.
- DO NOT touch, handle, or remove eggs from a nest.
- DO NOT attempt to ride the turtle back into the water.
- If you see a turtle that appears to be in trouble, DO NOT attempt to touch or move the turtle. Report the incident to the local park, beach, or police department.
- DO keep plastic bags out of the environment. Marine animals mistake them for a food source: jellyfish.
- DO watch out for and remove fishing line and other pollution hazards.
- DO extinguish city lights near beaches during turtle nesting and hatching season (June–October).
- DO beware of sea life when using motorboats, which cause a lot of damage to turtles and manatees.

The Turtle Awareness Project at Miami-Dade Parks Beach Operations (305-361-5421; 7921 Atlantic Way, where 79th Street meets Collins Avenue on Miami Beach) monitors nests from June through October, with a hatchling-release program in August and September.

Tour the Key Biscayne Heritage Trails on a bicycle, taking in early Tequesta Indian grounds, beach paths, the Cape Florida Lighthouse and keeper's cottage, the village of Key Biscayne, and more. There are bike rentals for children and adults, including bike seats, baskets, training wheels, helmets, and free maps. Open 9–6 Tuesday through Saturday and 10–6 Sunday. $–$$$$.

Sailboards Miami
305-361-7245
www.sailboardsmiami.com
Windsurfer Beach, 0.3 mile past the tollbooth on the south side of Rickenbacker Causeway

Owned and operated by U.S. Sailing Master Instructor Ovidio DeLeon, this company guarantees that it can teach people to sailboard in two hours—they say it's as easy as riding a bike. Sounds like fun, but if you're not so brave, they also rent single and double kayaks for exploring Biscayne Bay. Extreme-sport lovers also kite-board in this area. Open 10–6 daily (closed Wednesday) October through April and 11–7 daily (closed Wednesday) May through September. $$–$$$$.

Coconut Grove: Grave of the Groovy

Site of one of Miami's earliest settlements, this bayside community's roads and sites are named after the pioneers who first settled here, such as the Ingraham Highway, named for Flagler Railway scout James Ingraham. Some of the grand homes of the early 20th century still grace the shoreline, from Vizcaya to the Barnacle to the Deering Estate. Affectionately called "the Grove," the city served as an early Bahamian immigrant community, and in the 1960s it became quite popular with musicians and hipsters. Anyone who was there then will regale listeners with tales of intimate musical gatherings with David Crosby, Joni Mitchell, Fred Neil, and Jimmy Buffett. But the popularity of the community seemed to bring its downfall, as so often happens. In an effort to capitalize on the crowds, developers quickly swooped into the community with early versions of festival marketplaces—palaces of retail and restaurant trade designed to woo the music-loving public and to capture their dollars.

As it turned out, there wasn't a lot of money to be made from the hipsters of the 1960s, and the retail behemoths continue to pose a challenge for the community. But in the process the charming sense of a village atmosphere was lost and has never been fully recovered.

Nonetheless, the Grove maintains a hint of grooviness, and the streets of Coconut Grove still offer a plethora of kinky shops and sidewalk cafés of the sort that the hippies of yesteryear might have found interesting—including head shops and lingerie and sex-toy shops. Designer boutiques also line the streets, and mainstream shopping can be found at the Mayfair and Coco Walk. The Coconut Grove Playhouse is a delightful, small dual-stage theater that draws impressive national touring shows. The Grove may not be the same as wistful natives recall, but it's still a comfortable, casual place to enjoy an evening.

LODGING

Doubletree Hotel

305-858-2500

www.doubletree.com

2649 S. Bayshore Dr., Miami 33133

Renovated in 2003, this hotel, across from Biscayne Bay, offers fresh, comfortable, and chic rooms and suites at relatively reasonable rates. Amenities include Internet access, pool, fitness room, and whirlpool as well as a business center, restaurant, and lounge. $$$–$$$$.

Grove Isle Resort

305-858-8300

www.groveisle.com

4 Grove Isle Dr., Miami 33133

Crossing the causeway from Biscayne Boulevard to Grove Isle is like passing into a sub-tropical country. The man-made island houses Grove Isle Resort, such a luscious, exotic hideaway that you'll forget it's a big development once you're inside. With just 49 rooms, the hotel is intimate and distinctive, with an unusual monkey-themed décor that's whimsical and fun and leaves you wondering whether monkeys are somehow elite. Elegant yet comfortable, the Grove Isle is unique. $$$–$$$$.

Ritz-Carlton Coconut Grove

305-644-4680

www.ritz-carlton.com

3300 S.W. 27th Ave., Coconut Grove 33133

If goose-down comforters and sumptuous cotton linens are requirements when you travel, then the Ritz-Carlton is the place for you. Spacious rooms, fine furniture, luxurious appointments, and impeccable service are Ritz-Carlton hallmarks. Then there's the spa. Just a few years on the scene here in Coconut Grove, the hotel raises the bar in accommodations as well as dining options for the local community. Overlooking the bay, the hotel is within walking distance of the Grove's nightlife and shopping district. Perfection doesn't come cheap, however. $$$$+.

DINING

Baleen

305-857-5007

www.groveisle.com

Grove Isle Club and Resort, 4 Grove Isle Dr., Coconut Grove 33133

Gauzy curtains provide privacy when dining in the garden, a piano lends elegance inside, and the outdoor terrace overlooks Biscayne Bay. It's rich and far removed from Miami proper. Entrées include crab Benedict for breakfast, as well as tuna tataki, thinly sliced and seared, or Roquefort-crusted filet mignon. Happy hour; dog days on Sunday afternoons. $–$$$.

Scotty's Landing
305-854-2626
3381 Pan American Dr., Coconut Grove 33133

At this charming local favorite, enjoy live local music (I especially like Valerie Wisecracker and the 18 Wheelers) and fresh seafood on the outdoor patio overlooking the water. It's nothing fancy, but it's a great place for a sunny afternoon lunch or dinner. $–$$.

Tuscany Trattoria
305-445-0022
3484 Main Hwy., Miami 33133

This lovely Italian restaurant offers outdoor seating for those who enjoy crowd watching—a fun pastime in the Grove. The menu includes an exquisite tricolored salad with arugula, radicchio, and endive, as well as a delicious pasta pomodoro (pasta with a fresh tomato, basil, and garlic sauce). $$.

ATTRACTIONS, PARKS, AND RECREATION

The Barnacle Historic State Park
305-448-9445
www.floridastateparks.org/thebarnacle
3485 Main Hwy., Coconut Grove 33133

A yacht builder, Ralph Munroe bought his 40 acres of bayfront property in 1886 with $400 and a sailboat. The oldest home in its original location in the county, Munroe's Barnacle was built in 1891, long before air-conditioning relieved Florida's relentless summer heat. The Barnacle remains a fine example of environmentally friendly design, especially the home's roofline, which is raised in a cupola and vented in the center, helping to draw heat out of the home and enabling the fresh sea breezes to blow through the home from the many windows, many of which are shaded by an overhang. These were all successful techniques for making the home more livable in the warm summer months. Special events include Barnacle Under Moonlight, musical performances held under the full moon 6–9 monthly. The Barnacle is open 9–4 Friday through Monday; tours are at 10, 11:30, 1, and 2:30. $.

Museum of Science and Space Transit Planetarium
305-646-4200
www.miamisci.org
3280 S. Miami Ave., Miami 33129

Founded by the Junior League in 1950, the museum has grown continuously, nurturing the creative and scientific minds of children ever since. The museum pioneered a relationship with the Smithsonian Institution that resulted in long-term exhibitions of artifacts on loan from the national museum's collection. There's also a wildlife center with live animals and outdoor exhibits, star and laser shows at the planetarium, and a night-sky observatory with powerful telescopes. Museum open daily 10–6 (closed Thanksgiving and Christmas); observatory open Friday 8 PM–10 PM. $.

Vizcaya Museum and Gardens Greater Miami Convention and Visitors Bureau

Vizcaya Museum and Gardens

305-250-9133

www.vizcayamuseum.org

3251 S. Miami Ave., Miami 33129

This beautiful mansion was built on Biscayne Bay in 1916 by industrialist James Deering, whose brother also built a home nearby, the Charles Deering Estate. Vizcaya was created from stone in a Mediterranean Italian Renaissance style. The manse and acres of formal gardens continue to provide restful afternoons and a grand backdrop for gala events and weddings. Open daily 9:30–4:30 (except Christmas). $–$$.

CULTURE

Coconut Grove Playhouse

305-442-4000

www.cgplayhouse.com

3500 Main Hwy., Coconut Grove 33133

This small, prestigious, yet unpretentious theater is the venue for high-quality perform-ances. Tickets $$–$$$$.

SHOPPING

CocoWalk

305-444-0777
www.galleryatcocowalk.com
3015 Grand Ave., Coconut Grove 33133

This shopping center changed Coconut Grove from an artsy village to a modern destination. A frontrunner of the festival marketplaces, it's a complex of shops, restaurants,
and offices designed to resemble an Italian village, with Mediterranean-style stucco and
tile terraces. Trendy shops such as the Gap, Banana Republic, and Victoria's Secret draw
the crowds.

Organic Farmer's Market in Coconut Grove

305-238-7747
www.glaserorganicfarms.com
3300 Grand Ave. (at Margaret St.), Coconut Grove 33133

Come hungry to this wide spread of organic fruits, vegetables, nuts, seeds, juices, and prepared raw foods such as delicious sun patties (meat-free patties made of raw vegetables
such as beets, carrots, and sprouts), fruit pies, kim chi (fermented cabbage), curry-cashew
spread, and many more inventive and delicious dishes. Most of the food is grown and prepared by local farmers Tracy and Stan Glaser at their farm in Homestead. They bring it all
to market 10–6 every Saturday. Yum.

Coral Gables: Shaded and Sophisticated

Created from a bedrock of coral limestone in the early 1920s by developer George Merrick,
this city was carefully planned and laid out in keeping with the trend of the times to create
palatial living for America's elite. The historic city is called the City Beautiful for its 1920s
Mediterranean-style architecture nestled under towering oak, banyan, and royal poinciana
trees. It's a wonderful place for a meandering bike ride.

LODGING

The Biltmore Hotel

305-445-1926, 1-800-633-7313
www.biltmorehotel.com
1200 Anastasia Ave., Coral Gables 33134

The Biltmore was built by George Merrick,
founder of the city of Coral Gables, and
hotelier John McEntee Bowman just as the
Florida land boom was coming to an end in
1926. But the hotel was so grand that it was
fairly insulated against the economic down-
turns facing the masses. Its untouchable
clientele included the Duke and Duchess of
Windsor; high-living, high-profile criminal
Al Capone; Judy Garland; and Bing Crosby.
Today the hotel is a favorite of former
president Bill Clinton. Elegant water ballets
were performed at the pool—the largest
hotel pool in the nation—where *Tarzan* star
Johnny Weissmuller set diving records. The
hotel fell into disrepair after being converted into a veterans hospital during World War
II, but its glory was restored in the 1980s.
The incomparable grandeur of the past just
gets better with age. $$$$.

Doral Golf Resort and Spa
305-592-2000, 1-800-713-6725
www.doralresort.com
4400 N.W. 87th Ave., Miami 33178

This is a good place to get a grip on exactly what the magic is that drives hordes of successful men and women to hit and chase tiny balls into obscure holes in the landscape. Perhaps it's the chance to stroll among the trees and birds and bees on cushy, grassy knolls, enjoying the peace and quiet that nature provides. Or it could be the spa. Championship golf, restaurants, business center—this place is like a small resort city. $$$–$$$$.

Hotel Place St. Michel
305-444-1666, 1-800-848-HOTEL
162 Alcazar Ave., Coral Gables 33134

This quaint boutique property was revived and polished from its roots as a 1926 hotel. Its 27 rooms and suites are furnished uniquely with antiques, lending a European elegance. $$–$$$.

DINING

John Martin's
305-445-3777
www.johnmartins.com
253 Miracle Mile, Coral Gables 33134

John Martin's has an authentic Irish pub atmosphere and an impressive menu that features something for everyone: delicious pâtés and Irish stews, shepherd's pie, and Thai curries. Live music on weekends. $–$$$.

Le Provencal
305-448-8984
www.leprovencalrestaurant.com
382 Miracle Mile, Coral Gables 33134

This cozy French restaurant has old-country charm. Try foie gras or liver mousse pâté with creamy vichyssoise or a rich, hearty bouillabaisse, broiled salmon béarnaise, or yellowtail almandine. Enjoy your deep red table wine and dinner café-style on the sidewalk. $$.

Miss Saigon Bistro
305-446-8006
148 Girlada Ave., Coral Gables 33134

This small, lively dining establishment is in the downtown area of Coral Gables, where the post-office and pretheater crowds converge to enjoy the fresh and subtle flavors of Vietnamese fare. I like the spring rolls wrapped in lettuce, and the soups are fresh and delicious. Lemongrass and curry infuse the main dishes with Vietnamese flavors. $$.

Mundo's Norman Van Aken's New World Café
305-442-6787
The Village at Merrick Park, 325 San Lorenzo Ave., Coral Gables 33146

Enjoy Norman Van Aken's new cuisine at this casual, upscale restaurant. Serving a nice mix of small tapas dishes, the café allows diners to enjoy sampling and sharing a variety of flavors. Spicy sausages, tangy seviche, sesame tuna and sashimi, black beans, tamarind, and soy all combine to bring the best of each region to your table. Live music; nightly specials. $$–$$$.

Norman's
305-446-6767
www.normans.com
21 Almeria Ave., Coral Gables 33134

Norman Van Aken honed his fame here in Miami pairing unlikely elements to create unique and unforgettable flavor experiences known today as New American cuisine. He brings together the tangy tart and sweetness of tropical fruits such as mango and passion fruit with habanero peppers, ginger, citrus, and avocado. Spark and spice make for very nice dining. His restaurants generate acclaim from *Gourmet* magazine, *Wine Spectator,* and the *New York Times.* See what they're raving about. Closed Sunday, Memorial Day, and Christmas. Reservations recommended. $$$.

Ortanique on the Mile

305-446-7710
278 Miracle Mile, Coral Gables 33146

Chef Cindy Hutson has earned a fine reputation here with her new-world Caribbean dinners, in which she blends Jamaican, Asian, French, and traditional Florida elements to create "Cuisine of the Sun." Imagine: grouper, sea bass, snapper, or tuna infused with curries, passion fruit, mint, bananas, and rum. Reservations recommended. $$–$$$.

Palme D'Or

305-445-8066
www.biltmorehotel.com
Biltmore Hotel, 1200 Anastasia Ave., Coral Gables 33134

Palme D'Or offers fine dining in an elegant atmosphere of privilege. Create your own dinner from a tasting menu of more than 20 small plates featuring European flavors, or choose from a traditional menu of delicacies such as grilled tenderloin brochette in mustard sauce or wild striped bass in lemon sauce with thyme. Closed Sunday and Monday. $$$.

Titanic Brewery

305-667-ALES
www.titanicbrewery.com
5813 Ponce de Leon Blvd., Coral Gables 33146

A University of Miami fixture, the Titanic Brewery has seen a parade of famous customers and musicians over the years. The small pub holds the distinction of brewing its own beers and has a memorable menu to match: Brewmasters Meatloaf, steamed mussels fra diablo, steak salad, Dixie chicken steamed in Triple Screw Ale, crawfish, and andouille bisque are a few samples. It's a nice local spot for dinner and entertainment. $–$$.

ATTRACTIONS, PARKS, AND RECREATION

The Biltmore Golf Course

305-460-5366
1210 Anastasia Ave., Coral Gables 33134

The Biltmore golf course, built by Donald Ross in 1925, offers a challenging, par-71, 18-hole course with wide fairways and compact greens. The pro shop is particularly favored because of its wide selection of equipment. The course is home to the John Pallot Golf Academy. Open 6:45 AM–7 PM weekdays, 6:30 AM–7 PM weekends. $$$.

Deering Estate at Cutler

305-235-1668
www.deeringestate.com
16701 S.W. 72nd Ave., Miami 33157

Built by International Harvester heir Charles Deering at the turn of the 20th century, this stone home and boathouse were fully restored after suffering considerable damage during Hurricane Andrew in 1992. The estate provides a pleasant day reflecting on life in Florida's earlier days, of which there is a wealth of imformation supplied here. The 440-acre property

Venetian Pool Greater Miami Convention and Visitors Bureau

surrounding the estate is a natural preserve that represents a variety of ecosystems, including the globally endangered pine rockland habitat. Archaeological finds from the property include evidence of animal occupation one hundred thousand years ago, of humans ten thousand years ago, and a Native American burial mound. I met a manatee in the unique keyhole boat-turning basin. Canoe tours of the surrounding shoreline are available. Open 10–5 daily (except Thanksgiving and Christmas). $; admission includes parking and tour.

Fairchild Tropical Botanic Garden
305-667-1651
www.ftg.org
10901 Old Cutler Rd., Coral Gables 33156

A signature garden of Miami, Fairchild bears the fruits of the labor of Robert Montgomery and his friend David Fairchild, who traveled the world collecting exotic plants and seeds. Opened in 1938, the gardens represent Montgomery's collection of more than twenty-five thousand plants and four thousand species. Botanists and horticulturists conduct research at the garden and maintain a comprehensive database archive of information. Interesting gift shop. Kids' programs, special events, and plant shows are held throughout the year, including an International Mango Festival in July, orchid show in April, and "Ramble— A Garden Festival" each November. Open daily 9:30–4:30 (except Christmas). $.

Gold Coast Railroad Museum
305-253-0063
www.goldcoast-railroad.org
12450 S.W. 152nd St., Miami 33177

This train system is almost wholly responsible for the early population of Florida. Check out the old rail cars and learn about the path they cut through the hot, swampy wilderness. Train rides are offered on weekends. Gift shop. Open 10–4 Monday through Friday and 11–4 Saturday and Sunday. $.

Metrozoo
305-251-0400
www.miamimetrozoo.com
12400 S.W. 152nd St. (Coral Reef Dr.), Miami 33177

Roam the pathways of this tropical zoo and through the habitat zones of Komodo dragons, Bengal tigers, apes, baboons, and chimpanzees. You can also listen to and see the winged glory of three hundred rare birds from Asia as they roost and repast in the world's largest natural open-air aviary. Open 9:30–5:30 daily. $–$$.

Venetian Pool
305-460-5306
www.venetianpool.com
2701 De Soto Blvd., Coral Gables 33134

Originally the limestone quarry created as a source of native rock, which is the foundation of the community's Mediterranean architecture, the rock pit was transformed into a pool when the digging struck a spring. The fresh water still flows, filling the pool each night with more than 800,000 gallons of cool, fresh springwater. At this large, expansive pool with rock grottoes, caves, waterfalls, and lush greenery, visitors have been enjoying an invigorating dip here since 1924. Café open daily. Open 11–7 daily November through March; summertime hours vary. $.

CULTURE

Actors' Playhouse at the Miracle Theater
305-444-9293
www.actorsplayhouse.org
280 Miracle Mile, Coral Gables 33134

This delightful small theater, saved from the wheels of so-called progress by local activists, is one of the most esteemed theatrical houses in Miami. Tickets $$–$$$.

Coral Gables Congregational Church Community Arts Program
305-448-7421
www.coralgablescongregational.org
3010 De Soto Blvd., Coral Gables 33134

This incredibly durable old pioneer church, first occupied in 1925, today is frequently used for cultural events as well as Sunday services. Tickets $–$$$.

GableStage

305-445-1119
www.gablestage.org
1200 Anastasia Ave., Coral Gables 33134

Formerly known as the Florida Shakespeare Theatre, GableStage presents a series of five or six plays each season at the Biltmore Hotel. The theater boasts a long list of awards for its productions, which often have controversial or provocative themes. Tickets $$$.

SHOPPING

Books & Books

305-442-4408
www.booksandbooks.com
265 Aragon Ave., Coral Cables 33134

Books and Books earned its reputation as a haven for bibliophiles during its early years in a small, multiroom shop with a loft, each cubby lined floor to ceiling with books. A few years ago this book lovers' paradise expanded into a fresh new space, many times larger than its original home, adding a central courtyard and café. This store is a premier stop for national author tours—check the calendar for special events. Open 9 AM–11 PM daily.

Downtown Coral Gables and Miracle Mile

305-569-0311
www.shopcoralgables.com
224 Miracle Mile, Coral Gables 33134

Acclaimed restaurants, fine-art galleries, antiques shops, jewelry stores, beauty salons, and bridal boutiques, as well as many independent, international, and exclusive couture and gift shops, line the wide, stately streets of this upscale downtown, a haven for shoppers. Stores include Ma Vie en Lingerie, Jennie's Furs, Leather World, Mr. and Mrs. Wigs, and the Dog Bar.

Gem Galleries Antiques at the Colonnade Hotel

305-443-1196
2333 Ponce de Leon Blvd., Coral Gables 33134

Here you'll find a broad collection of furnishings and accessories, from the incredibly massive and gorgeous chandeliers to the little naked netsukes practicing their lessons from the *Kama Sutra*. Open 10–10 daily.

Miami Twice

305-666-0127
www.miamitwice.com
6562 Bird Rd., Coral Gables 33155

This shop has an incredibly fun collection of vintage clothes and antiques and specializes in hippie gear and garb from the 1960s and '70s—but there's also everything else you could ever think of to decorate bones and home. Open 10–7 Monday through Saturday and noon–6 Sunday.

The Village at Merrick Park

305-529-0299

www.villageofmerrickpark.com

358 Avenue San Lorenzo (at Ponce de Leon Blvd.), Coral Gables 33146

Here you'll find boutique shopping in a grand center and grand shops in a marketplace setting. Although this outdoor mall was not welcomed as being architecturally inviting by locals, the adage from *Field of Dreams*, "If you build it, they will come," proved true. In spite of poured-concrete walls the size of big-box stores and the push-push of supply-side economics screaming in your face, it's a bit intoxicating to shop the designer shops and top-rate department stores. Close your eyes and pretend you're in Spain, Italy, or France, and you'll wake up at Swarovski, La Perla, or Jimmy Choo. Open 10—9 Monday through Saturday and noon—6 Sunday.

Homestead, Florida City, and South Miami: Farms, Everglades, and Alligators

Homestead, a farming community that is distinctly different from Miami, boasts a vintage village that's currently being revitalized with brick streets and renovation projects. Several antiques shops and a few authentic Mexican restaurants (thanks to a high population of farm workers and former farm workers) can be found in the downtown area, but the real jewels of this community are still in the backcountry. Driving the back roads west and north of town during the winter growing season, you'll find many little farm stands, each selling its own local produce, whether tomatoes, strawberries, corn, melons, flowers, citrus, or tropical fruits. It's a world away from the city shorelines.

LODGING

Baymont Inn and Suites

305-278-0001

10821 Caribbean Blvd., Cutler Ridge/Miami 33189

I always choose Baymont when I can. I like the reliably clean, newly furnished rooms with pillowtop mattresses, the desks with Internet connections, the laundry facilities, and the complimentary breakfast. Pets are welcome, and the prices are always right. Children 18 and younger stay free with an adult. $–$$.

Everglades International Hostel and Tours

305-248-1122, 1-800-372-3874, fax 305-245-7622

www.evergladeshostel.com

20 S.W. Second Ave., Florida City 33034

The Everglades Hostel provides laid-back lodging for those more interested in function than style. Located in the heart of the Redland farm area, the hostel is convenient to many attractions at the southern tip of the state, including Everglades National Park, Biscayne National Park, the Keys, and South Miami. The hostel provides Internet access, free national phone calls, a movie room, a full kitchen with complimentary pancake

*The Everglades International Hostel
has a relaxed bohemian atmosphere.*

ingredients (you're the cook), free parking, and laundry facilities. You may camp in the garden, rent a bed in a dorm room with five others (there's a small extra fee for air-conditioning in the summertime), or choose a semiprivate or private room with shared bath. Nonmembers of Hostelling International USA (www.hiusa.org) pay a little more. Priority is given to inter- national travelers over locals as a means of ensuring that explorers on a budget get a room for the night. $–$$.

Redland Hotel
305-246-1904, 1-800-595-1904
www.redlandhotel.com
5 S. Flagler Ave., Homestead 33030

Built in 1904, this building, which has suffered fires and poverty and nearly met the wrecking ball, was discovered and saved by Katy and Rex Oleson with the help of friends Nancy and Jerry Gust in 1997. Today the restored hotel has 22 rooms, a vintage bar, and an expansive veranda. $–$$$.

Dining

Keys Seafood House
305-247-9456
404 S.E. First Ave., Florida City 33034

Frozen or fresh, at this casual restaurant or at home, the fare at the Keys Seafood House is the gourmet's answer to low-cost and high-quality Florida Keys seafood. Beer and wine. $.

Rosita's Restaurante
305-246-3114
199 W. Palm Dr., Florida City 33034

Fresh authentic Mexican fare is served in this friendly—if rather too bright—atmosphere. Rosita's has the best salsa in town, great prices, friendly service, and a clean dining area. Beer is available with meals only. $.

ATTRACTIONS, PARKS, AND RECREATION

Biscayne National Park
305-230-7275
www.nps.gov/bisc
9700 S.W. 328th St., Homestead 33033

Explore this national underwater park's coral reefs and mangrove shorelines. It's popular for boating, sailing, fishing, snorkeling, diving, and camping, or take the glass-bottom boat cruise over the coral reefs and a shipwreck or artificial reef. The three-hour park-tour boat trips depart at 10 daily for the living coral reefs or the nearby Elliott or Boca Chita Keys, depending on the weather. Four-hour snorkel/Scuba trips depart at 1:30. The visitors center is open 9–5 daily; the park is open 7:30–5:30 daily. Free admission.

Coral Castle
305-248-6345
www.coralcastle.com
28655 S. Dixie Hwy., Miami 33033

This incredible sculpture garden was created by jilted lover Edward Leedskalnin, who spent his life hoisting and honing these multi-ton chunks of coral rock into a dining table and chairs, bathtub, gate, telescope, generator—a home for the bride of his dreams. How he moved these hunks of stone remains a mystery. Visit the garden at sunset, when the setting sun casts romantic shadows. Open 7 AM–8 PM daily. $.

Biscayne National Park

I asked park ranger Maria Beotegui what the most pressing environmental concern facing the park was, and she replied, "Oh, do I have to choose just one? Water quality, the coral reef, and overfishing." What can we do? "Awareness is the key to solving these problems. If people think about where their water comes from and where it goes when it leaves their homes, they might be more careful about how they dispose of wastes and more careful about what goes in the landfills, too. And even in their driveway, the oil from their cars runs into the water supply. Water treatment ends up putting so much excess nutrients in the water, causing an overgrowth of algae.

"People need to make the connection, and when they come to the park and see that there aren't as many fish here as they remember, or that the coral reefs are dying, then maybe they'll make the connection and we can begin to change the way we handle our water and natural resources.

"I don't want to give up hope yet."

Biscayne National Park is a popular place to go diving. Biscayne National Park

Swamp Walk: Our "Muckabout"

I laid awake all night the night before, worrying about encountering snakes and gators on my walk through the Everglades swamps with Clyde and Niki Butcher, who hold an annual "Muckabout" Swamp Walk, a three-day event held over Labor Day weekend at their Big Cypress Gallery, located about 30 miles west of Miami on the Old Tamiami Trail, US 41. The gallery is set on a 10-acre piece of swamp where the Butchers live and work. Clyde's black-and-white photos of the Everglades are internationally famous, and he lends them to help raise awareness of the dire environmental issues facing the River of Grass. During the Swamp Walk you venture into water up to your waist or higher, knowing full well that alligators and snakes live in these parts and that you're invading their territory. It sounds crazy, but the proceeds of the Swamp Walk go to charity. The real purpose, the Butchers say, is to raise awareness of the delicate Everglades ecosystem and to inspire its preservation.

Anxious yet excited, I dressed in jeans and tough old shoes to ward off any sharp teeth, and we—myself; my husband, Jim; and his brother, Gary—were off. After driving for an hour from Fort Lauderdale into the Everglades, we found the Butchers' gallery. A few gators lay placidly in the front-yard pond. We paid the fee, signed a waiver, and set off on the path. We were all issued broomsticks before we set out, and while no one said they were for fending off attacks, what else could they be for?

I didn't want to end up at the back of the line—or the front—but I ended up third from the back, Jim and Gary behind me. With trepidation, we stepped off the trail and down into the water. I expected to sink into muddy muck, but we didn't. The water was brown, stained with tannins from the inland pine trees. As we stepped into the murky water, there was no way of knowing whether a snake

Everglades Alligator Farm

305-247-2628
www.everglades.com
40351 S.W. 192nd Ave., Florida City 33034

Everyone who comes to Florida seems to want to see a real alligator, and there are certainly plenty of opportunities at the Everglades Alligator Farm, home to more than three thousand alligators, as well as baby alligators and snakes (which visitors can hold). This is also a commercial farm that provides those gator bites seen on menus throughout the state. Visitors can take an airboat ride through the Everglades and see the gators on their home turf and natural habitat, the River of Grass. Watch out for that sawgrass—the rough edges of the graceful green blades will tear your fingertips to shreds. Alligator shows are held at 11, 2, and 5 daily; alligator feeding at noon and 3. Open 9–6 daily (except Christmas). $–$$.

Everglades National Park

305-242-7700
www.nps.gov/ever/index.htm
40001 FL 9336, Homestead 33034

Travel west on Palm Drive to 192nd Avenue (the Robert Is Here roadside market is on the corner), go south, and then follow signs to the park entrance. The Everglades are

You can see real live gators at the Everglades Alligator Farm. Everglades Alligator Farm

unique. This park was created in 1947 thanks to Marjory Stoneman Douglas, who created awareness of the "River of Grass," and to former president Harry S. Truman, who designated its national park status. Activity is limited to quiet pastimes and explorations. Peaceful visitors who don't disturb or frighten the wildlife are likely to see alligators and, during the migratory seasons, rare birds. Other creatures who call the 'Glades home, such as Florida panthers, bobcats, dolphins, and manatees, tend to remain scarce to humans. Environmental concerns remain important: the Everglades are considered to be endangered today because of encroaching development and agriculture and diminishing water supply and quality. Open 24/7. $.

Fruit and Spice Park

305-247-5727

24801 S.W. 187th Ave., Homestead 33031

Want to taste something different while you're in subtropical Miami? This 35-acre park cultivates more than five hundred varieties of exotic fruits, herbs, spices, and nuts from around the world. Daily tours allow sampling of ripe produce, and related products, cookbooks, and plants are sold in the gift shop. Tours are given daily at 11, 1:30, and 3. $.

Pinecrest Gardens

305-669-6942

www.pinecrest-fl.gov/gardens.htm

11000 Red Rd., Pinecrest 33156

Pinecrest Gardens was once home of the famous Parrot Jungle and Gardens, but when the attraction moved to Watson Island, the city of Pinecrest managed to hang onto the lushly planted tropical garden. A popular spot for weddings, birthdays, and musical performances, the garden provides a peaceful backdrop for whatever momentous occasion or relaxing event you have in mind. $.

or gator might lie beneath the surface. But as I looked around at the crowds of happy humans, I realized—and hoped—that most of the wildlife had probably gone on a hike of their own when we came on the scene. If we just kept moving, we'd probably be okay. But we weren't moving. We were just standing in place waist deep in this impenetrable water, listening to some silly park ranger tell bad jokes about swamp life. (Okay, maybe he was imparting important facts in a humorous way. I was a little nervous and not paying the closest attention.)

Finally we got moving again, and soon Jim was yards ahead of me. I looked back at Gary for protection, but he was way behind, chatting up the lady ranger in the back. At least we were moving. This couldn't take too long now. With no one to talk with, I began to notice the beauty of the wet woods, and I realized how clean the water felt, even if it was murky from so many hikers. The air was fragrant with orchids and other plants. The sun shone stunningly through the overhead canopy. Other than a few birds and butterflies, there wasn't a wild creature in sight. I relaxed enough to enjoy the rest of the walk, though I wasn't disappointed when it came to an end before too long. But by then I'd tasted nuts growing on the trees and tried to take pictures with my underwater camera.

When we got out, I didn't even care whether we changed from our wet clothes. They felt good somehow. We said hello to Clyde and looked at some books for sale, perused the gallery, ate delicious gator bites and grouper sandwiches, and listened to a little Cracker music performed by lifelong local Valerie Wisecracker. What a wonderful day it turned out to be. Would I do it again? Why tempt fate? But I'm glad I did it once, and I'll continue to do what I can to help protect this last vestige of the beautiful, mysterious, and essential Everglades.

SHOPPING

Gardner's Market
305-255-2468
www.gardnersmarkets.com
8287 S.W. 124th St., Pinecrest 33156

Great food and wine since 1912. This most delightful market has the finest of foods, wines, cheeses, fresh-baked breads and pastries, fresh meats and seafoods, and all the eclectic ingredients a discriminating cook could desire. Farmer's market on Sunday morning during the local growing season (November–April). Open 8–8 Monday through Saturday and 8–6 Sunday.

Knauss Berry Farm
305-247-0668
15980 S.W. 248th St., Homestead 33031

A visit to this better-than-average farm stand always anchors my visits to the Redland. The German Baptists who farm the Homestead fields during the fall and winter months produce delicious herbs, greens, tomatoes, strawberries, and flowers. As an added bonus, fresh-baked pies and breads are always available and in demand at this popular spot, as are the fruit milk shakes that have made the place famous. Open 8–5 Monday through Saturday from Thanksgiving through Easter.

Robert Is Here
305-246-1592
19200 S.W. 344th St., Homestead 33034

This roadside market offers a wide variety of local and exotic fare, with samples displayed alongside the most unusual. There are bottled sauces, jellies, jams, and honey as well as fruit milk shakes. Take a walk in back of the market to see the family's reptile collection of turtles and iguanas. If you're on the road to Everglades National Park, this is a great place to fill up the cooler with boating snacks and picnic fare, especially if you're planning to stay a night or two.

ANNUAL EVENTS

January
Art Miami
305-573-1388, 1-866-727-7953
www.art-miami.com
Miami Beach Convention Center, 1901 Convention Center Dr., Miami Beach 33139

Parties and perspectives mark this four-day festival, which has formed the foundation of an arts reputation that is fast becoming Miami's own. Artists from around the world display their wares at edgy new galleries. $$.

Miami International Film Festival (MIFF)

305-348-5555

www.miamifilmfestival.com

Various locations throughout Miami-Dade County

This film festival showcases some of the best in world cinema, and the rich cultural environment of Miami provides a winning venue. MIFF is always a much-anticipated series, with showings over several weeks at multiple locations. Many film events are attended by producers, directors, and actors. $–$$.

Orange Bowl Football Game

305-371-4600

Pro Player Stadium, 2269 N.W. 199th St., Opa Locka 33056

This college football championship has been hosted in Florida since 1935, usually on New Year's Day. $$$$.

Redland Natural Arts Festival

305-247-5727

www.miamidade.gov/parks

Fruit and Spice Park, 24801 S.W. 187th Ave., Homestead 33031

The Redland is the rich farmland that is a south Florida heritage—for decades, this was the land that fed the nation during the cold winter months. Celebrate the plants, arts, crafts, and music of the growers who settled this land a century ago and whose families still work to feed the world. $.

February

Coconut Grove Arts Fest

305-447-0401

www.coconutgroveartsfest.com

Along S. Bayshore Dr. in downtown Coconut Grove

One of the nation's most successful outdoor art festivals, this has grown over more than 40 years to host hundreds of artists who sell millions of dollars' worth of work over the three-day festival. Children's activities, live music, and food vendors help maintain the pleasant atmosphere that draws such an appreciative audience. $.

Miami International Boat Show

305-441-3220

www.discoverboating.com/miami

Miami Beach Convention Center, 1901 Convention Center Dr., Miami Beach 33139

Thousands of the hottest boats on the market are on display at this world-renowned festival of seafarers' dreams. Featuring a fishing tournament, photo contest, dock parties and block party, educational seminars, and super sales, the Miami Boat Show is one hot ticket in the neighborhood. $$–$$$.

March
Callé Ocho Festival
305-644-8888
www.carnavalmiami.com
Between 4th Ave. and 27th Ave.,
on S.W. Eighth St.

The annual Callé Ocho Festival, a
Latin cultural celebration that draws
an estimated million partyers, is
billed as the premier Hispanic event
in the United States. The pinnacle
event of Carnaval Miami, it's a street
festival that features huge pans of
paella, a Cuban dish of rice, seafood,
and sausage; music; and fun. Free
admission; food and events $–$$.

PGA Ford Championship, Doral Golf Resort and Spa
305-477-4653
www.fordchampionship.com
4400 N.W. 87th Ave., Miami 33178

This premier national golfing event
features top-rated players on championship courses. $$$$.

Callé Ocho Festival Greater Miami Convention and Visitors Bureau

April
International Orchid Festival
305-667-1651
www.ftg.org
Fairchild Tropical Garden, 10901 Old Cutler Rd., Coral Gables 33156

Orchid lovers converge on the garden for this festival of flowers—buyers can find bargains
from far and wide. It's hard to resist carrying out boxes full of hopeful beginnings after
seeing the gems on display at this delightful festival. Educational lectures and exhibits
provide a wealth of information, along with the incomparable beauty of so many thousands
of orchids blooming throughout the gardens. $.

Miami Gay and Lesbian Film Festival
305-534-9924
www.mglff.com
Various locations throughout Miami Beach

This festival is all about bringing the gay experience into the open with grace, humor, and
dignity. Film perspectives examine gay life and issues at two weeks' worth of film events at
several venues. $–$$.

July
International Mango Festival
305-667-1651
www.ftg.org
Fairchild Tropical Garden, 10901 Old Cutler Rd., Coral Gables 33156

Celebrate the luscious pink, purple, green, and gold fruit of subtropical Florida with aficionados of the sweet and tangy fruit. Try mango punch, mango pastries, mango pie, and mango brunch. Sample the many varieties of the fruit, buy bags full, buy mango trees and learn to care for them, and learn how to prepare the fruit. This is one of south Florida's most popular festivals. 9:30–4:30 Saturday and Sunday. $.

August
Miami Spice Restaurant Month
305-539-3000
www.miamirestaurantmonth.com
Restaurants throughout Miami and Miami Beach

Enjoy prix fixe menu specials at select area restaurants throughout the month of August.

November
Ford Championship Weekend NASCAR Nextel Cup Series
305-230-RACE
www.homesteadmiamispeedway.com
Homestead-Miami Speedway, 1 Speedway Blvd., Homestead 33035 (preshow on Las Olas Blvd., Fort Lauderdale)

At the final race in the annual NASCAR series, racers and fans gather at this end-of-the-world raceway to share a few days of race mania and then launch out on journeys to the Keys or on cruises to celebrate a long season of oval tracks and turns. $$–$$$$.

Miami Book Fair International
305-237-3258
www.miamibookfair.com
300 N.E. Second Ave., downtown Miami, Miami-Dade College, Wolfson Campus

This premier celebration of books features titles and authors from South America and the islands as well as the U.S. mainland. A week of events leads up to a festival weekend of high-profile lectures and demonstrations, including a children's arena and colorful book sale stalls. Free admission and lectures, but bring a little cash for snacks, drinks, and book bargains.

December
Art Basel Miami Beach
305-674-1292
www.artbasel.com/miami_beach
Miami Beach Convention Center, 1901 Convention Center Dr., Miami Beach

This huge art party, a gallery hop that stretches from South Beach to the Design District, brings a bit of Switzerland to Miami. $$.

EMERGENCY NUMBERS

In an emergency, dial 911.
Poison information: 1-800-222-1222

HOSPITALS

Aventura Hospital and Medical Center
305-682-7000
www.aventurahospital.com
20900 Biscayne Blvd., Aventura 33180

Baptist Health South Florida
305-661-0363
www.baptisthealth.net
6855 Red Rd., Suite 600, Coral Gables
33143

Bascom Palmer Eye Institute
305-326-6000
900 N.W. 17th St., Miami 33136

Homestead Hospital
786-243-8000
160 N.W. 13th St., Miami 33136

Jackson Memorial Hospital
305-585-1111
1611 N.W. 12th Ave., Miami 33136

Mount Sinai Medical Center
305-674-2121
4300 Alton Rd., Miami 33140

South Miami Hospital
305-661-4611
6200 S.W. 73rd St., Miami 33143

University of Miami Hospital and Clinic
305-547-6418
1475 N.W. 12th Ave., Miami 33136

NEWSPAPERS

Daily Business Review
305-377-3721
www.dailybusinessreview.com
1 S.E. Third Ave., Suite 900, Miami 33131

The Miami Herald
305-350-2111
www.herald.com
1 Herald Plaza, Miami 33132

South Florida Business Journal
954-359-2100
www.southflorida.bizjournals.com
1000 East Hillsboro Blvd., Suite 103,
Deerfield Beach 33441

TRANSPORTATION

Admiral Limousine & Transportation Service
305-899-9320
www.admirallimousine.com
13255 W. Dixie Hwy., N. Miami 33161

Amtrak
305-835-1222
www.amtrak.com

Aventura Limousine
305-770-5466
www.aventuralimo.com
20251 N.E. 15th Ct., N. Miami 33179

Avis Rent-a-Car
1-800-331-1600
2330 N.W. 37th Ave., Miami 33142

Enterprise Rent-a-Car
305-534-9037, 1-800-325-8007
www.enterprise.com
2211 Collins Ave., Miami Beach 33139

Exotic Toys Car Rental
305-888-8448
www.exotictoyscarrental.com
4801 N.W. 36th St., Miami 33166

Metrobus
305-770-3131
www.miamidade.gov/transit
Metromover
305-770-3131
www.miamidade.gov/transit

Metrorail
305-770-3131
www.miamidade.gov/transit

Miami International Airport
305-876-7000
www.miami-airport.com
4200 N.W. 21st St., Miami 33122

Ocean Drive Limousine
305-374-7182
www.oceandrivelimousine.com
555 N.E. 15th St., Miami 33132

Tri-Rail stations
305-836-0986, 1-800-TRI-RAIL
www.tri-rail.com

Golden Glades station (16000 N. FL 9,
   Miami 33169)
Hialeah Market station (1200 S.E. 11th Ave.,
   Hialeah 33010)
Metrorail Transfer station (2567 E. 11th Ave.,
   Hialeah 33013)
Miami Airport station (3797 NW 21st St.,
   Miami 33142)
Opa Locka station (480 Ali Baba Ave.,
   Opa Locka 33054)

TOURISM CONTACTS

Coconut Grove Chamber of Commerce
305-444-7270
www.coconutgrove.com
2820 McFarlane Rd., Coconut Grove 33133

**Greater Miami Convention & Visitors
Bureau**
305-539-3000
www.miamiandbeaches.com
701 Brickell Ave., Suite 2700, Miami 33131

Historic Miami: Dade Heritage Trust
305-358-9572
www.dadeheritagetrust.org
190 S.E. 12th Terr., Miami 33131

**Miami Beach Latin Chamber of Commerce
Visitor Information Center**
305-674-1414
www.miamibeach.org
510 Lincoln Rd., Miami Beach 33139

Miami Beach Visitor Center
305-672-1270
1920 Meridian Ave., Room 831,
Miami Beach 33139

Monroe County, Florida's Keys

The Conch Republic

Ponce de Leon is credited as the first explorer to encounter the Florida Keys, although when he found them on May 15, 1513, they were populated with native tribes of Calusa and Tequesta Indians. Since the islands were difficult to access, most activity for the following three hundred years reflected the life of the sea. Pirates occasionally inhabited the islands and often crashed into the coral reefs lining the shores. A flourishing wrecking industry was established to collect pirates' treasure and the bounties of cargo ships caught between the Caribbean islands and Europe and South America. Key West became the wealthiest city in the nation in the late 1800s and early 1900s, and it quickly developed into a more bustling city than any other in slow-growing south Florida. Pioneers from Palm Beach to Miami and Fort Myers visited Key West for supplies and to connect with the distant worlds of Washington, D.C., New York City, and Europe. Meanwhile, sponging, cigar making, and farming industries emerged in the Keys.

Henry Flagler is credited with opening up the Florida Keys to wealthy vacationers as well as the general public thanks to his "railroad that went to sea." The project took twenty thousand men seven years and cost $50 million. During construction 250 lives were lost, and there were three hurricanes. The sponge trade died when a blight killed the sea creatures, and the farmers were put out of business when Flagler's railway made it possible to feed America's northern cities more cheaply with produce from Cuba. Alas, the train was laid to rest at sea by the Labor Day hurricane of 1935, which wiped out the railroad bridge along with most of Islamorada. The combination of the Depression era and the loss of revenue from Flagler's railway tumbled the fortunes of the Keys. Franklin Delano Roosevelt helped to reemploy local residents by commissioning the building of the Overseas Highway, which helped reestablish the Keys tourism industry and revived the local economy.

Today tourism is the leading industry in the Keys, where visitors can revel in the laid-back atmosphere and enjoy the perpetual sunshine and crystal blue sea with the nation's only living coral reef. Residents strive to protect the natural resources that make the Florida Keys the premier place in the nation for sport fishing, scuba diving and snorkeling, boating, and relaxing. The tiny chain of islands represents a fragile and unique ecosystem that provides habitats to many species of wildlife, marine life, and botanicals, all of which create the Keys paradise visitors and residents enjoy. More than 2,800 square nautical miles of water surrounding the island chain are designated as the Florida National

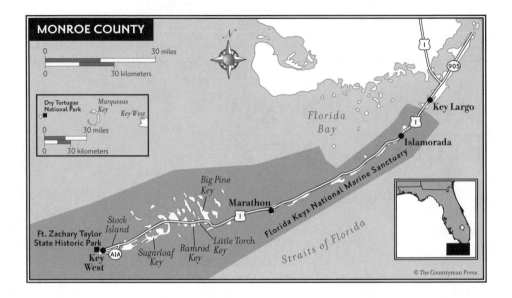

Marine Sanctuary, where sea life, plants, and coral reefs are protected from destruction and pollution. The National Wildlife Refuges of the Florida Keys protect 416,000 acres of land and sea, as well as the many plants and animals that depend on these unique habitats.

Key Largo (mile marker 118–90.7)

One of the reasons I love islands is that they often have a laid-back atmosphere that feels very away-from-it-all. The Keys are famous for that, and Key West, the farthest key from the mainland, is the extreme example. Key Largo, at the beginning of the long chain of islands, is a transitional sort of place. It has a strong sense of island charm, where boating and fishing are mainstays of activity, and its convenience to the mainland draws a big weekend tourist crowd. Yet since it is closest to the mainland, its atmosphere is still very traditional, very businesslike. There is a great deal of commerce and business here, and many residents commute to the mainland to work. Some might say Key Largo is the best of both worlds.

LODGING

Amy Slate's Amoray Dive Resort

305-451-3595, 1-800-426-6729, fax 305-453-9516
www.amoray.com
Mile marker 104, US 1 bayside
104250 Overseas Hwy., Key Largo 33037

This is the place for divers and wannabes. Since 1978 Amy Slate has offered cozy shelter, instruction, and boat trips for those anxious to enjoy the beautiful coral reefs, shipwrecks, stingrays, sharks, sea life, and dolphins. Single rooms and waterfront apartments are available. $–$$$$.

Florida Keys National Marine Sanctuary Regulations

The Florida Keys National Marine Sanctuary, designated in 1990, is 2,800 square nautical miles that encompass the entire 125-mile chain of islands in the Florida Keys and the waters surrounding them. Including the Key Largo National Marine Sanctuary, it is the second largest marine sanctuary in the United States. Sanctuary regulations prohibit the following:

* spearfishing

* handling or standing on coral formations

* removing or damaging natural features living or dead (including coral, shells, sea biscuits, sea fans, sponges, star fish, and so on)

* damaging natural features by watercraft or anchors

* removing or damaging archaeological, cultural, or historical resources

* collecting tropical marine life

* tampering with or damaging markers, mooring buoys, or scientific equipment

* discharging trash or other pollutants

* using wire fish traps

* dredging, filling, excavating, or building activities

* sand mining for popular "beach renourishment" projects

Violators are subject to penalties. For more information contact the Florida Keys National Marine Sanctuary (305-743-2437; P.O. Box 500368, Marathon 33050).

Coconut Palm Inn

305-852-3017, 1-800-765-5397,
fax 305-852-3880
www.coconutpalminn.com
Mile marker 92, bayside
198 Harborview Dr., Tavernier 33070

This spacious bayside inn has a beach, two docks for your boat or rental, a heated pool, barbecue grills, and hammocks. Restored and expanded from a 1930s hotel, the resort offers comfortable lodging at reasonable prices. Rooms and suites. No pets. $$$–$$$$.

Holiday Inn Key Largo

305-451-2121, 1-866-240-6311,
fax 305-451-5592
www.holidayinnkeylargo.com
Mile marker 100, US 1 oceanside
99701 Overseas Hwy., Key Largo 33037

Here you'll find reliably standard rooms, a pool, a fitness center, a restaurant, a tiki bar, and a dock. $$–$$$.

Jules' Undersea Lodge

305-451-2353
www.jul.com
51 Shoreland Dr., Key Largo 33037

Ever want to just submerge in the deep blue sea and not come up for a while? Here's your chance: take a room in the world's only undersea lodge, a two-bedroom submarine 30 feet below sea level. Scuba divers only need apply, and several safety rules are in force for those daring enough to plan a vacation, wedding, or honeymoon in the Undersea Lodge. Originally a research laboratory that aided scientific studies of both space and sea, the lodge has hosted such celebrities as rock star Steve Tyler,

Jules' Undersea Lodge |ules' Undersea Lodge

scientists Dr. Sylvie Earl and Dr. Eugenie Clark, Jean Michel Cousteau, astronauts Vladimir Titon and Jean-Loup Chretien, and Robin Leach, host of the television show *Lifestyles of the Rich and Famous.* The lodge is fully staffed and will deliver by scuba a gourmet dinner or late-night snacks, including pizza from a local parlor. This is definitely the thing if you're looking to do something different—and your budget allows. Dive courses available (instruction or prior certification required for entry to the lodge). $$$–$$$$.

Key Largo Resorts—Marina Del Mar

305-453-7150
www.keylargoresorts.net
Mile marker 100, US 1
99701 Overseas Hwy., Key Largo 33037

The Marina Del Mar offers clean, spacious rooms in a traditional hotel setting, with fitness center; Internet access; boat dock and marina; snorkel, dive, and fishing charters; and even a casino boat. Pet friendly. $$–$$$$.

Kona Kai Resort & Gallery

305-852-7200, 1-800-365-7829, fax 305-852-4629
www.konakairesort.com
Mile marker 97, US 1 bayside
97802 Overseas Hwy., Key Largo 33037

Owned by Joe and Ronnie Harris since 1991, in 2003 Kona Kai became a member of the Charming Hotels, an international organization reserved for independent luxury hotels. Cottages are simple, clean, and elegant, each with a view of the bay, beach, or gardens. Fresh fruit and flowers from the surrounding jungle frequently find their way to the guest rooms. There's also an on-site art gallery. The word here is *relax.* $$$–$$$$.

Neptune's Hideaway

305-451-0357, 1-888-251-4813, fax 305-451-1504
www.neptuneshideaway.com
Mile marker 104.5, US 1 bayside
104180 Overseas Hwy., Key Largo 33037

Simple, clean, and affordably priced lodging is available here, along with free dockage for those whose interest in the Keys is all about water. The tiki bar on the waterfront is a central place to share fish tales and libations while watching another of the Keys' incredible sunsets over the Gulf. $–$$$.

Ocean Pointe Suites at Key Largo

305-853-3000, 1-800-882-9464, fax 305-853-3007
www.oceanpointesuites.com
Mile marker 92.5, oceanside
500 Burton Dr., Tavernier 33070

The oceanfront tiki bar at Neptune's Hideaway

Snorkeling in the Keys

There is something simply magical about boating in the Keys, and snorkeling is like entering another world. We'd been out all day, jumping from spot to spot, and we were all getting too hot. Finally we found a spot we thought looked good for a dip, and I jumped in. It felt so marvelous in the warm, buoyant, salty water as I went in search of coral or a shipwreck I thought might be nearby. I saw a huge starfish on the sea bottom and reveled in the glorious seawater. At the next stop I marveled at the coral undersea gardens and the hundreds of fish slipping from side to side. A fierce foursome of barracudas hung menacingly nearby, baring their teeth. I giggled at them, wanting to let them know that I was no threat. Maybe they got it. I was quickly surrounded by so many different, colorful fish of all sizes that I couldn't see beyond the clouds of them. I became a little uneasy but felt strangely protected and safe. Then from the corner of my eye I saw a big, dark, forked tail swimming away from me, down near the ocean floor. I'm still not sure whether it belonged to a dolphin or a shark, but I was a bit unnerved. Even though it was swimming away, I decided I'd seen enough of the sea for the day. I have swum with both dolphins and sharks in the wild, and I'm in complete awe of them. But we needn't tempt fate.

This oceanfront all-suites resort, which provides a bit of the upper crust for the masses, has a heated pool, a spa, tennis and volleyball courts, a marina and boat ramp, a beach, and boat and kayak rentals. Sleep up to four in a one-bedroom suite with sofa bed. Breakfast included. $$$.

The Sheraton Beach Resort

305-852-5553, fax 305-852-3530
www.keylargoresort.com
Mile marker 97, US 1 bayside
97000 S. Overseas Hwy., Key Largo 33037

Internet access, bike rentals, beauty salon, free parking, two hundred rooms and suites—what more do you need? Single rooms, Jacuzzi suite for four. $$$–$$$$.

Tavernier Hotel

305-852-4131, 1-800-515-4131,
fax 305-852-4037
www.tavernierhotel.com
Mile marker 91.8, US 1 oceanside
91865 Overseas Hwy., Tavernier 33070

This striking historic building will catch your eye as you motor down US 1 through the Keys, whether or not you plan to stop and stay here. Built in 1928, the former movie theater is painted pink and stands out against the roadside. Rooms are simple and quaint, decorated in 1970s chic, with singles, doubles, and a cottage with kitchenette. The prices can't be beat. On-site restaurant; pets allowed. $–$$.

DINING

Copper Kettle Restaurant at the Tavernier Hotel

305-852-4131, 1-800-515-4131,
fax 305-852-4037
www.tavernierhotel.com
Mile marker 91, US 1 oceanside
91865 Overseas Hwy., Tavernier 33070

Breakfast, lunch, and dinner are served inside in a cottage atmosphere or out in the tropical courtyard. Conch chowder, seafood specials, liver and onions, and award-winning Key lime pie are just a few of the menu offerings. $–$$.

ATTRACTIONS, PARKS, AND RECREATION

Florida Bay Outfitters and Paradise Paddlers Kayak and Canoe Club
305-451-3018, fax 305-451-9340
www.kayakfloridakeys.com
Mile marker 104, US 1 bayside
104050 Overseas Hwy., Key Largo 33037

This family-operated paddlers' resource shop and club has worked with the federal office of Greenways and Trails to establish the Florida Keys Overseas Heritage Trail and Paddling Trail, now officially designated as a National Recreations Trail. Paddlers can buy or rent boats and gear here, receive instruction on kayaking and canoeing, join an eco-tour trip, or attend a summer kids camp. Owners Frank and Monica Woll and their seasoned staff are dedicated to exploring, enjoying, and sharing the wonders of the Keys waterways. Open daily 8:30–6 (except Thanksgiving, Christmas, and New Year's Day). Canoe and kayak rental $$–$$$$; tours and instruction $$$$.

Florida Keys Wild Bird Center
305-852-4486
Mile marker 93.6, US 1 bayside
93600 Overseas Hwy., Tavernier 33070

Nestled among the mangrove trees on the shoreline of the Florida Bay is a complex of cages and habitat areas for rescued and recovering birds found in the Florida Keys and beyond. These birds have had their wings broken or injured by fishing line, have ingested plastic filament or fishing hooks, have been poisoned, or have been physically injured by a variety of known and unknown causes. When possible, the birds are nursed back to health and released back into the wild to resume their natural lives, while others become permanent residents of the center because of their injuries. Visiting the center is a great way to meet ospreys, hawks, and roseate spoonbills up close, learn about the dangers facing wild birds and what can be done to help them. An average of one thousand birds are rescued by the center each year, with 40 percent returning to the wild. All are cared for at this nonprofit center by a largely volunteer staff and interns. The center was founded in 1991 by Laura

Sea Grass
Sea grasses on the ocean floor are an integral part of the marine ecosystem and need to be protected. The grasses provide nesting areas, food, and protection for sea life and help maintain the sandy bottom of the sea. Boaters, Jet Skiers, and swimmers should take care to avoid running aground in sea grasses as well as on coral to avoid damaging this fragile ecosystem. Sea grasses are also frequently damaged by the dredge-and-fill activities that accompany the development of coastal cities. Sea grasses are the nurseries for the game fish that bring the Keys worldwide fame and millions of tourist dollars—the local economy and sport fishing industry depend on their protection. Bonefish sport fishing alone contributes approximately $1 billion annually to the Florida economy, making sport fishing more valuable than commercial fishing in today's market, according to the Rosenstiel School of Marine Science at the University of Miami. Visit www.dep.state.fl.us/coastal/habitats/seagrass/ for more information on sea grasses.

Quinn, a former teacher who announced her retirement in 2004. Although she put the center up for sale, its life is expected to continue through grants from the Village of Islamorada and support of the Florida Fish and Wildlife Commission, which owns the surrounding property. Gift shop. Open daily sunrise–sunset. Free; donations welcome.

John Pennekamp Coral Reef State Park

305-451-1202, fax 305-853-3555, camping information 1-800-326-3521
www.pennekamppark.com
Mile marker 102.5, US 1, Key Largo

Award-winning John Pennekamp Coral Reef State Park was the nation's first undersea park, established in 1963. The park, part of the Florida Keys National Marine Sanctuary that extends 3 miles into the ocean along 25 miles of coastline, comprises 178 nautical square miles of Atlantic Ocean and Biscayne Bay, including amazing vistas of coral reef and shipwrecks. Snorkeling, scuba diving, glass-bottom boat tours, equipment, instruction, and boat rentals are available daily. The park shoreline is not particularly scenic because it's lined with mangrove trees, whose roots form tangles in the shallow water that help prevent erosion and provide a safe habitat for numerous sea creatures. Mangroves are protected from removal by state and federal mandates because of their importance to the food chain and their erosion-control properties. Open daily 8:30 AM–sunset. $.

CULTURE

Kona Kai Resort & Gallery

305-852-7200, 1-800-365-7829,
fax 305-852-4629
www.konakairesort.com
Mile marker 97, US 1 bayside
97802 Overseas Hwy., Key Largo 33037

Veronica and Joe Harris, owners of the resort, have established an on-site gallery that features original art, and Joe coordinates a permanent exhibit of locally inspired art and creative works for the local hospital wellness clinic, the Mariners Hospital Medical Arts Center. The gallery is open to the public daily from 9 to 7 and by appointment. There is no admission fee, but many of the original works of art are for sale.

Protecting Living Coral

The coral reef in the Florida Keys is the nation's only living reef. Developed over five to seven thousand years, the coral reef looks like rock formations in many different shapes, but it's actually composed of living animals, called polyps, growing from the ocean floor. The reef provides habitat and protection for many ocean creatures, including sponges, shrimp, crabs, turtles, lobsters, eels, and fish. Scientists estimate that as much as 90 percent of the world's reefs have died, in spite of government protection declarations. Reefs are threatened by poor-quality water with unnaturally high nutrient values from farm fertilizer runoffs and sewage contamination, poisons from pesticides and herbicides, global warming, and even from those who wish to observe the coral in shallow waters: the animals die when touched by human hands, fins, boats, or propellers. Officials estimate that scuba divers average six hard contacts with the reef, each hit killing coral polyps and causing reef damage. Cruise ships are said to cause tremendous damage from the release of untreated sewage into the oceans. Touching or standing on coral is prohibited, and boaters must take care to avoid anchoring in coral. Buoys are provided so boaters can tie to the attached ropes for snorkeling and diving the reef areas. For more information on how to protect the coral reef, contact Reef Relief (305-294-3100, fax 305-293-9515; www.reefrelief.org; 201 William St., Key West 33040), a nonprofit organization dedicated to doing just that.

Islamorada (mile marker 90.7–63)

Early settlers began farming the islands of Islamorada in the 1800s, and wreckers also did a big business in the settlement's earliest days. Henry Flagler began pushing his railroad from Miami to Key West in the early 1900s, creating an industry of construction and quarrying for the islands that lasted for a quarter century. The railroad put an end to the farms of Islamorada by introducing the accessibility of competing produce from Cuba, where cheap labor rendered local efforts obsolete. Completed in 1912, a year before Flagler's death, the railway served the Keys for 23 years until the Labor Day hurricane of 1935, which wiped out years of progress as well as most of Islamorada.

Small concrete houses were quickly built by the Red Cross to house hurricane victims, and many of them still stand today. Two years after the hurricane the federal government created the Overseas Highway, opening up tourism to Key West. Water and electricity from the mainland followed in the early 1940s.

A monument to those lost in the 1935 hurricane stands at mile marker 81.5, bayside. Created from the polished keystone harvested from the coral quarries at Windley Key, the monument is a memorial to the more than five hundred who died in the hurricane as well as to war veterans.

Now called Islamorada, Village of Islands, the town was incorporated by its residents on December 31, 1997, and now includes four islands in the middle keys from Plantation to Lower Matecumbe, comprising 6 square miles with about seven thousand residents. The incorporation enabled the community of relatively wealthy residents to keep a larger share of its considerable tax base for local improvements rather than lending unbalanced support to the higher-traffic tourist zones such as Key West. One such local improvement is Founders Park, which has a beach, Olympic-size pool, playground, and dog park. Town officials also work together to develop responsible development regulations and a plan to address infrastructure and environmental issues, such as the need to upgrade septic and wastewater treatment systems to protect local waterways from contamination. Incorporation also helps protect the community, a stretch 18 miles long and a mile wide, from rampant overdevelopment, a big problem in the Keys in the past few decades.

Islamorada is known as the sport fishing capital of the world and hosts many tournaments throughout the year. It's not surprising that the World Wide Fisherman and Islamorada Fish Company complex has grown to epic proportions over the past decade or two.

Islamorada is known as the sport fishing capital of the world. Monroe County Tourist Development Council

LODGING

Casa Morada

305-664-0044, 1-888-881-3030,
fax 305-664-0674
www.casamorada.com
Mile marker 82.2, US 1 bayside
136 Madeira Rd., Islamorada 33036

You've passed by the mom-and-pops, fishermen's hideaways, and party centrals—and for good reason. The alternative is Casa Morada, which combines sun-drenched Keys ambience with chic New York style. Guests at Casa Morada can relax in their private patio hot tubs, call for a massage, retreat to the bayfront island gazebo, or bask in the sun by the beachside pool. The renovated 1950s hotel suites feature cool terrazzo floors, crisp white cotton—dressed queen and king beds, dark Mexican wood, and rattan furniture. It's a perfect getaway for those who don't want to leave the luxury of a charmed life behind. $$$–$$$$.

Cheeca Lodge & Spa

305-664-4651, 1-800-327-2888,
fax 305-664-2893
www.rockresorts.com
Mile marker 82, US 1 oceanside
81801 Oceanside Hwy., Islamorada 33036

This self-contained, nationally acclaimed resort is the perfect getaway for those who require privacy yet desire the utmost in service and amenities. Cheeca, established as an inn in 1946, offers 27 acres of ultra-manicured fun for celebrities such as former president George H. W. Bush, for whom the lodge's grandest suite is named. The resort is currently renovating the rooms, and some units will be sold as condo-hotel suites. In addition, a new private club is under construction for owners and members to enjoy, along with other member-exclusive privileges such as preferred pricing on amenities, a private beach, and dining areas. With a palm-lined beach, sunset cruises perfect for weddings, and long, lighted dock, Cheeca easily lives up to its trademark "barefoot elegance." $$$–$$$$.

Environmental Awareness at Cheeca Lodge

Impressively, and perhaps in view of the fact that Keys resorts such as Cheeca depend upon a healthy environment, Cheeca Lodge actively promotes environmental awareness and maintains environmentally conscientious practices, including recycling (which saved the lodge $20,000 in its first year); on-site wastewater treatment and gray-water reuse for landscaping; low-flow showers and toilets; xeriscaping; use of biodegradable, low-phosphate, and recycled materials in multiple applications; a ban on Jet Skis to protect sea grasses; and land preservation through a butterfly garden. The lodge dims beach lights during turtle nesting season, and the restaurant refrains from serving endangered species, offering farm-raised seafood seasoned with fresh herbs from the restaurant garden. Guests are educated about local and global environmental issues through a nationally acclaimed children's eco-camp and in-room awareness booklets. An interpretive nature trail winds through the grounds, and signs on the fishing dock help anglers determine species-specific environmental regulations. More tips are posted on the lodge's designated "catch and release" pier. Cheeca Lodge holds an Earth Day celebration and contributes to environmental causes including the Save-a-Turtle and Reef Relief foundations. Recognizing the importance and value of protecting our environmental well-being benefits not only the birds and fish that depend on the Keys habitat, but humans as well. And by protecting the environment that makes the Florida Keys an attractive destination, Cheeca Lodge is investing in its own future.

Chesapeake Resort
305-664-4662, 1-800-338-3395,
fax 305-664-8595
www.chesapeake-resort.com
Mile marker 83.4, US 1 oceanside
83409 Overseas Hwy., Islamorada 33036

If you like the well-ordered life, you'll like
the well-organized, self-contained retreat
at Chesapeake Resort. Offering standard
rooms overlooking the gardens and two-
bedroom oceanfront suites, the Chesapeake
enjoys a reputation as being reliably well
cared for. Amenities include boat docks
with charters for fishing and diving, a
beach with oceanfront Jacuzzi, and a pool.
$$$–$$$$.

Coconut Cove Oceanfront Resort and Marina
305-664-0123
Mile marker 84.8, US 1 oceanside,
Islamorada 33036

A few 50-year-old concrete block cabins
provide adequate shelter, and although a new
building is under construction, a permitting
controversy promises delays. There are two
tiki bars, but they're not operational; the
swimming pool is under construction; and
the advertised free kayaks have holes in
them. There are additional fees for every-
thing from dogs to dirty dishes. $–$$.

Coral Bay Resort
305-664-5568, fax 305-664-3424
Mile marker 75.6, US 1 bayside
75690 Overseas Hwy., Islamorada 33036

Quaint yet well maintained, this laid-back
bayside resort is popular for its tropical
foliage, sunset views, and atmosphere and
style reminiscent of yesteryear. It's very
popular with anglers due to the local population of bonefish, tarpon, snapper, and
grouper. Bring your own boat for dockage
in the protected harbor. No pets. Standard
rooms and cottages are available. $$–$$$$.

Holiday Isle Beach Resorts and Marina
305-664-2321, 1-800-327-7070,
fax 305-664-2703
www.holidayisle.com
Mile marker 84, US 1 oceanside
84001 Overseas Hwy., Islamorada 33036

This place is legendary for its tiki bar,
which serves tropical rum runners and piña
coladas all day and night to the hundreds
who've chosen to stay here or in the near
vicinity (there is a complex of hotels, shops,
and restaurants clustered here). The
atmosphere is big and busy, loud and fun—
it's a place where anglers, boaters, tourists,
and kids coexist in a crowd of ticky-tacky
fun. Stay at Harbor Lights, 0.5 mile from
the tiki bar ($$ for a single), or on the
ocean at Holiday Isle ($$$$ for the presi-
dential suite).

The Moorings Village and Spa
305-664-4708, fax 305-664-4242
www.mooringsvillageandspa.com
Mile marker 81.6, oceanside
123 Beach Rd., Islamorada 33036

The Moorings is simply the most beautiful
and peaceful collection of oceanfront cottages
in the Florida Keys. Situated on 18 acres with
1,100 feet of Atlantic coastline beach, the
Moorings is composed of 18 wooden Keys-
style cottages that feature colorful shutters,
tin roofs, and plantation verandas looking
over the ocean or into lush tropical gardens.
The property was once a coconut plantation, and the cottages are nestled quietly
among tall palms, hardwoods, and flower-
ing, fragrant, and fruit trees. Each cottage
is fully modernized and elegantly appointed, some with Jacuzzi tubs and complete
kitchens. (There is no room service at the
Moorings, and housekeeping is optional.)
Amenities include spa treatment and mas-
sages (held at the two-story tiki hut), daily
yoga sessions, kayaking and sailboarding,
and a pool and tennis court. $$$–$$$$.

Pelican Cove Resort

305-664-4435, 1-800-445-4690,
fax 305-664-5134
www.pcove.com
Mile marker 84.5, US 1 oceanside
84457 Old Overseas Hwy., Islamorada
33036

This oceanfront resort has a little bit more
style than most in this party zone area of
the middle Keys, where boaters gather at an
offshore sandbar with coolers, chairs, and
even their dogs to just chill together in the
summer sun. The resort offers a small
restaurant and bar on the ocean, a pool and
hot tub, and boat and water sport rentals on
the shore. Two- and three-bedroom suites
are available. No pets. $$–$$$$.

The Ragged Edge Resort

305-852-5389, 1-800-436-2023
www.ragged-edge.com
Mile marker 86.5, oceanside
243 Treasure Harbor Rd., Islamorada
33036

Ragged Edge fits its reputation as the best
clean, low-budget oceanfront accommoda-
tions in Islamorada, except it's not really so
no-frills. An oceanfront pool and boat dock
complement this off-the-highway hide-
away, where old-fashioned shuffleboard
and biking are popular. Single motel rooms
with refrigerators; deluxe two-bedroom
apartments with two baths and a kitchen.
No pets. $–$$$.

DINING

Caribbean Café and Catering

305-664-0004
www.islamoradaweddings.com
Mile marker 80.9
80925 Overseas Hwy., Unit 5, Islamorada
33036

Open only for lunch because owners
Debbie Pierog and chef David Mansen

run a catering business in the evening, this
is a don't-miss spot. The roadside restaurant sports just a half dozen tables, often
full, of course, but you can pick up a lunch
to go if necessary. Try macadamia-crusted
chicken salad with mandarin oranges, avocado, red onion, and cumin; grilled veggie
panini with Brie and sundried-tomato
pesto; or Happy Hour chicken, sautéed with
apricots, mangos, ginger, and herbs and
served over jasmine rice and topped with
toasted coconut. The Caribbean jerked tuna
sandwich with Chef David's secret sauce
(soon available at local Winn-Dixie gro-
ceries and online) is unforgettable. Diners
are invited to bring their own beer or wine,
and well-behaved dogs are even welcome to
settle beneath their feet. $.

Islamorada Fish Company

305-664-9271, 1-800-258-2559
www.islamoradafishco.com
Mile marker 81.5, US 1 bayside
81532 Overseas Hwy., Islamorada 33036

This small but tenacious roadside fresh-
fish market, which opened in 1948, affiliated with Bass Pro Shops in 1998 and
evolved into a huge and thriving partner
to World Wide Sportsman. It's still the
best place to buy fresh seafood in the middle Keys, and now there is a consistently
packed outdoor dining area. Fresh seafood
and sushi are served at the Marlin Bar, and
this is the place to buy perfect Keys pink
shrimp, as well as any other local seafood to
enjoy during your stay or to take home for
later. Fresh seafood can be ordered via the
Web site as well. $$.

Kaiyō

305-664-5556
www.kaiyokeys.com
Mile marker 82
81701 Old Hwy., Islamorada 33036

The atmosphere here is invitingly dark, yet
it glows in golden light that sparks off the

Kaiyō |Jim Wurster

fresh sorbet in guava, mango, and pickled ginger flavors. All are served on handcrafted ceramic plates and platters made by local artist Beth Kaminstein, which are available for sale at the restaurant or online. Closed Sunday. Reservations accepted; catering and carryout available. $$–$$$.

Lorelei Restaurant and Cabana Bar
305-664-4656
Mile marker 82, US 1 bayside,
96 Madeira Rd., Islamorada 33036

You can't miss the giant mermaid sign, which is like a siren beckoning you in to sample the basic but hearty seafood fare at this longtime Keys institution. Dine overlooking the water or outdoors on the waterfront. Live music nightly. $$.

Morada Bay Beach Café
305-664-0604
Mile marker 81.6, US 1 bayside
81600 Overseas Hwy., Islamorada 33036

Known for its bayside beach café, sunset dining, and full-moon parties, Morada Bay serves sophisticated breakfast, lunch, and dinner fare on its porch, in the Moroccan- and Tibetan-furnished dining room, or upstairs in the more formal Pierre's restaurant. Relax with a cigar and cognac in the Green Flash Lounge after a continental dinner. $$.

glass mosaics and handcrafted functional ceramic pieces that grace each table. Creative drinks served here include sake-tinis, sake Maria, sake mojito, and Kaiyō Kolada, made with blue saké and fresh pineapple. Chef Dawn Sieber, formerly of Cheeca Lodge just down the street, serves up creative cuisine such as Key lime rolls; Islamorada roll with tuna, avocado, and mango; baby barbecue ribs; and single servings of sushi and sashimi, which allows for customized variety plates. Desserts include

ATTRACTIONS, PARKS, AND RECREATION

Anne's Beach
Mile marker 73.5, US 1 oceanside, Islamorada

Owned, upgraded, and maintained by the Village of Islands, this beach is the last stop before leaving Islamorada. It's been a roadside attraction for decades, with its small patch of sand and pull-off lot, but in recent years the village has installed a boardwalk to protect the ground vegetation, rest rooms, and a parking lot and has expanded the beach. The shallow water and smooth bottom makes this a nice place for children, and friendly dogs have been seen romping in the surf, too. It's a great place to cool off in the middle of the long drive to or from Key West. Open sunrise to sunset. Free.

Avanyu Spa at Cheeca Lodge

305-517-4485
Mile marker 82, US 1 oceanside
81801 Oceanside Hwy., Islamorada 33036

Relax your back and brain at this full-service spa open to the public. Enjoy an Avanyu
Swedish massage or several different variations, with or without the fragrance of essential
oils, or invigorate your circulation with a salt scrub, mud wrap, or hydrotherapy. There are
facials, sun-damage treatments, and special services for kids and teens, too. $$$$.

Bump and Jump Boat Rental

305-664-9494, 1-877-453-9463
www.keysboatrental.com
81197 Overseas Hwy., Islamorada 33036

Owner Gilles Fumat personally delivered my boat to my hotel dock the night before my big
day at sea, and he carefully introduced me to all aspects of its use and care. He made boat
rental super easy. He also provides sailboats, sailboards, kayaks, bikes—whatever you need
to best enjoy the Islamorada area. $–$$$$.

The Florida Keys Memorial

Mile marker 81.8, US 1 oceanside, Islamorada

Also called the Hurricane Monument, this memorial was erected by the WPA in 1937 in
honor of the hundreds killed by the Labor Day hurricane of 1935 and veterans of World
War I. The ashes of some three hundred hurricane victims are buried in the crypt of the
monument. Keystone, coral rock from the Windley Key Quarry, was used to face the edifice.

The Florida Keys Memorial Jim Wurster

Founders Park

Founders Park
305-853-1685
Mile marker 87, US 1 bayside
87000 Overseas Hwy., Islamorada 33036

Transformed from an old resort, the Plantation Yacht Harbor, the park is an effort to improve recreational resources for residents by the newly incorporated Village of Islands. With an Olympic-size pool, bayfront beach, dog park, tennis and basketball courts, amphitheater, kiddie water playground, and skate park, the park has something for every-one. Visitors are welcome to use the park for free—ask for a pass at any Islamorada hotel. Open sunrise to sunset daily. $.

Indian Key State Historical Site
305-664-2540
Mile marker 78.5, US 1 oceanside, Islamorada

Visible from the Overseas Highway, this small, 10-acre island looks like it's fully covered in brush, with a dock, but there's more here than bushes. The public is welcome to come ashore and explore this island, now a Historic State Park. A thriving settlement during the glory days of shipwrecking and even the Dade County seat during the early 1800s, the island community was attacked and wiped out by Indians in 1840. The hotel where John James Audubon visited during his journey to paint birds of the Keys was among the many buildings burned to the ground and destroyed, and many residents were killed. One of those who met their fateful demise in the attack was Dr. Henry Perrine, a well-known physician and botanist who planted groves of tropical plants, including agave and tamarind on the island and nearby. Today those trees are thriving over the ruins and narrow roadways left on the island. Ranger tours are available at 9 and 1 Thursday through Monday, and maps and brochures are available for free self-guided tours. Accessible by boat only; round-trip tour-boat service is available from Robbie's Marina (mile marker 77.5, bayside; call 305-664-9814 a half hour before the tours start; $$). Open daily 8–sunset. $.

Lignumvitae Key Botanical State Park
305-664-2540
Mile marker 78.5, 1 mile west of US 1, bayside; access by boat only

This botanical preserve is the scene of the Matheson House, a self-sufficient home built in 1919 featuring a windmill for power and a roof cistern to collect rainwater to meet household water needs. It's surrounded by a virgin tropical forest: wear shoes and expect bugs! One-and-a-half-hour guided walks are conducted at 10 and 2 Thursday through Monday. Call 305-664-9814 for advance reservations and tour-boat information. Open 8–5 Thursday through Monday. $.

Robbie's Marina
305-664-9814, 1-877-664-8498
www.robbies.com
Mile marker 77.5, US 1 bayside, Islamorada

Here you can rent boats, hire a fishing guide, go on a tour, or even dine at the Hungry Tarpon Restaurant, but the really big deal here is that you can feed the tarpon. The schools of huge fish that hover under the docks and wait for the nearly constant handouts have made Robbie's famous. The fun began in 1986 when marina owners Robbie and his wife, Mona, found an injured tarpon under their dock. The fish needed stitches for a slash in his jaw, and the couple nursed him back to health for six months before releasing him. Dubbed Scarface, the fish came back to visit and brought his fish pals along, and soon the feeding tradition was established. Open daily 8–6. Tarpon feeding $; boat tours $$; boat rental $$$$.

The Shipwreck of the SAN PEDRO

If you have or rent your own boat, you may want to check out one of the shipwrecks that likely brought riches to the Indian Key island dwellers—perhaps Calusa Indians at the time. Just 1.25 miles southeast of the island lie the remains of the SAN PEDRO, a ship that sank in a hurricane on July 15, 1733, and was one of a fleet of Spanish treasure ships. Much of the recovered bounty was later housed in Art McKee's Treasure Village, a castlelike building that today serves as a collection of shops by the same name. All that's left of the SAN PEDRO are piles of round ballast stones (remember, these are archaeological treasures in the National Marine Sanctuary—don't touch or take them) and some replica cannons, all in 18 feet of water and surrounded by white buoys for easy identification and mooring.

Windley Key Fossil Reef State Geologic Site
305-664-2540
Mile marker 85.5, US 1 bayside, Windley Key

This is the remains of a quarry from which coral rock and limestone were cut to provide building blocks, as well as fill and polished keystone, for area homes, buildings, and Henry

Flagler's railroad. The quarry continued to operate until the 1960s, and today it provides a unique glimpse into the geology of the coral reefs as well as a broad sample of ecosystems on the property, from wetlands to hardwood hammocks that feature more than 40 types of trees. Several paths are available for self-guided tours; guided walks are held at 10 and 2 daily. Open 8–5 Thursday through Monday. $.

CULTURE

Rain Barrel

305-852-3084
Mile marker 86.7, US 1 bayside
86700 Overseas Hwy., Plantation Key
33036

This rustic gallery, like a walk in the rain forest, is where ten local artists display their wares at indoor/outdoor booths and shops among lush plants, ponds, and trickling waterfalls. Ceramics, glassware, jewelry, and musical chimes are among the offerings. Open 9–5 Monday through Friday and 9–6 Saturday and Sunday.

Rain Barrel Jim Wurster

SHOPPING

Ms. Cellaneous Quality Consignments

305-517-9990
Mile marker 82.7
82751 Overseas Hwy., Islamorada 33036

Owner Rae Cavanaugh presents a marvelously eclectic collection of bargain consignment items, gifts, clothing, and artwork. My daughter Rachel found a beautiful multihued crocheted skirt-and-sweater ensemble here that she wore in Key West. Open 10–5 Monday through Friday and 11–4 Saturday.

Treasure Village Courtyard Shops

305-852-0511
Mile marker 86.7, US 1 bayside
86729 Old Hwy., Plantation Key 33036

You can't miss the giant lobster standing sentry over this castlelike shopping village, originally built to store and display shipwreck salvage items by treasure salvor Art McKee. The treasures found here today are still worth a look if you have some time. Open 9–6 daily.

A giant lobster stands sentry over Treasure Village.

World Wide Sportsman
305-664-4615, 1-800-327-2880
www.worldwidesportsman.com
Mile marker 81.5, US 1 bayside
81576 Overseas Hwy., Islamorada 33036

In 1998 Johnny Morris's Bass Pro Shops of Springfield, Missouri, came to town and joined forces with the Islamorada Fish Company, a family-owned market since 1948. Morris's skill in developing fishing lures turned his expertise into a full-service sporting-goods concern. Today the fish market sits next to World Wide Sportsman, a warehouse-size supplier of all things outdoors (many of the other shops in the Bass Pro chain are called Outdoor World). All your fishing equipment, guides, and a bayside marina are on-site. Open 9–8:30 Sunday through Thursday and 9–9 Friday and Saturday.

Marathon (mile marker 63–47)

Marathon, composed of several incorporated islands, marks the point where the island chain turns and heads west instead of south, and also the point where the islands are formed from limestone residue rather than coral heads. Here the islands have extended beyond Florida Bay, so rather than being referred to as bayside, properties are called gulfside, indicating that they are on the west side of the highway, bordering the Gulf of Mexico, opposite the Atlantic Ocean.

Much wider than the islands from Largo to Islamorada, Marathon boasts an airport and is home to a strong population of working fishermen. From Marathon to Big Pine and Sugarloaf Keys, the islands have more of an "everyman" feel to them than the resort areas of Islamorada and Key West. Locals continue to preserve the charm of yesteryear that characterizes the Keys, with many small motels and resorts from the 1950s restored and still thriving as some of the best places to really enjoy the Keys and what makes them unique. Big development and corporations pose a challenge to these small, mostly independent proprietors, but some persist, with the conviction that if they should let drop their stance, the Keys will become like any other shoreline destination, losing the character that brings the tourists in the first place. There is concern that locals can't keep up with increasing real estate and living expenses as corporations move into the area. Many servers work two and three jobs to stay afloat, and some large resorts have begun importing cheap labor from Miami, running daily bus service for maids, landscapers, and waitstaff. Someday the Keys won't even need locals, will they?

LODGING

Banana Bay Resort and Marina
305-743-3500, 1-800-226-2621
www.bananabay.com
Mile marker 49.5, US 1 gulfside
4590 Overseas Hwy., Marathon 33050

A family resort with 62 units, a restaurant, dockside services and charters, and two small meeting rooms, one theater style, Banana Bay is nestled under a canopy of banana, breadfruit, and poinciana trees. In addition, the resort owns Pretty Joe Rock, a private island

The cottage on Pretty Joe Rock, Banana Bay's private island

with a two-bedroom cottage that's fully equipped with water, electricity, Jacuzzi tub, glass-walled shower, and even a full bar. The island paradise rents for a long weekend or per week and includes a boat. $$–$$$$.

Black Fin Resort and Marina
305-743-2393, 1-800-548-5397
www.blackfinresort.com
Mile marker 49.5, US 1 gulfside
4650 Overseas Hwy., Marathon 33050

The clean, basic, old-style Keys rooms here have coffeepots and data ports, and the apartments have full kitchens. Dining, kayaks, and marina available; sandy beach area with volleyball near the dock. Pets welcome for a small fee. $–$$$.

Captain Pip's Marina and Hideaway
305-743-4403, 1-800-707-2844
www.captainpips.com
Mile marker 47.5, US 1 bayside
1410 Overseas Hwy., Marathon 33050

It pays to stay at a fishing marina: Captain Pip's offers the use of an 18- or 21-foot boat

during your stay, which is a big savings on boat rental. Crafted of rustic whitewashed Dade County pine and shaded with colorful blue awnings, the rooms have refrigerators, microwaves, and toasters, while suites have oceanfront views and full kitchens. There are also efficiencies, apartments, and suites, some available by the week only. The lowest rates are from September to December. $$$–$$$$.

Coconut Cay Resort
305-289-7672, 1-877-354-7356,
fax 305-289-0186
www.coconutcay.com
Mile marker 51, US 1 gulfside
7196 Overseas Hwy., Marathon 33050

These colorful cottages, painted lime green, watermelon pink, sunshine yellow, and sky blue, jump out at passing travelers. The rooms themselves received a modern makeover by owners Jim Rhyme and Pam and Randy Baad and now have cool tile floors, floor-length muslin drapes, and sleek but casual furnishings. Rooms in the resort area border around the pool and cabana, while the dockside rooms at the marina behind the resort offer free boat slips for guests. If you don't have your own boat, you can rent one from the marina. Standard rooms, two-bedroom/kitchen cottages; pets allowed in a few units. $$–$$$$.

Conch Key Cottages

305-289-1377, 1-800-330-1577
www.conchkeycottages.com
Mile marker 62.3, US 1 oceanside
62250 Overseas Hwy., Walkers Island
33050

This private retreat has one- and two-bedroom cottages on the ocean, a lushly landscaped pool, a marina, fishing charters, and complimentary kayaks. The remote island atmosphere is laid back, and the cottages reflect Keys character with pine paneling, tile, Florida casual furniture, and cool tropical colors. There are updated gourmet kitchens for those who prefer to prepare their own holiday seafood feasts with the day's catch. Efficiency apartments with kitchenette up to two-bedroom oceanfront cottages are available; minimum stays required during holidays. $–$$$$.

Coconut Cay Resort

Hawk's Cay Resort

305-743-7000, 1-800-432-2242
www.hawkscay.com
61 Hawk's Cay Blvd., Duck Key 33050

Originally a small resort, this property on Duck Key has drawn famous vacationers since the 1950s. Renovated and expanded by a Maine developer known as Pritham Singh, Hawk's Cay is now a huge complex occupying 60 acres on Duck Key, a collection of five islands connected by bridges. Villas, called Conch Houses, are built in rows of two-story side-by-side buildings, painted in pastel colors with Disneyesque landscaping and atmosphere. Guests can visit the spa, play tennis, golf, or, of course, fish. Boating charters are available, or kayak, canoe, or sail. Hawk's Cay conducts a popular dolphin encounter program with captive dolphins. (It's hard to spend time with these beautiful, intelligent creatures and not feel that they should be allowed to live freely, rather than as money-makers for a wealthy resort.) Standard rooms and villas are available; three- to five-night minimum stays required at peak times. $$$–$$$$.

Hidden Harbor Motel

305-743-5376, 1-800-362-3495
www.hiddenharbormotel.com
Mile marker 48.5, US 1 gulfside
2396 Overseas Hwy., Marathon 33050

Your basic no-frills fisherman's motel, Hidden Harbor has simple and clean rooms, some with kitchenettes and kitchens, scattered over a spacious piece of gulf-front land with a boat launch and slips. This quiet spot has enhanced security: guests are protected behind an electronic gate and 6-foot fence. There's a nice pool and dock with picnic tables and grills along the water, but the real treasure here is the Turtle Hospital (see Attractions, Parks, and Recreation). $–$$$.

Jolly Roger Trailer Park
305-289-0404
Mile marker 59, US 1 gulfside

Although Keys campers may find bigger, fancier RV parks than this one, Jolly Roger is a favorite among those who prefer a quiet atmosphere with nature as the main attraction. This park has 131 tent and RV sites, some waterfront, with water, electric, and sewer hookups. Showers and laundry facilities, swimming area, snorkeling, boat ramp, and dock. $–$$.

Rainbow Bend Fishing Resort
305-289-1505, 1-800-929-1505
www.rainbowbend.com
Mile marker 58, US 1 oceanside
57784 Overseas Hwy., Grassy Key, Marathon 33050

Rainbow Bend offers a variety of room options, from a standard hotel room to two-bedroom oceanfront suites and several in between. In business for three decades, Rainbow Bend maintains its authentic Keys charm with rooms that are clean and neat though not fancy. Fees include half-day use of a small motorboat, free kayaks and sailboats, and free breakfast daily. As an added bonus, Rainbow Bend is home to the award-winning Hideaway Café, open for breakfast and dinner. Pets under 40 pounds permitted for an extra fee; children three and older and additional adults in the room are extra. $$–$$$$.

Seabird Key
305-669-0044
www.seabirdkey.com
Marathon

How about your own private 10-acre island for your Keys getaway? There's room for eight in this privately-owned home, with two double bedrooms and baths plus a loft for kids with four bunk beds and another bath. There are also two outdoor showers

---

Safe Boating Tips

Protecting the fragile coral reefs and sea-grass beds in the Florida Keys is essential to preserving the ecological habitat as well as the pleasures visitors come to the Keys to enjoy. If you take time to learn a few rhymes, you're likely to have a better time:

Brown, brown, run aground. Coral and sea grass in shallow water appear brown, so avoid taking a boat into water that looks brown.

White, white, you'll be there all night. Sandbars in shallow water appear white, and the water may be more shallow than it looks. Be careful not to get caught on a sandbar in shallow waters.

Green, green, nice and clean. The beautiful clear green waters of the Florida Keys indicate clear sailing for small craft in deep water free of reefs or sea-grass beds. Consult your NOAA marine chart to plot a safe course.

Blue, blue, cruise on through. The deep ocean waters appear a deep blue color and are generally safe, but be cautious and on the lookout for reefs that may rise suddenly from the water.

If you run aground, turn off your boat engine and try to raise the motor so it does not sit on or hit the reef, sandy, or grassy bottom, all of which could seriously damage the marine habitat. Allow the tide to help you drift into deeper water, or call for help using your boat radio.

Don't anchor on the reef. Mooring buoys are provided near many coral reefs for snorkelers and divers. Tie your boat onto the rope that is attached to the top of the buoy and be careful of shallow waters, sea-grass beds, and coral reef formations.

The eco-house on Seabird Key

Adam and Eve at Seabird Key

"This is our little place to get away from the world and just enjoy each other," says JoAnn Ellis, who has celebrated her wedding anniversary on Seabird Key with husband Charlie every year since their honeymoon there in 1996. "We like to play Adam and Eve for a whole week." Ellis says they get lobsters and grouper right off the dock and lie on the dock to watch parrotfish and stingrays swim past. "It's like being in heaven."

Caretaker Jeff Davis is busy at work building a boardwalk out into the mangroves on the island. "Most people don't know anything about the mangroves. The walkway will take them into the mangroves and under the canopy. In wintertime herons and other birds roost in the trees overhead. This gives them a chance to see the roots of the mangroves—the tiniest start of the food chain grows in the swampy water around these roots. This is where all life begins."

Adam and Eve are on to that.

and a white-sand beach. This ultimate eco-resort relies on solar power (with backup generators) for electricity. Built from river-dredged cypress, the tropical cottage is raised high off the ground to capture ocean breezes, and floor-to-ceiling louvered window shades help keep the air flowing through the home, so no air-conditioning is needed. Most other conveniences of modern life are available, though, including a telephone, microwave oven, and even a coffee-bean grinder, and music is piped all the way to the beach. Rainwater is collected in a cistern, and laundry wastewater is recycled for irrigating the lush tropical gardens. Yard wastes and seaweed are recycled as compost, and table scraps are fed to fish and wildlife or composted. You'll have your own 19-foot boat (which would otherwise cost a bundle for the week) and Sunfish sailboat, as well as snorkeling,

swimming, and fishing gear. A library of books, CDs, and videotapes is on hand, or make your own music at the piano. The island is a five-minute boat ride from Marathon and an hour's drive from Key West. Summer specials are sometimes available. $$$$.

Seascape Ocean Resort
305-743-6455, 1-800-332-7327,
fax 305-743-8469
www.seascaperesort.us
1075 75th St. (off US 1 oceanside),
Marathon 33050

Originally a private estate built in 1953, this tropical paradise has been renovated into nine rooms and suites by owners Bill and Sara Stites. Each is beautifully decorated with original artwork, some created by Sara herself and offered for sale. Removed from the busy commercial area of Marathon, the island is truly a retreat from civilization. An oceanside pool and marina, kayaks, and tropical gardens occupy guests. Kitchenettes are available in some rooms, and Bill can recommend a list of local dining establishments. This relaxing and luxurious getaway offers privacy and style unparalleled at large resorts or roadside hotels. $$$–$$$$.

Tropical Cottages
305-743-6048
www.tropicalcottages.com
Mile marker 50.5, gulfside
243 61st St., Marathon 33050

Owned by Banana Bay Resorts, these historic cottages are being renovated from no-frills fishermen's getaways to romantic, adults-only honeymoon cottages with Egyptian cotton sheets, Turkish bath sheets, new bathrooms, and gardens. Unrenovated units $; new units $$–$$$$.

DINING

Barracuda Grill
305-743-3314
Mile marker 49.5, gulfside
4290 Overseas Hwy., Marathon 33050

Here you'll find cool barracuda décor and delicious food, but weary, unhappy waitstaff. The grilled grouper with Key lime butter and caper sauce and grilled rare yellowfin tuna with wasabi drizzle and seaweed salad were both delectable, but the signature soup, a cream of tomato, was huge and simply too rich. $$–$$$.

Chiki Tiki Bar & Grille at Burdines Waterfront
305-743-9204
www.burdineswaterfront.com
Mile marker 50, US 1 oceanside
1200 Oceanview Ave., Marathon 33050

This family-owned restaurant on the water

in Boot Key Channel is popular with locals and boaters who come and go through Burdines Waterfront Marina. Try the green chile–cheese sandwiches; grilled, fried, or blackened fresh catch (yours or theirs); quesadillas and salsa; or Key lime pie. $–$$.

Hideaway Café
305-289-1554
www.hideawaycafe.com
Rainbow Bend Resort, mile marker 58,
US 1 oceanside
57784 Overseas Hwy., Marathon 33050

After a few days in the laid-back fishermen's paradise of the Keys, you may find yourself in the mood for a little finery. Perhaps a little coq au vin, escargots, or beef Wellington? Residents say that the Hideaway Café, a five-star restaurant with patio dining overlooking the ocean, is the place to go. Hosted by Robert Gray, husband of chef Jacqueline Gray, the award-winning restaurant has tables dressed with white linen tablecloths and fresh roses, and waiters in shirts and ties—a rarity in the Keys. Numerous recommendations for the rack of lamb proved true, and the fresh Keys pink shrimp were delicious, but the filet mignon medallions didn't impress. Other entrées included smoked salmon, zuppa di clams (a soup made of a rich broth, vegetables, and clams), and chateaubriand. Open for breakfast and dinner; sunset specials 4:30–5:30 daily. $$–$$$.

Keys Fisheries Market and Marina
305-743-4353, 1-866-743-4353
www.keysfisheries.com
Mile marker 49, gulfside
35th St., Marathon 33050

Groups of up to six can join a commercial lobster or stone crab boat crew for a taste of a working day at sea, learning about the industry and the history of the Keys from your captain, a professional commercial fisherman. At day's end, the bounty of the

Enjoy a dockside dinner at the Keys Fisheries restaurant.

day can be prepared for your dockside dinner at the Keys Fisheries restaurant. The restaurant offers all varieties of fresh local fish—grilled, blackened, or fried— along with crab cakes, crab Alfredo, and Key lime pie. The Famous Lobster Reuben is a huge sandwich of chunks of lobster bathed in Thousand Island sauce, smothered with Swiss and sauerkraut and slapped between two massive slices of Texas toast. Huge and tasty. Place your order at the counter, along with the name of your favorite criminal or celebrity (so when the servers call out "Jesse James" or "Marilyn Monroe," you'll know when they're looking for you), and then dine at picnic tables while birds and tarpon volley for handouts. The market also offers fresh fish to go or will ship it far and wide. $$.

Sombrero Marina and Dockside Lounge
305-743-0000
Mile marker 50, US 1 oceanside
35 Sombrero Blvd., Marathon 33050

A local favorite. At Sombrero's boaters can stop by to grill their catch and do their laundry, pick up supplies at the liquor store, relax with friends at the Tiki Dock, or dine at the Dockside Lounge, a local hot spot with live music nightly and Sunday local open-jam sessions. Casual fare includes pizza, wings, burgers, and local seafood. $$–$$$.

ATTRACTIONS, PARKS, AND RECREATION

Crane Point Hammock and Museum
305-743-9100
www.cranepoint.org
Mile marker 50.5, US 1 gulfside
5550 Overseas Hwy., Marathon 33050

Named for Francis and Mary Crane, a Massachusetts couple who bought the property in 1949 and helped to preserve the natural area, Crane Point provides a great opportunity to learn about Keys wildlife and history. The 63-acre preserve includes a wild bird rescue center and a historic home, the Adderly House, the oldest house in all the Keys (except Key West), built by Bahamian settlers at the turn of the 20th century. Nature trails wind through a tropical hammock, and a children's museum with educational exhibits as well as a museum of natural history are open for visitors. *Whaling Wall #27*, one of one hundred wall murals worldwide painted by environmental artist Wyland and donated to communities in hopes of inspiring greater awareness for marine mammal conservation, is in the children's museum. Also on exhibit at Crane is a horribly beat-up Styrofoam boat, the homemade raft that in 1992 carried to the Keys four Cubans who were rescued 24 miles off the coast of Marathon. The gift shop offers an interesting collection of Keys souvenirs, books, and jewelry, and if you're lucky, you'll meet Giggles, a Pomeranian who works there and likes to play with the nautical plush children's toys. Also, be sure to check out the amazing wonderland rain forest—the perfect place to catch a refreshing mist while exploring the grounds. Samples from the tropical plant collection are for sale on weekends. Open 9–5 Monday through Saturday and noon–5 Sunday. $.

Marathon Kayak at Sombrero Resort
305-743-0561
www.marathonkayak.com
Mile marker 50, US 1 oceanside
19 Sombrero Blvd., Marathon 33050

Explore the near shore and backwaters of the Florida Keys, where fish rest and feast in mangrove roots, birds roost in the island trees, and manatees and dolphins cruise the shallow waters. Rent your own kayak, or join an eco-tour or sunset tour. Instructions, life jackets, maps, and delivery are available, as well as half-day rentals, full-day rentals, and tours. Open 9–5 daily. $$–$$$.

Wild-Bird Protection Tips
The Marathon Wild Bird Center at Crane Point rescues and rehabilitates wild birds and also educates anglers and others about bird protection. The following are some suggestions for ensuring birds' safety:

- Never throw out large fish bones for birds—they may puncture the birds' throats and digestive systems.
- Be careful with fish hooks and monofilament line. Dispose of them properly, not in the water. If a bird should get caught on a fish hook, be sure to remove any fishing line that could entangle him.
- If a bird swallows a hook or is entangled, call the center at 305-743-8382 or bring the bird to Knight's Key Campground, at mile marker 47 in Marathon.

Pigeon Key Monroe County Tourist Development Council

Sombrero Beach

Pigeon Key

305-289-0025, 305-743-5999

Mile marker 48, US 1 gulfside, Marathon

It's hard to cross the 7-mile bridge along the Overseas Highway to Marathon and beyond without looking down at Pigeon Key and wanting to explore. The quaint-looking little 5-acre island was once a residential station for laborers of Flagler's famous Florida East Coast Railway. Many of the wooden cottages that made up the workers' village remain today, and they have earned the designation of National Historic Site. Serving as a marine science and educational research camp, the Pigeon Key Foundation was formed in 1992 and works to preserve the island and its history. A museum displays artifacts that help tell the story of the island's past, and the gift shop offers Key lime treats and Keys artwork, treasures, and history books. Day visitors can explore with the help of a guide or self-guided tour. Plan to stay a few hours, or bring a picnic and snorkeling gear and stay all day. Access Pigeon Key from the Pigeon Key Visitor's Center and Gift Shop on Knight's Key, in an old railroad car parked at about mile marker 48 on the ocean side of US 1. A shuttle bus makes the trip each hour daily beginning at 10 and ending at 3. Boaters may access the Key with permission to dock (ask at the visitors center). $.

Sombrero Beach

305-743-0033

Mile marker 50, US 1 oceanside

Sombrero Rd. at the ocean, Marathon

This formal, quiet patch of sandy beach is popular with local families. Donated by Marathon pioneers Stanley and Wanda Switlik, who also built nearby Sombrero Country Club, the park includes grills and play equipment. Well-behaved, leashed dogs are welcome. Open daily until dark.

The Turtle Hospital

305-743-6509
www.theturtlehospital.org
Mile marker 48.5, US 1 bayside
2396 Overseas Hwy., Marathon 33050

Rescue, rehabilitation, and *release* are the key words for this unique hospital—the only one in the world exclusively for sea turtles. Terrorized by monofilament fishing line, boat propellers, and polluted waters, turtles are brought here for surgeries and treatment. Amputations are sometimes necessary due to entanglement in fishing line, but the most common surgery performed is on tumors, found on nearly half the green turtles in the Keys and present worldwide. Affiliated with the University of Florida, the hospital's researchers are working to determine the cause of the tumor-producing illness. The facility, founded by hotel owner Ritchie Moretti, treats up to 70 turtles each year and has released 750 back into the wild since opening in 1986. Housed at the Hidden Harbor Hotel, the hospital gives public tours daily at 10 and 4:20. Reservations are requested for an educational visit (call 305-743-2552). $–$$.

CULTURE

Bougainvillea House Gallery

305-743-0808
Mile marker 53.5, US 1 oceanside
12420 Overseas Hwy., Marathon 33050

Local artists' paintings, ceramics, pottery, blown and stained glass, photography, and jewelry are displayed and are for sale. Open 10–6 daily November through April. Summer hours vary, so call ahead. Free admission.

Marathon Community Theatre

305-743-0994
www.marathontheater.org
5101 Overseas Hwy., Marathon 33050

Seeking culture of the stage variety? Take in a play or musical with local actors. Matinees are at 3 and evening performances are at 8; doors open a half hour early, and seating is preferred 15 minutes in advance. In operation since 1944, the theater also runs a cinema (call 305-743-0288 for titles and times). Tickets $–$$$.

SHOPPING

Anthony's Ladies Apparel

305-743-5855
5800 Overseas Hwy., Marathon 33050

This ladies' fashion shop offers the quintessential bikinis and swimsuits as well as more formal dresses, silk blouses, and slacks. A popular shopping stop on the Overseas Highway for decades, this still-popular small chain reflects little influence of pop culture.

Anthony's has shops in Key Largo and Islamorada as well. Open 9:30–5:30 Monday through Saturday and noon–5 Sunday.

J&J Jewelry
305-743-0912
2299 Overseas Hwy., Marathon 33050

Jerry Kranz and his partner, Jacquie, import, cut, and set Australian opals and do repair work as well. A volunteer plant curator at Crane Point Hammock, Jerry also sells rare tropical rain forest plants through the shop. Open 10–5 Monday through Friday and 10–1 Saturday.

The Lower Keys and Stock Island (mile marker 47–4)

THE LOWER KEYS: BIG PINE KEY, RAMROD KEY, LITTLE TORCH KEY, AND SUGARLOAF KEY
Perhaps the least touristy islands of the Keys, the Lower Keys certainly offer many places to stay, boat, fish, and play, but these islands are also very residential and are among the most affordable for Keys living. Most activities center around nature in this part of the Keys, with less emphasis on shopping and restaurants than in the more tourist-oriented areas such as Islamorada and Key West. Here are popular diving areas such as Looe Key and wildlife preserves including the National Key Deer Refuge.

LODGING

Big Pine Key Fishing Lodge
305-872-2351
Mile marker 33, US 1 oceanside
33000 Overseas Hwy., Big Pine Key 33043

This family-owned lodge has been in business since 1972, serving fishers, boaters, divers, campers, and vacationers. Boat and fishing charters are available at the marina, and fishing, diving, camping, and snorkeling supplies are available at the lodge store. On the water in Spanish Harbor, the lodge includes docks and a swimming pool. Campsites for tents and RVs available. $–$$$.

You may see Key deer grazing on the lawn at Deer Run Bed & Breakfast.

Casa Grande Bed and Breakfast on the Ocean
305-872-2878
Mile marker 33, oceanside
1619 Long Beach Dr., Big Pine Key 33043

A sense of privacy pervades the atmosphere at this Spanish-style guest house, which has family quarters in one wing and three guest rooms in another, both joined by a sitting room with fireplace and second-story screened porch with a hot tub overlooking the sea. Rooms for two include an 8:30 breakfast. No children, pets, or credit cards. $$–$$$.

Deer Run Bed & Breakfast
305-872-2015, fax 305-872-2842
www.floridakeys.net/deer
Mile marker 33, oceanside
P.O. Box 431, Long Beach Dr., Big Pine Key 33043

Sit on the beach in back of the house while Key deer graze the lawn of this bed & breakfast. Comfortable and quiet, peaceful and pleasant, rooms offer oceanfront or garden views. Bike or canoe; relax in the ocean, in the hot tub, or in a beachfront hammock; or fish and barbecue your catch for dinner. No children or pets; three-night minimum on holidays. $$.

Little Palm Island
305-872-2524, 1-800-343-8567,
fax 305-872-4843
www.littlepalmisland.com
Mile marker 28.5, US 1 oceanside
28500 Overseas Hwy., Little Torch Key 33042

One of the most ultra-luxurious hideouts in the lower Keys, Little Palm Island has been a favorite of superstars for its seclusion and exclusivity. Accessible only by boat or seaplane, the resort maintains a launch at mile marker 28.5 on Little Torch Key, where boats run hourly at the half hour 7:30–10:30 and by request around the clock for resort and dinner guests. Thatched-roof duplex bungalows provide privacy, and for added peace, there are no phones or televisions on the island, but data ports are available in the rooms. What's your pleasure: Russian caviar and champagne? Massage oil, fresh strawberries, and whipped cream? Chips, salsa, and cold beer? Your choice of refreshments will be waiting when you arrive at your bungalow. Enjoy the spa, water sports, classic library collection, Zen garden, or life-size chess, as well as the award-winning cuisine. A Saturday-night treat features Big Dipper Bill, a retired university professor who gives astronomy highlights under the stars dockside. $$$$+.

Looe Key Reef Resort and Dive Center
305-872-2215, 1-800-942-5397,
fax 305-872-3786
www.diveflakeys.com

Mile marker 27.5, US 1 oceanside
27340 Overseas Hwy., Ramrod Key 33042

Currently under renovation, the rooms are basic motel rooms for those with diving in mind. Back doors open onto the dock, and the pool is used for diver certification classes. Snacks and tropical refreshments can be had at the cash-only tiki bar and at Julio's Grill. Prices vary from single to six-person suites; some may require a minimum three-night stay. $–$$$$.

Old Wooden Bridge Fishing Camp
305-872-2241
www.oldwoodenbridge.com
Mile marker 30.5, bayside
1791 Bogie Dr., Big Pine Key 33043

This collection of 13 efficiency cottages has evolved from a 1943 fishing camp beneath a long-gone wooden bridge. All of the cottages, which have recently been renovated, are waterfront and have one or two bedrooms and kitchens. Two-night minimum stay; pets permitted. $–$$.

Parmer's Resort
305-872-2157, fax 305-872-2014
www.parmersresort.com
Mile marker 28.5, oceanside
565 Barry Ave., Little Torch Key 33042

With 45 motel rooms, efficiencies, and apartments spread in several small buildings over the 5-acre waterfront property, at Parmer's you won't feel crowded. The grounds are lushly landscaped and feature several aviaries for the tropical bird collection. The putting green and clubs are free, but bikes, kayaks, and paddleboats are for rent. Ice chests and pets are forbidden in the rooms, and you'll be subjected to a hefty fee if you break the rules. The rooms are large, and the atmosphere is very peaceful and relaxed. Dockage available. $–$$$$.

Sugar Loaf Lodge

305-745-3211, 1-800-553-6097,
fax 305-745-3389
www.sugarloaflodge.com
Mile marker 17, US 1 oceanside
17001 Overseas Hwy., Sugarloaf Key 33042

Owned and operated by the Good family for
decades, Sugar Loaf has seen its fair share
of Keys characters and excitement and does
show a little wear and tear. The lodge has its
own marina and a private airstrip, offering
charter planes, rides (Fantasy Dan's Air-
plane Rides, 305-745-2217), and skydiving
(Sky Dive Key West, 305-745-4386). The
dining room and tiki bar will keep you in
fresh seafood and tropical drinks. All
rooms look out at the bay. $–$$$.

DINING

Little Palm Island Dining Room

305-872-2524, 1-800-343-8567,
fax 305-872-4843
www.littlepalmisland.com
Mile marker 28.5, US 1 oceanside
28500 Overseas Hwy., Little Torch Key 33042

Guests are welcome to utilize the resort
launch for dinner if reservations are made
in advance. Dine indoors by candlelight; on
the terrace overlooking the grounds, where
Key deer and birds are frequent visitors; or
at torchlit tables on the beach. At the top-
rated restaurant, diners enjoy Executive
Chef Anthony Keene's imaginative cuisine,
which features Key lime, coconut, curry,
and ponzu sauces paired with tropical fruits
and fresh seafood. $$$–$$$$.

Mangrove Mama's Restaurant

305-745-3030
Mile marker 20, US 1 oceanside
19991 Overseas Hwy., Sugarloaf Key 33042

This is a great place to stop for a fresh
salad, seafood special, or cold beer when
you're staying in the lower Keys. Indoor and
patio seating; friendly pets welcome. Happy
hour. $–$$.

No Name Pub

305-872-9115
Mile marker 30, gulfside
N. Watson Blvd., Big Pine Key 33043

This peaceful pub is full of friendly locals,
including anglers, bikers, boaters, artists,
and writers, who all congregate for a little
laid-back fun on the waterside. Pub fare
includes pizza, grouper sandwiches, and
grilled Cuban sandwiches. $–$$.

ATTRACTIONS, PARKS, AND RECREATION

Bahia Honda State Park

305-872-2353, 1-800-326-3521
www.bahiahondapark.com
Mile marker 37, US 1 oceanside
36850 Overseas Hwy., Big Pine Key 33043

Named the world's best beach in 1992 by Dr. Beach, Florida International University professor Stephen Leatherman, Bahia Honda State Park offers the rare opportunity to camp
on the oceanfront beach, with private sites separated by sea grapes, palms, and gumbo
limbo trees. Cabins are also available on the park's inlet and dock, where you may park
your boat, rent a kayak, or catch a scuba, snorkeling, or fishing tour. Fishing, diving, and
snorkeling equipment is available for rent, along with snacks and gifts in the campground
shop. Open 8–sunset daily. $.

Bat Tower

Mile marker 17, bayside
Bat Tower Rd., Big Pine Key

Known as "One Man's Folly," the imposing structure was built by entrepreneur Richter Perky in 1929 as a peaceful means of combating mosquitoes, but no bats have ever chosen to roost in the elaborate wooden tower. Free.

Florida Keys Exotic and Wild Bird Rescue

305-872-1982
1388 Avenue B, Big Pine Key 33043

Director Maya Totman, a nurse, was inspired by the plight of birds worldwide during her travels and has dedicated herself to helping the wild birds in the Keys since 2000. Volunteers help Totman rescue birds injured by fish bones tossed aside by anglers, as well as those tied up in fishing line and caught in plastic six-pack debris. Educational programs are available on- and off-site; volunteers and donations appreciated. Open daily 8–6. Free.

Fish Carcasses Kill Birds

Mary Totman, director of Florida Keys Exotic and Wild Bird Rescue, houses about 80 rescued wild birds while they await their eventual recovery and, hopefully, return to the wild. Totman is clearly upset as she describes the horror she's seen when birds die from internal injuries caused by fish bones tossed aside during fish cleaning. "The Keys are a beautiful place for visitors and residents, but people just don't realize how many bird injuries are caused by discarded fishing line and fish bones. You wouldn't feed those razor-sharp bones to your dog or cat because you know they're dangerous. But people don't think about the birds looking for a meal. The fish carcasses and fish scraps will kill them. The bones puncture their internal organs, and they die an agonizing death, slowly bleeding internally. Please dispose of fishing line in the cans we've put out along the bridges or in trash cans, and please, don't feed sea birds fish carcasses—it will kill them."

Looe Key Reef Resort and Dive Center

305-872-2215, 1-800-942-5397, fax 305-872-3786
www.diveflakeys.com
Mile marker 27.5, US 1 oceanside, Ramrod Key 33042

Dive instruction, equipment, and charters are available here. Open 7:30 AM–9 PM daily. $$$$.

National Key Deer Refuge

305-872-2239
http://nationalkeydeer.fws.gov
Mile marker 31, US 1 bayside (turn at Key Deer Blvd.)
Visitors center headquarters: 305-872-0774; Big Pine Shopping Center, mile marker 30.5, US 1 bayside, Big Pine Key

The refuge comprises 8,542 acres on Big Pine and No Name Keys—you'll know you've entered the zone by the high fence along the Overseas Highway and the warning speed-limit signs reducing travel to 45 mph during the day and 35 mph at night. It's not unusual, especially at dawn and dusk, to see the tiny dog-size deer grazing on roadsides, a perilous activity for the endangered fauna, which weigh an average of 75 pounds and stand just about 2 feet tall. Protective efforts such as the fence, reduced speed limits, and establishment of the refuge land preserve have helped to reestablish the deer population in recent years. Relatives of the Virginia white-tailed deer, these deer are specific to the Keys. You can drive (slowly, please) into the refuge area by turning northwest at Key Deer Boulevard, mile marker 30. Hike the 0.6-mile Jack C. Watson Trail or the 800-foot handicapped-accessible Fred Manillo Wildlife Trail to meet the deer. Remember, it's illegal to feed or entice wildlife. The walking trails are located at Blue Hole, an abandoned limestone quarry that's the largest freshwater lake in the Keys—and the birds, fish, turtles, and alligators know it. Swimming is not advised, but an observation tower provides a lookout over the water. Open 8–4:30 daily. Free.

Sky Dive Key West
305-745-4386
www.skydivekeywest.com
Sugarloaf Airport, mile marker 17, Sugarloaf Key 33041

How long does it take the average human to drop 10,000 feet? You'll have only forty seconds of free dive plus five minutes with a parachute to fret—and if you're lucky, you'll be in awe instead. First-time divers are strapped to an instructor. Open daily 10–7 by appointment. $$$$.

Shipwreck Trail
In cooperation with several Keys foundations, the Nature Conservancy, and Florida Heritage, the Florida Keys National Marine Sanctuary and area chambers of commerce have prepared a Shipwreck Trail guide to nine historic dive and snorkel shipwreck sites. Each site is marked with a buoy, and dive-shop operators or the chambers of commerce can assist boaters in locating the ships. Ask for the guide at boat-rental marinas and dive shops. Shipwrecks serve as artificial reefs, which offer shelter and good growing conditions to sea life. Snorkelers and divers are reminded to avoid touching or taking any remnants of ships—it's illegal. Monroe County Tourist Development Council

STOCK ISLAND

Donated to the city of Key West in 1914 as a recreational area, Stock Island is the last piece of land before the island of Key West. Today it provides space for the local community college, a golf course, a wildlife care center, a botanical garden, a police station, boat docks, and trailer homes. Some artists, no longer able to afford Key West life, have taken up residence in warehouse bays along the docks on Stock Island, creating a quiet and pleasant artists' community. A few restaurants can be found on Stock Island, a world away from the tourist venues of Key West.

Lodging

Boyd's Key West Campground

305-294-1465, fax 305-293-9301
www.boydscampground.com
Mile marker 5, oceanside
6401 Maloney Ave., Key West 33040

This campground on Stock Island has evolved from a rustic place to pitch a tent on the waterfront to a full-service and much fancier RV and tent campground over the past few years. Family-owned and family-operated, Boyd's still offers an economic alternative to local hotels. Most pets allowed. $$.

Dining

The Hickory House

305-292-2211
Mile marker 5, oceanside
5948 Peninsula Ave., Stock Island 33040

If you'd like a taste of Key West before the crowds set in, be sure to make your way around to this little restaurant on Stock Island. Built in the Bahamas and floated to its current location in the 1940s, the restaurant offers dockside dining with a sunset view, as well as live jazz Friday, Saturday, and Sunday nights. Delicious fare includes fresh seafood right off the docks. Try the fantastic jerked shrimp, fresh and perfectly cooked, and the huge salads. Enjoy dinner with a signature margarita, and follow it with black-bottom Key lime pie or warm chocolate-walnut pie. Sunday brunch includes crab Benedict, seafood omelet, and Chicken Mojo sandwich. $–$$.

Attractions, Parks, and Recreation

Florida Keys Community College (FKCC)

305-296-9081
www.fkcc.edu
5901 College Rd., Stock Island, Key West 33040

In operation since 1965, FKCC is the southernmost college in the United States. Although it has satellite locations in Marathon and Coral Shores, this campus is particularly

Dateline: Full Moon, Key West

We went swimming with dolphins today.

"It was so different than I thought it would be," said my son Bud. "They don't look like the cartoon figures we've seen. They slide by so fast, click, click, clicking. They're so . . . mystical."

It seemed only minutes had passed before a big, noisy cruiser broke the magical spell that surrounded us. The dolphin scampered off, and our captain, Victoria Impallomeni, beckoned us back to the boat. Our time was up. We didn't want to get out of the water—or even off the boat—when we made it back to the dock.

I had scheduled this trip with Captain Victoria, a wilderness educator and lifelong Key resident who's found a spot she calls the bedroom, a playground in the placid blue waters off Key West where dolphin gather to sleep, play, and procreate. She'll take you there to snorkel and dive and—if you're lucky—to frolic with the friendly sea mammals in their natural habitat. She's one of at least five Keys boat captains who provide charters to swim with dolphins in the wild. Of course, none can guarantee an encounter with the wild and free, but Victoria says she finds them 90 percent of the time.

Victoria also offers snorkel instruction, dropping hints that the dolphin may be more responsive to those with the least artificial equipment. She explains bits of biology and ecology, pointing out sea grasses that produce calcium (which becomes sand), explaining that the waters are being overburdened with the nutrient-rich cocktail of agricultural runoff. Fertilizers finding their way into the ocean cause overgrowths that damage the ecosystem and rob the water of oxygen.

Although she describes the clear, shallow area she takes us to as a dolphin playground, she's quick to remind the adventure-minded that it's not an amusement park for humans. While she lives to share the incredible experience with others, she shudders to think of thrill-seekers who envision themselves cutting through the waves on the sleek gray backs of the wild creatures or otherwise exploiting the good nature of the gentle mammals. The dolphins are too smart for that anyway, she says.

There are many places where people can pay to swim with dolphins, but they're not free, they're captive. Most places call the swim programs educational, citing the law that prohibits people from harassing or feeding wildlife, but many wilderness educators and some scientists believe this is an ill-advised way to experience the dolphins. The National Marine Fisheries Service says that more than half of all dolphins captured die within two years, and the rest live an average of 5.8 years in captivity. While wild dolphins have a life expectancy of up to 40 years, those kept in tanks average only 20.

International Dolphin Watch, founded by Dr. Horace Dobbs, encourages individuals and organizations to campaign against captivity. For more information, log on to www.idw.org. For more information about booking a trip with Captain Victoria, call 305-304-7562 or 1-888-822-7366, or log on to www.captainvictoria.com.

pleasant, with recently renovated, brightly colored buildings on the waterfront. Many student works of art decorate the campus and its new Tennessee Williams Fine Arts Center.

Key West Golf Club

305-294-5232

6450 E. College Rd., Stock Island, Key West 33040

Designed by golf legend Rees Jones, this 18-hole, 6,500-yard course on 200 acres is open to the public daily. The course offers a pro shop, rental equipment, a dining room, and instruction. $$$-$$$$.

Key West Tropical Forest and Botanical Garden
305-296-1504
www.keywestbotanicalgarden.org
5210 College Rd., Stock Island, Key West 33045

The only "frost-free" tropical moist forest garden in the continental United States, this 11-acre garden is all that's left from the original 55 acres designated in 1936 by the Federal Emergency Relief Act. The garden fulfilled its purpose of helping the community overcome the Depression, becoming one of south Florida's biggest attractions. Although it has dwindled since losing ground to a hospital in World War II, the garden's recovery has been helped by the Key West Botanical Garden Society, a nonprofit organization that maintains the attraction. Boardwalks carry guests through several ecosystems in this wildlife habitat and butterfly sanctuary, which features more than 30 endangered species of fauna. Open 10–4 daily (closed Wednesday and September). Free; suggested donation $.

Mango Pango Boat Rentals, Inc.
305-294-2113, 1-800-342-2001
www.mangopangoboats.com
Murray Marine Tackle and Dive Shop, 5710 US 1, mile marker 5, Stock Island 33040

Here you can rent your boat of choice, including a 14-foot skiff, a party pontoon for 14 with porta potty and grill, or a 23-foot cabin cruiser, which are all available at half-day prices, with discounts for weeklong rentals. $$$$.

CULTURE

Tennessee Williams Fine Arts Center
305-296-1520
www.tennesseewilliamstheatre.com
Florida Keys Community College, 5901 W. College Rd., Stock Island, Key West 33040

The newest and largest theater south of Miami presents dramatic productions and also hosts the Key West Pops, the Florida Keys Chorale, and the Key West Symphony Orchestra. Performances are given winter through spring. Tickets $–$$$$.

Key West (mile marker 4–0)

Key West is one of the most unusual cities in the country and one of the most visited, although a high proportion of visitors spend a very limited time in town—just long enough to hike from one end of legendary Duval Street to the other, buy a T-shirt, and have a beer at Sloppy Joe's before jumping back aboard their cruise ship.

This cruise-ship tourism was denounced by former mayor Shirley Freeman as a costly exploitation of the island, and indeed, the ambient spirit that has drawn artists and writers here since before the days when Hemingway made Key West his home in the 1930s does seem to be dwindling at the expense of a hustle to survive. The intense proliferation of hotels, guest houses, and restaurants catering to a well-heeled crowd with pockets full of money is driving real estate prices through the roof, displacing local residents to other islands. Paradise runs the risk of losing its artistic cultural backbone, giving way to carbon-copied galleries, chain restaurants, and hotels.

I encourage you to take the time to find and enjoy the flavors of Key West that can't be found anywhere else in the world. Spend time musing, writing, painting, and nourishing your own artistic soul while visiting, enjoying, and at the same time replenishing the spirit that makes the place special. Come drink a toast to Ernest Hemingway with thousands of white-bearded men during Hemingway Days in July, or don (or should I say remove?) your Mardi Gras garb for the wildest Halloween masquerade you've ever seen during Fantasy Fest in October.

The Keys of Yesteryear

If you're unfamiliar with the spicy flavor of the Keys of the past, check out PROFILES OF KEY WEST (Poho Press, 1996), written by Dr. Alma Halbert Bond, a psychoanalyst and author who lived in Key West for more than a decade after retiring from Manhattan. The book is composed of articles she penned for newspapers and magazines about the interesting and artistic citizens drawn to the creative "soul magic" of the Keys. Without care, Key West could soon take on the sheen of any other city, its spirit snuffed by money.

Key West is home to a wealth of exemplary cuisine and charming guesthouses with luxuriously appointed rooms. Duval Street is lined with pubs busy from early in the day to late into the night. The creative community welcomes gay and lesbian members, and many businesses and activities cater to gays, such as Women Fest and Fantasy Fest, celebrations held in September and October. Drag shows provide exceptional entertainment for all persuasions, and an easygoing atmosphere ensures fun for all. Key West ascribes to a philosophy dubbed One Human Family, a public declaration adopted on October 17, 2000, that all people everywhere are entitled to equal rights, respect, and dignity and lives free from violence, prejudice, and harassment.

The Conch Republic

Perhaps you've heard of the Conch Republic, noticed the blue and yellow flags flying, or spotted the unique passports available in gift shops. All of these are inspired by the week of independence declared in 1982, creating an independent island nation for a few days. It all started when the U.S. Border Patrol set up a roadblock on US 1 as it exited the Keys in Florida City, searching all cars as they left the islands on a Sunday afternoon. The federal agency said the goal of the roadblock was to apprehend illegal aliens entering the country, yet in four days only four illegals were found, while three thousand were recorded coming into Miami Beach. The car searches also turned up about 3 pounds of pot, which turned out to be another of the Border Patrol's objectives.

But the fiasco had a greater impact on the Keys. A traffic jam 19 miles long greeted those returning from Keys vacations and discouraged potential visitors. The negative effect on the Keys biggest industry, tourism, was significant. When U.S. citizens were stopped and asked for proof of citizenship before being allowed to pass onto the mainland, Key West officials became angry. Then the mayor decided to take action: since the Keys were being treated like a foreign country, the islands would secede from the nation. A mock ceremony was held at Mallory Square, drawing international attention to the border fiasco.

Called a creative approach to a serious problem, the publicity stunt worked, and the roadblock was removed after five days. The event is commemorated each year in April at the ten-day Conch Republic Independence Celebration. Its motto: "We seceded where others failed."

LODGING

Ambrosia House
800-535-9838
www.ambrosiakeywest.com
615, 618, and 622 Fleming St., Key West
33040

Smartly decorated in cool, island styles,
Ambrosia House and Ambrosia Too offer
suites, town houses, and a cottage clustered
around tropical pools set in tropical gardens. It's close to Old Town, yet just far
enough away to be nicely secluded in its
own lush ambience. $$–$$$$.

Artist House Key West
305-296-3977, 1-800-582-7882,
fax 305-296-3210
www.artisthousekeywest.com
534 Eaton St., Key West 33040

Stepping into the Artist House, said to be
one of the most authentically restored
Victorian guest houses in Old Town, is like
stepping back in time. And some say that
not everyone has left the premises from
days gone by—is the turret room haunted?
$$–$$$$.

Atlantic Shores Resort
305-296-2491, 1-800-598-6988,
fax 305-294-2753
www.glresorts.com/asr
510 South St., Key West 33040

A throwback to 1950s fun, this gay-friendly
beachfront paradise welcomes all—guests
and nonguests—to its party-time fun. Free
films on the beach each Thursday night;
Wednesday and Sunday outdoor dance parties—everything is open to the public at this
fun-for-all resort. Pets welcome. $$.

Authors of Key West Guesthouse
305-294-7381, 1-800-898-6909,
fax 305-294-0920
www.authorskeywest.com
725 White St., Key West 33040

This private compound of conch-style cot-
tages, suites, and rooms is reminiscent of
the many writers who have made Key West
home. Bring pen and notebook and settle
into the quiet atmosphere and peaceful
gardens to pen your masterpiece, or just
enjoy a few nights in style. Rooms and cot-
tages; no pets. $–$$.

Avalon Bed and Breakfast
305-294-8233, 1-800-848-1317,
fax 305-294-9044
www.avalonbnb.com
317 Duval St., Key West 33040

Once a Cuban club at the quiet end of Duval
Street, this bed & breakfast offers clean,
quiet rooms with cool wood floors and net-
canopied beds for guests seeking privacy
and perhaps a little romance. Built in 1895,
the Avalon is listed on the National Register
of Historic Places. $$–$$$.

Banana Bay Resort Key West
305-296-6925, fax 305-296-2004
www.bananabay.com
2319 N. Roosevelt Blvd., Key West 33040

Set apart from the action at Sloppy Joe's,
but close enough to walk or bike into town,
this resort caters to adults, with romantic
rooms, a tropical pool, and fitness and
business centers. A beachside gazebo is
standing by for weddings, snorkel guides
and wild dolphin charters are available,
and if you bring your own boat (less than
25 feet), you can dock here for a daily fee.
Fully equipped rooms; no kids under 16
or pets allowed. $$–$$$$.

Center Court Inn and Cottages
305-296-9292, 1-800-797-8787
www.centercourtkw.com
915 Center St., Key West 33040

A collection of several historic properties
scattered through Old Town; each has been
renovated to sleek perfection. Most include

gardens, hot tubs, pools, and kitchens, and many are pet friendly. Rooms and cottages; breakfast included with some accommodations. $$–$$$$.

Crowne Plaza La Concha

305-296-2991, 1-800-745-2191,
fax 305-294-3282
www.laconchakeywest.com
430 Duval St., Key West 33040

Built in 1925 during Key West's heyday as the wealthiest city in the nation, La Concha is the tallest building on the island, with seven stories. The rooftop offers a popular lookout over Duval Street at the Top of La Concha Bar. With all the extra amenities you'd expect from Crowne Plaza resorts, rooms are standard issue with fine appointments, data ports, and room service at the push of a button. La Concha provides for those whose trust relies on familiar service. $$$–$$$$.

The Curry Mansion House

305-294-6777, 1-800-633-7439,
fax 305-294-5322
www.curryhousekeywest.com
806 Fleming St., Key West 33040

Romantic rooms are clustered around the pool of this restored historic Victorian mansion and offer a relaxing vacation reminiscent of a nearly forgotten era. European breakfasts, pool, hot tub, and daily cocktail parties enhance the romance. If you should happen to hear a sad-sounding trombone blaring into the night—that would be the ghost of Miss Petunia, who whiled the hours waiting for her captain to come home from sea by playing her instrument from the Curry House widow's walk. Rumor has it she was felled by a stray cannon blast, but everyone wonders, was it the miserable horn that cost her her life? Very reasonable rates in Key West terms. $$–$$$.

Duval House Key West

305-294-1666, 1-800-223-8825,
fax 305-292-1701
www.duvalhousekeywest.com
815 Duval St., Key West 33040

Put yourself on the edge of the middle of the action. Duval Street, lined with all the shops and pubs of Key West, is the strip to stroll when twilight fades and the lights take over the night. If you like to be in the thick of things, yet shielded by a white picket fence with a pool in a hidden garden for respite from the excitement of the city, this is the place for you. Small rooms to two-bedroom suites. $$$–$$$$.

Eaton Lodge

305-294-9870, 1-800-305-9870
1024 Eaton St., Key West 33040

Owned and operated by divers who love Key West so much they couldn't leave after an underwater wedding, Eaton Lodge offers some of the most affordable options for overnight travelers. Small, clean rooms are brightened with tropical fish décor. $–$$$.

Eaton Lodge Historic Inn and Gardens

305-292-2170, 1-800-294-2170,
fax 305-292-4018
www.eatonlodge.com
511 Eaton St., Key West 33040

A blend of Victorian restoration and modern comfort, the Main House, built in 1886, and the William Skelton House, built in 1832, offer plush beds in fresh, sunny rooms, many with verandas. The private tropical garden offers a restful escape from the heart of Duval Street, just a block away. Rooms and the two-bedroom Suite William are available. $$–$$$$.

Eden House

305-296-6868, 1-800-533-5397,
fax 305-294-1221
www.edenhouse.com
1015 Fleming St., Key West 33040

Owned by Mike Eden since 1975, the Eden House is Key West's oldest hotel, circa 1924. The fully renovated rooms are fresh and airy with clean tile and wood paneling. A second-story sun deck overlooks the pool and treetops. Prices go up incrementally with enhancements such as private bath, TV, refrigerator, kitchenette, porch, Jacuzzi, and extra bedroom. Guests receive a complimentary cold drink on arrival, and there's also complimentary happy hour daily. Eden House has a small restaurant, Cafe Med, offering convenient dinners with Mediterranean flavors. $$–$$$$.

Frances Street Bottle Inn

305-294-8530, 1-800-294-8530,
fax 305-294-1628
www.bottleinn.com
535 Frances St., Key West 33040

Built in 1879, the building that is now the Frances Street Bottle Inn has a history as colorful as that of Key West itself, serving over the years as private home, grocery, church, boardinghouse, flop house, TV show set, and finally the renovated guesthouse that it is today. Named for owner Mary Beth McCulloch's antique bottle collection, the inn offers rooms that are cool and colorful, bright and breezy. A hot tub patio, continental breakfast, and social hour complement a comfortable stay. Pets welcome. $$–$$$.

Gardens Hotel

305-294-2661, 1-800-526-2664,
fax 305-292-1007
www.gardenshotel.com
526 Angela St., Key West 33040

Possibly the most luxurious Old Town guesthouse in Key West, the Gardens Hotel has rated inclusion in *Condé Nast Traveler*'s list of the world's best places to stay for several years, including 2004. For more than 30 years it was a private mansion with a carefully cultivated botanical garden, and in the 1990s the property was purchased and ren-

ovated into a hotel. It was recently purchased by Kate Miane, owner of Ambrosia and Ambrosia Too, for an unprecedented multimillion-dollar price tag, and neighbors wait with bated breath to see whether Ms. Miane can be as successful with this expansive and beautiful property as she has been with Ambrosia. Confidence is inspired by her first order of business—refreshing the gardens and bringing back the butterflies. Fresh, elegant, modern rooms and suites. $$–$$$$.

The Grand Key West

305-294-0590, 1-888-947-2630
www.thegrandguesthouse.com
1116 Grinnell St., Key West 33040

Called one of the best deals in Key West, the Grand offers clean, simple rooms with refrigerators. Five blocks from Duval Street in historic Old Town, the Grand had been a private home and rooming house before its current incarnation as a small hotel. $$.

Heron House

305-294-9227, 1-800-294-1644,
fax 305-294-5692
www.heronhouse.com
512 Simonton St., Key West 33040

Lush, charming, and exclusive, Heron House has a private, sheltered atmosphere, as if complicit in sharing your secrets. Once inside its stone privacy wall, guests can gather around the pool or retreat on a private sun deck. A four-crown, four-diamond inn, Heron House is just a block off Duval Street. Rooms and suites available. $$–$$$$.

Hilton Key West Resort and Marina

305-294-4000, 1-800-445-8667,
fax 305-294-4086
www.keywestresort.hilton.com
245 Front St., Key West 33040

If you're looking for an oceanfront room in Key West, most choices are waterfront hotels rather than guesthouses, such as the Hilton. Backed by the Hilton Marina, the hotel frequently has large cruise ships docked behind it, so be sure to ask about the view from your room when you book. Rooms are spacious, cool, and luxuriously appointed with up-to-the-minute amenities for discriminating travelers. The location on the waterfront puts visitors in the thick of activity around the clock, as the hotel is surrounded by museums, shops, and restaurants. Rooms and suites available. $$–$$$$.

Hog's Breath Guesthouse

305-296-4222, fax 305-292-8472
www.hogsbreath.com/guesthouse.htm
310 Elizabeth St., Key West 33040

In need of a full house for a large group? The Hog's Breath Guesthouse is often used to provide housing for entertainers at the popular nightclub. The two-story house has three bedrooms plus two-bedroom lofts and is fully furnished with washer and dryer, kitchen, private garden, and pool. It's located near the waterfront and Mallory Square, just a few blocks from Duval Street. Three-night minimum. $$$$.

Key Lime Inn

305-294-5228, 1-800-549-4430
www.keylimeinn.com
725 Truman Ave., Key West 33040

A historic hotel with buildings that date from the beginning of the 20th century, the renovated Key Lime Inn offers crisp tropical accommodations for couples in a private compound with lush trees and a pool. Standard and deluxe queen rooms include continental breakfast. $$.

La Mer Hotel & Dewey House

305-296-6577, 1-800-354-4455,
fax 305-294-8272
www.lamerhotel.com
506 South St., Key West 33040

One of the few beachfront historic properties in Key West, La Mer and Dewey House, built as a turn-of-the-20th-century guesthouse and private home, have been meticulously renovated by Southernmost Resorts. Both include continental breakfast and afternoon tea served on the oceanfront veranda and a morning paper. $$$–$$$$.

LaTeDa Hotel and Bar

305-296-6706, 1-877-528-3320
www.lateda.com
1125 Duval St., Key West 33040

The sultry and sophisticated nightclub here has a 30-year tradition of fame and is said to have the best drag show in town. The décor of the standard, deluxe, and luxury rooms includes traditional home-style furnishing and sleek wood floors, tile, mahogany furnishings, French doors that open onto the garden, Roman tubs (in the luxury rooms), data ports, and refrigerators. $$–$$$$.

Marquesa Hotel

305-292-1919, 1-800-869-4631
www.marquesa.com
600 Fleming St., Key West 33040

This complex of conch houses in Old Town has been transformed into award-winning luxurious rooms and suites with the finest amenities, from elegant marble baths to plush bathrobes. Lush gardens surround two refreshing pools, and a notable restaurant serves dinner on the premises if walking a block to Duval has lost its appeal. $$$–$$$$.

Old Customs House Inn

305-294-8507, fax 305-292-2780
www.oldcustomshouse.com
124 Duval St., Key West 33040

This historic home is set off the street through a gate right on Duval, yet it's private and charming thanks to gardens and trees that shade the porches and balconies. White wicker offsets the white picket fencing around the balconies, and rooms gleam with hardwood floors, tile accents, and Dade County pine furnishings. Studios and suites feature kitchenettes. Pets welcome, but call first. $$–$$$.

Olivia by Duval

305-296-5169, 1-800-413-1978
www.oldtownsuites.com
511 Olivia St., Key West 33040

The spacious, renovated rooms clustered around the wood-decked pool make guests feel comfortable and at home during their stay on Olivia Street. Some rooms have kitchens; others have coffeemakers, refrigerators, and microwaves. $–$$$.

Simonton Court Historic Inns and Cottages

305-294-6386, 1-800-944-2687
www.simontoncourt.com
320 Simonton St., Key West 33040

A wide range of accommodations make up Simonton Court, from sleeping rooms in a manor or mansion to quaint cottages and elegant town houses, the largest with four bedrooms. Attention to details, décor, ambience, and atmosphere shows through such touches as tropical gardens, white linens, and natural wood floors. Hot tubs, pools; continental breakfast included. $$$–$$$$.

Southernmost Hotel and Resorts

305-296-6577, 1-800-354-4455
www.oldtownresorts.com
1319 Duval St., Key West 33040

This 127-unit hotel is indeed the southernmost hotel in the United States. Built in the 1950s, the hotel has been through major renovations to keep up with the fast-growing tourist industry on the island, so guests get a blended feeling of 1950s motel with 21st-century style. Some people prefer

the group atmosphere, reliability, and service that's professional yet maintains the guests' privacy and anonymity. The Southernmost Hotel provides a fine alternative to the many similarly priced guesthouses, and it's across the street from the beach. $$–$$$.

The Southernmost House Grand Hotel and Museum

305-296-3141, 1-866-764-6633
www.southernmosthouse.com
1400 Duval St., Key West 33040

Built in 1896, the Southernmost House is a stunning piece of Victorian architecture on the beach, saved from disintegration by a 1996 restoration costing $3 million. The house has hosted five presidents of the United States and has many museum pieces that reflect that history. Today guests can stay at the hotel, tour the museum, or spend the day enjoying the beachfront pool and bar. An all-day pass ($) includes museum tour, use of the pool, beach, and a drink. Tours are held daily. Rooms are decorated in period antiques and offer oceanfront or garden views. $$$–$$$$.

Southernmost on the Beach Hotel

305-296-6577, 1-800-354-4455,
fax 305-294-8272
www.southermostonthebeach.com
508 South St., Key West 33040

This midscale hotel on the beach offers clean, comfortable, waterfront rooms at reasonable rates. Children under 18 sleep free with parents, and facilities at the Southernmost Hotel (including pool, tiki bar, Internet access, and Jacuzzi), just across the street, are available to guests. $$–$$$$.

Suite Dreams

305-292-4713, 1-800-730-2483
www.oldtownsuites.com
1001 Von Phister St., Key West 33040

The luxury accommodations offered by Old Town Suites, which also owns Olivia by Duval, Suite Dreams is a gated home far removed from the hustle of Duval Street, in a suburban setting several blocks away from the tourist crowds. There's a small pool and fishpond on the shared patio and a private pool and gourmet kitchen for the three-bedroom Super Suite. The beach is just a few blocks away. $$–$$$$.

Sunset Key Guest Cottages
305-292-5300, 1-888-477-7786, fax 305-292-5395
www.sunsetkeycottages.hilton.com
245 Front St., Key West 33040

Relieve yourself of the congested pubs, restaurants, and shops clustered along Duval Street by staying a boat ride away. Ocean Properties Ltd. of Delray Beach bought what was once known as Tank Island and built a modern island-style village for your private retreat. Now called Sunset Key and franchised by Hilton Hotels, the island offers clusters of cottages, all freshly appointed to ensure your comfort, even including a shopping service to stock your cottage with your favorite foods. Some are beachfront, others have views, and some look upon the pool instead, giving parents a nice chance to remain close while their children play. Tennis and basketball courts are on the grounds, in addition to a spa, and there are water sports and other activities. Guests may utilize the launch day and night to partake of city pleasures and then return to quiet island life. Guests may also request the services of a private chef to cook in their cottage, or the Latitudes Beach Café provides oceanside Caribbean dining for guests as well as visitors. If you like Sunset Key so much you don't want to leave, you don't have to. Single- family residences are available for sale. Sunset Key has been rated as the second best place to stay in the United States and Canada by *Travel + Leisure*. Minimum stays may apply. $$$$.

Wyndham Casa Marina Resort
305-296-3535, 1-800-626-0777, fax 305-296-9960
www.casamarinakeywest.com
1500 Reynolds St., Key West 33040

Originally built by Henry Morrison Flagler for the tourists his train brought to town, this hotel now offers 311 rooms on the oceanfront, with a wide amount of beach-front set aside for guests' use. Rooms are carefully maintained to ensure that guests can enjoy the privilege and service they have come to associate with the Wyndham brand. $$$–$$$$.

DINING

Alice's at LaTeDa
305-296-5733
www.aliceskeywest.com
1125 Duval St., Key West 33040

Called New World Fusion Confusion by *Bon Appétit*, Alice Weingarten's cuisine has won a long list of awards. Alice creates an always beautiful blend of Mediterranean, tropical, and traditional flavors and styles for break-fast, lunch, and dinner. Try a seviche martini with gazpacho sidecar for a pair of flavors that are hard to choose between, or a pure passion salad with mango, goat cheese, almonds, and berries over fresh baby greens and topped with passion-fruit vinaigrette. Desserts are not to be bypassed, and don't forget the after-dinner show in the Crystal Room—it's the hottest drag show in the city. $$–$$$.

Blue Heaven
305-296-8666
www.blueheavenkw.com
305 Petronia St., Key West 33040

Blue Heaven is mostly outdoors, with chickens running underfoot and a hanging rope swing to entertain diners awaiting their brunch, lunch, or dinner. A rooftop dining area gets a breeze from surrounding trees, while those below benefit from shade provided by sails spread from the tree limbs. Caribbean flavors spice up the fare, reflecting perhaps this restaurant's location in Bahama Village. Its popularity came like wildfire, netting national acclaim from all angles, but the fame hasn't changed the atmosphere or spawned a chain. You can still enjoy a refreshing drink while watching the kids chase chickens and swing in the trees. $$–$$$.

Café Marquesa

305-292-1919, 1-800-869-4631
www.cafemarquesa.com
600 Fleming St., Key West 33040

Chef Susan Ferry has made a name for herself and Café Marquesa that permeates the city like the fine sauces she creates to accompany the creative dishes she concocts. The small restaurant exudes its charm even when closed and empty, beckoning passersby to come in and enjoy such treats as heirloom eggplant, corn, and tomato salad with Brie or goat cheese, walnut-crusted rack of lamb, and Key lime napoleon with fruits and berries. Open for dinner only. $$–$$$.

Crabby Dick's

305-294-7229
www.crabby-dicks.com
712 Duval St., Key West 33040

You can while away the afternoon here downing inexpensive draughts and nibbling cheap chicken wings, enjoying the breeze on the outdoor patio or the cool bar. $.

The Green Parrot Bar

305-294-6133
601 Whitehead St., Key West 33040
The Green Parrot has been serving cocktails, cold beer, and great music to locals since 1890, but there's no food to be had

Blue Heaven   Monroe County Tourist Development Council

here. No cover charge; happy hour 4–7 PM.; music usually begins about 10 PM.

Hog's Breath Saloon

305-292-2032
www.hogsbreath.com
400 Front St., Key West 33040

How about a Hog's Breath T-shirt, hat, or beer cup? This Keys club has become a famous brand. It's a fine place for a semi-outdoor evening drink and a little admirable live music. (It's the home of the Key West Songwriters Festival each May; www.keywestsongwritersfestival.com). Enjoy fine wings and fish dip—spiced up with Hog's Breath own hot sauce—burgers, or fish of all kinds. Remember, Hog's Breath is better than no breath at all! $$–$$$.

Kelly's Caribbean Bar and Grill

305-293-8484, fax 305-293-9405
www.kellyskeywest.com
301 Whitehead St., Key West 33040

Instead of rocketing to celebrity fame after appearing in *Top Gun,* Kelly McGillis came back to her hometown of Key West and opened a top-flight restaurant, where in the early days she could often be found serving as hostess. With a local writers' library and its own brewery, Kelly's provides a relaxing atmosphere for those seeking a higher plane. Impressive gourmet fare includes seafood dishes with Caribbean flair, such as sesame seared tuna and yellowtail snapper served with tropical fruit, or keep it simple with chicken fettucine or prime rib. McGillis has opened another restaurant, Kelly's Duval Beach Club, on the beach at 1405 Duval. $$$–$$$$.

Latitudes Beach Café
305-292-4313
On Sunset Key—catch the launch at 245 Front St., Hilton Marina

Looking for a boat ride? Catch the launch to Sunset Key for a breakfast omelet; fresh, local snapper or wahoo; pink shrimp; or spiny lobster with your choice of sauce and salsa, or a salad, sandwich, or petite filet for lunch. Splurge for dinner on the Land and Sea—crab-stuffed lobster tail with petite filet or rack of lamb—or keep it cool with grilled vegetables. $–$$$$.

La Trattoria
305-296-1075, fax 305-293-8169
www.latrattoria.us
524 Duval St., Key West 33040

Considered by many to be Key West's best restaurant, La Trattoria has earned a basketful of People's Choice Awards. La Trattoria seduces diners with a sophisticated atmosphere and then fattens them with stunningly delicious treats. And it's not your standard-issue Italian: here you'll find superb blends of garlic, olive oil, tomato, and basil with ravioli, tortellini, penne, and gnocchi. After dinner be sure to make your way to the back of the restaurant, where you'll be delighted to find a hidden

little jazz bar, Virgilio's, famous for its chocolate martinis. $$–$$$.

Louie's Backyard
305-294-1016
www.louiesbackyard.com
700 Waddell Ave., Key West 33040

The elegant indoor dining room looks out at the ocean, or dine outside, which is a bit more casual. It's even more casual at the on-site Afterdeck Bar, where well-behaved, leashed dogs are welcome. Sandwiched between Dog Beach and an apartment once rented by Jimmy Buffett, this mansion, built at the turn of the 20th century by a wealthy wrecker, now offers inspired cuisine. Try the cracked conch roll with horseradish aioli or grilled scallops with spicy mango ketchup—you won't soon forget it. $$$.

Mangoes
305-292-4606
www.mangoeskeywest.com
700 Duval St., Key West 33040

As you stroll up and down Duval Street, Mangoes is one of the restaurants you can't help noticing. It stands out with its white picket fence and trees towering over the dining area, and there is a sense that something special must lurk within. The wild mushroom martini with white truffle is luscious and a nice complement to a fresh salad, or try passion snapper crusted with coconut and mango, jerk pork, or island paella. Whatever your choice— dining alfresco or seeing and being seen— it's part of the scene to enjoy at Mangoes. $$–$$$$.

Margaritaville Café
305-292-1435
www.margaritaville.com
500 Duval St., Key West, 33040

Slide into Jimmy Buffett's Margaritaville Café to sample some conch chowder, squid

Some of the contestants in the annual Hemingway look-alike contest at Sloppy Joe's

Monroe County Tourist Development Council

rings and couch potatoes, Cuban seafood enchiladas or New Orleans–style sausage, red beans and rice. Parrot Heads congregate in this Margaritaville Café to pay tribute to the conch that started it all. In turn, Jimmy Buffett never forgets to thank his fans with fun, pleasure . . . and the occasional surprise appearance. 10 AM– 1 AM daily. $-$$.

Sloppy Joe's

305-296-2388
www.sloppyjoes.com
201 Duval St., Key West 33040

Put on your Hemingway beard, grab your pen and paper, and have a drink just like Papa used to. This bar owes its fame to the fact that it (or perhaps a facsimile) belonged to Ernest's friend Joe Russell, who opened the place on December 5, 1933—the day Prohibition was repealed.

The bar has sponsored the Hemingway look-alike contest in mid-July every year since 1933. Sloppy Joe's offers the seafood the Keys are famous for, such as calamari, Key West shrimp, conch fritters, and conch chowder, and also has traditional bar foods such as potato skins and wings. Other entrées include island delights such as the Jamaican jerked chicken sandwich, grilled Cuban sandwich, fried grouper, and, of course, a Sloppy Joe. Open late. $-$$.

Turtle Kraals Bar and Restaurant

305-294-2640
www.turtlekraals.com
1 Lands End Village, Key West 33040

It's hard to eat here without reflecting on the fact that this was once a turtle cannery, but just remind yourself that those days are over now. Order a salad, gazpacho, or spinach and artichoke dip if it makes you feel better. Enjoy the open-air view of the waterfront and seaport, and relish the historic charm that emanates from the walls. Or go ahead and indulge in the Cuban- and Southwest-flavored seafood that's famous here, like lobster chiles rellenos or mojo grilled shrimp. Wash it down with a bottle of Key West Sunset Ale, and relax in the salty breeze. $$.

ATTRACTIONS, PARKS, AND RECREATION

Audubon House Museum, Tropical Gardens, and Fine Art Gallery

305-294-2116, 1-877-281-2473, fax 305-294-4513
www.audubonhouse.com
205 Whitehead St., Key West 33040

Though called the Audubon House after painter and ornithologist John James Audubon, this house was actually the residence of Capt. John J. Geiger in the early 1800s. A wealthy wrecker, Geiger is said to have hosted Audubon when he traveled to the Keys, documenting the bird life—which he did in a rather cruel way by killing dozens of birds to use as models for the now-famous renderings. The house has been restored to its full glory and includes an acre of tropical city garden for wandering and imagining life in Key West's heyday. The Audubon House Fine Art Gallery features a permanent collection of John James Audubon limited-edition prints for display and sale. Open 9:30–4:30 daily. $; admission includes audio tour.

Conch Tour Train

305-294-5161
www.conchtrain.com
303 Front St., 3850 N. Roosevelt Blvd., and 901 Caroline St., Key West

Take a 90-minute tour of the historical highlights of Key West, from Indian days through the romance of the 1930s, '40s, '50s, and '60s to the social and cultural hot spots of today. Pass by Ernest Hemingway's home, Harry S Truman's Little White House, and the Audubon House. Tours depart every 30 minutes, 9–4:30 daily. $$.

The Conch Tour Train Monroe County Tourist Development Council

Curry Mansion Museum and Inn

305-294-5349, 1-800-253-3466, fax 305-294-4093
www.currymansion.com
511 Caroline St., Key West 33040

This restored Victorian mansion was the home of Key West's first millionaire, William Curry, in 1869. Its restoration and impressive collection of period antiques are the work of Edith and Al Amsterdam, who bought the place, virtually empty, in 1974. Tour 15 rooms and the common areas of the 25-room property, or stay a few nights. Open for tours 10–5 daily. $.

Discovery Glass Bottom Boat Tours

305-293-0099
www.discoveryunderseatours.com
251 Margaret St., Key West 33040

This is a chance to submerge in the depths of the coral reef without getting wet and view the beautiful blue world of colorful tropical fish, sharks, dolphins, and sea turtles as they swim amid corals of all colors. The two-hour trips run in the morning, in the afternoon, and at sunset, when boaters can climb on deck to watch the rosy orange glow over a champagne toast to celebrate another beautiful day in the Florida Keys. $$–$$$.

Dry Tortugas National Park

305-242-7700
www.nps.gov/drto/
P.O. Box 6208, Key West 33041

It's clear the Florida Keys have been providing happy days for anglers and tourists for more than a century, and the population and plethora of commercial enterprises are the evidence. If you're wondering what the Keys looked like in days past, consider a tour of the Dry Tortugas National Park, seven islands about 70 miles west of Key West. Difficult to access, the islands are home to Florida's own Alcatraz, Fort Jefferson, which served insufficiently as both fort and prison before being abandoned and consigned to the park service. Visitors can camp on the virtually unoccupied islands or just visit for the day. Travel there by ferry, seaplane, or private boat ($$$$). Park admission $.

East Martello Fort and Museum

305-296-3913l
www.kwahs.com
3501 S. Roosevelt Blvd., Key West 33040

Built in 1862 for protection during the Civil War, the East Martello battery was never used for battle because of obsolete construction methods, although it has been used to house and train soldiers. Today it serves as a suitable repository for historical artifacts, including those from Native American times, from shipwrecking, from the Keys' wealthy days as a U.S. port of entry, from sponging and fishing, and more, through the past few decades of island history. Open 9:30–4:30 daily (except Christmas). $.

Ernest Hemingway's home Monroe County Tourist Development Council

Ernest Hemingway Home and Museum
305-294-1136, fax 305-294-2755
www.hemingwayhome.com
907 Whitehead St., Key West 33040

One of Key West's most popular attractions, the home of Ernest Hemingway lends insight into the creative life inspired by the islands' charm and special artistic energy. Hemingway spent many years at this island retreat, creating a legend that endures. Writers will enjoy seeing the charming home and lush environment in which the master produced several memorable works, including *A Farewell to Arms* and *For Whom the Bell Tolls*. Today a National Historic Landmark, the home was built in 1851 and was occupied by Hemingway during the 1930s and '40s, and then sporadically until his death in 1961. The property is populated by about 60 cats, many polydactyl, which look as if they have thumbs. Some are the descendants of Hemingway's own pet. Open 9–5 daily. $.

Flagler Station
305-295-3562
901 Caroline St., Key West 33040

The *Miami Herald* proclaimed Flager's East Coast Railway the "eighth wonder of the world" in January 1912, and a few days later Flagler arrived in Key West aboard his train from New York City. Begun in 1905, it was finished seven years, three hurricanes, and $50 million later, after hundreds of lives were lost. Flagler died in 1913, leaving this as his greatest life achievement. Today known as the railroad that went to sea, it lasted only until it was blown off track in the Labor Day hurricane of 1935. Tour a train car and hear the story at Flagler Station. Open 9–6 daily. $.

Fort Zachary Taylor Historic State Park
305-292-6713
South end of Southard St., through Truman Annex, Key West

The beach here is frequently referred to by locals as "the only one I'd go to." Water quality is a constant concern because overpopulation and overdevelopment causes frequent contamination. This beach tends to score better, apparently, than others in the area. In addition to a quiet, tree-lined beach is Fort Zachary Taylor, a massive fort built between 1845 and 1866 to protect the new state of Florida. It served as a critical outpost for Union troops in the Civil War, and it served the nation in the Spanish-American War as well. Renovated but rarely used over the next 80 or more years, it was excavated by volunteers in the late 1960s and stands today as an impressive National Historic Landmark and testament to ingenuity. Take time to tour the fort (which was deserted when I stopped by) and drink in the fabulous view of sailboats in the surrounding sea from the same spot where soldiers probably once spied marauders. You can almost hear the whispers of centuries past. Open 9–5 daily; tours at noon and 2. $.

Ghosts and Legends of Key West

305-294-1713
www.keywestghosts.com
Porter Mansion, 429 Caroline St., Key West 33040

Learn about the legends of Key West on these spooky evening tours of Old Town. Tours held at 7 and 9 daily; reservations required. $–$$.

Harry S. Truman's Little White House

305-294-9911
111 Front St., Key West 33040

Florida's only presidential museum, this home, now on the National Register of Historic Places, provided quarters for the 33rd president for 175 days during his term of office, and it also hosted subsequent presidents Eisenhower, Kennedy, and Carter. Truman had the

Harry S. Truman's Little White House Monroe County Tourist Development Council

right idea: working from paradise. A two-bedroom suite with sun deck is available for vacation accommodations ($$$). Tours are given daily 9–5. $.

Island City Strolls
305-294-8380
www.seekeywest.com
534 Fleming St., Key West 33040

Historian and artist Sharon Wells arrived in Key West in 1976 and has been charting the territory ever since. She provides personalized walking or bike tours through her company Island City Strolls and is also author of *Sharon Well's Walking and Biking Guide to Historic Key West*, available free at locations all around town for those who prefer to make their own way. Either way, if you've taken a liking to Keys architecture or are interested in the old cemetery, literary sites, grand homes and gardens, or gay highlights of Key West, Wells will help you find them. Wells's paintings and photographs of Key West and beyond are displayed at her gallery, KW Light Gallery, at 534 Fleming Street. Tours $$; four-person minimum.

Key West Aquarium
305-296-2051
www.keywestaquarium.com
1 Whitehead St. (at Mallory Square), Key West 33040

Opened in 1934, the Key West Aquarium was the Keys' first official tourist attraction, a move that turned the local economy around and in a positive direction that may have reached its peak by now. The aquarium has fish, sharks, stingrays, and more. Open 1–6 daily. $.

Key West Butterfly and Nature Conservatory
305-296-2988, 1-800-839-4647
www.keywestbutterfly.com
1316 Duval St., Key West 33040

Walk among hundreds of captive butterflies, and buy butterfly books, art, and gifts. Open 9–5 daily. $$.

Key West Cruisers
305-294-4724, 1-888-800-8802
1111 Eaton St., Key West 33040

Rent a two- or four-seater electric car to get around. The kids can drive, too. Open 8–4 daily. $$$$.

Key West Diving Society
305-292-3221
www.keywestdivingsociety.com
Conch Harbor Marina, 955 Caroline St., Key West 33040

Voted the friendliest dive operator in Key West. Open 10–6 daily. $$$$.

Key West 1847 Cemetery

www.keywest.com/cemetery.htm

Margaret and Angela Streets, Key West

This is an interesting if a bit creepy collection of aboveground crypts and gravestones, many moved here in 1847 after an underground cemetery flooded in a hurricane, scattering bodies and tombstones. Those daring enough to explore will see quirky monuments and creative epitaphs. Free.

Key West Lighthouse and Keeper's Quarters Museum

305-294-0012

www.kwahs.com/lighthouse.htm

938 Whitehead St., Key West 33040

Built in 1847 as an early lighthouse to protect approaching ships from the island shores, the lighthouse and museum, on the edge of the Old Town area, are now home to a collection of maritime relics and history. You can climb the 88 steps to the top of the 92-foot lighthouse for a nice view of the island. Open 9:30–5 (last entry at 4:30) daily. $.

Key West Lighthouse Monroe County Tourist Development Council

Key West Marine Park

305-294-3100

www.reefrelief.org

William St. at historic Seaport, Key West

The marine park consists of three designated buoyed areas for swimming and snorkeling that are closed to motorized vessels and are protected "no-take" zones. Established by the city of Key West in cooperation with Reef Relief, the marine park gives snorkelers and divers the opportunity to observe sea life and the living coral reef. (Reef Relief also educates about the dangers facing the coral reefs and raises awareness about coral reef and ocean life protection.) Open 9–5 Monday through Saturday. Free.

Key West Museum of Art and History at the Custom House

305-295-6616

www.kwahs.com

281 Front St., Key West 33040

Built in 1981 to process incoming cargo and treasures from shipwrecks, this imposing red-brick structure now serves as a museum of Key West's cultural past. Admission, which includes an audio tour, also includes discounts and combo tickets to other area museums (including the Key West Lighthouse and Keeper's Quarters Museum and the East Martello Fort and Museum). Open 9–5 daily (except Christmas). $.

Key West Shipwreck Museum

305-292-8990

www.shipwreckhistoreum.com

1 Whitehead St., Mallory Square, Key West
33040

Storytellers will take you back to relive the
history of the *Issac Allerton*, a ship sunk on
its trip from New York to New Orleans. It
was partly recovered in 1856, but not fully
discovered and reclaimed until 1985—by
descendants of the original wrecker who
claimed the loot in 1856! Open 9:40–5
daily. $.

Mel Fisher Maritime Museum

305-294-2633

www.melfisher.org

200 Greene St., Key West 33040

See and imagine the piles of treasure
dredged up from the sea by maritime
entrepreneur and modern-day wrecker Mel
Fisher, now a millionaire thanks to his
grand find. Replicas and authentic loot are
for sale. Open 9:30–5 daily. $.

Moped Hospital

305-296-3344

601 Truman Ave., Key West 33040

Here you can rent mopeds and bikes—great
ways to make your way around Key West.
Open 9–5 Monday through Saturday and
10–5 Sunday. $$–$$$$.

Nancy Forrester's Secret Garden

305-294-0015

www.manaproject.org

1 Free School Lane, Key West 33040

Local Hero: Nancy Forrester

Nancy Forrester moved to Key West with her
parents when she was 11 years old, and in 1969
she bought an acre of land for $25,000. It
had been used by townspeople as an unregu-
lated dump for one hundred years, but Nancy
and her sister hauled off the trash and began
caring for the hardwood hammock that had
previously gone unnoticed, adding to the for-
est over the years until she realized she'd cre-
ated a wild garden reminiscent of a rain forest,
with paths for visitors, sitting areas for con-
templation, and even a clearing that's hosted
a few weddings.

"I am an environmental artist," Nancy
explains. "My passion is to activate people to
take care of the environment. But most peo-
ple are here in Key West to shed their prob-
lems—eat, drink, relax—and are not as
interested in helping the environment as I'd
hoped.

"What motivates this economy is building
these homes that max out. They pave over the
land, and everybody puts a pool in their back-
yard. There are no indigenous animals here
anymore. But this isn't for saving the indige-
nous animals. This is for saving the environ-
ment, for cutting back on materialism. It's sad
if it doesn't happen here in Key West. This is
my home."

Nancy invites visitors to let her know what
sort of environmental projects they're working
on at home, "because I can't do this job
alone—I need your help."

Nancy Forrester, owner and curator of the last acre of undeveloped land in Key West, works
hard to protect the status of her land. Enjoy a walk through the wild jungle paths and chat
with resident parrots for a precious reminder of the importance of preserving nature and
learning to live harmoniously with our environment. She also offers her property as an
artists' retreat, and sometimes she rents out the small, Bahamian cottage in the garden—
it's lovely, with a porch and kitchenette, but it also has no air-conditioning. Open 10–5
daily. $ donation requested from first-time visitors.

Old Town Trolley Tours

305-296-6688
www.historictours.com
Mallory Square, Key West

Catch the Old Town Trolley at any of the stops along its route, including the Historic Key West Seaport, the La Concha Crowne Plaza hotel, the Bahama Village Market, or the Southernmost Point. Your guide will point out historic sites, restaurants, and other places of significance along the way, and if something catches your fancy, hop off and check it out— you can pick up another trolley at the same location every 30 minutes. Tours are offered 9–4:30 daily. $$.

Seaplanes of Key West

305-294-0709, 1-800-950-2359, fax 305-296-4141
www.seaplanesofkeywest.com
Key West Airport, 3471 S. Roosevelt Blvd., Key West 33040

If you have only half a day but twice the money, you may prefer to visit the Dry Tortugas via seaplane. You'll still get nearly four hours on the island, but you'll spend only half an hour each way in transit. And those who've had the experience describe it as especially amazing—the short flight stays low over the sea, so it's possible to see sharks, sea turtles, and reef formations from the air. Polarized sunglasses are recommended for best visibility. Open 7 AM–10 PM daily. $$$$.

Sebago Watersports

305-294-5687
www.keywestsebago.com
Historic Key West Seaport, 201 William St., Key West 33040

Sebago offers parasailing, snorkeling, reef and eco tours, and champagne sunset sails. Business office open 9–5 Monday through Friday. $$$.

Southernmost Point Monroe County Tourist Development Council

Southernmost Point
Whitehead and South Streets, Key West

Who visits Key West without stopping for this photo op? A familiar marker stands by, announcing that it's just 90 miles from Cuba at this southernmost point of the United States.

Subtropic Dive Center
305-296-9914
1605 N. Roosevelt, Key West 33040

Snorkel or dive the clear Keys waters to find beautiful coral, sea creatures, and mysterious shipwrecks. Instruction and equipment are available. Morning, afternoon, and evening trips are offered daily, weather permitting, at 9 AM and 1:30, 2, and 6 PM. There are also night dives by appointment. $$–$$$$.

Sunny Days Catamarans
305-293-5144, 1-800-236-7937
www.sunnydayskeywest.com
At Elizabeth and Greene Streets at the Historic Seaport

Among the other boat trips available, you can enjoy continental breakfast on board the *Fast Cat II* catamaran and a buffet lunch at Fort Jefferson. Snorkeling gear and tour included. Departs at 8 AM. $$$$.

Sunset Celebration
Hilton Pier, Mallory Square, Key West

A fun tradition has established itself in Key West: hundreds of people gather at Mallory Square each evening to admire and celebrate another beautiful Key West sunset. The event has become a tradition that includes a festival-like atmosphere, with artists peddling their wares, flame throwers, and carnival acts to entertain tourists and passers-by. It's a great way to mark the transition from day into evening. Prefer to watch the fun from afar? Take in the scene from the second-floor Sunset Bar at the Hilton, overlooking the pier and western sky. Free, but there's plenty to buy here, so bring a few bucks.

YANKEE FREEDOM II Dry Tortugas and Fort Jefferson Ferry Service
305-294-7009, 1-800-634-0939
www.yankeefreedom.com
240 Margaret St., Key West 33040

The daily daylong trip includes gourmet snacks and lunch during the two-hour transit time each way, a 45-minute tour of Fort Jefferson, and snorkeling gear for use during the four-hour visit to the island. Departs at 8 AM. $$$$.

CULTURE

Gingerbread Square Gallery
305-296-8900
1207 Duval St., Key West 33040
Key West's oldest gallery features work by local artist Sal Salinero. Open 10–6 Sunday through Thursday and 10–10 Friday and Saturday. Free admission.

Harrison's Gallery
305-294-0609
www.harrison-gallery.com
825 White St., Key West 33040

Helen Harrison, award-winning wood sculptor, has owned this gallery since 1990 and specializes in showcasing the artwork of Key West locals as well as her own. Open noon–5 daily—please ring the bell. Free admission.

Helio Gallery
305-294-7901
www.heliographics.com
814 Fleming St., Key West 33040

Owned by local artists Reen Stanhouse, Dawn Wilkins, and Leslie Kantor, the gallery specializes in "FUNctional" local art: furnishings, clothing, ceramics, and more. Open 10–6 Monday through Saturday. Free admission.

Joy Gallery
305-296-3039
www.joy-gallery.com
1124 Duval St., Key West 33040

Original paintings and sculpture from local and international artists are displayed here. Open 11–5:30 daily. Free admission.

Key West Film Society
305-295-9493
www.keywestfilm.org
Tropic Cinema, 416 Eaton St., Key West 33040

Sprung from a communal desire to embellish local film options, the Key West Film Society presents a wide range, from mainstream films and controversial films to independent, foreign, and alternative films. The society aims to generate discussion as well as entertain. $–$$.

KW-Light Gallery
305-294-0566
www.kwlightgallery.com
534 Fleming St., Key West 33040

Displayed here are photos, paintings, and limited-edition Giclée prints by Sharon Wells and Alan Kennish. Open 11–6 Tuesday through Saturday. Closed September. Free admission.

Luis Sottil Studios

305-292-6447
716 Duval St., Key West 33040

Here you can view original artwork from Luis Sottil and other international artists. Open 10–10 Sunday through Thursday and 10 AM–11 PM Friday and Saturday. Free admission.

Mary O'Shea's Glass Garden

305-293-8822
www.keywestglass.com
213 Simonton St., Key West 33040

Here, at the largest glass studio/gallery in Key West, you'll see glass creations of jewelry, dishes, artwork, and more. Open 10–5 Monday through Saturday. Free admission.

Montage

305-295-9101
512 Duval St., Key West 33040

Scenes and signs shot around Key West are emblazoned on fiberboard to create a permanent memento of your island dream vacation. Take home an image of the road that ends at mile marker 0, an epitaph from the Key West Cemetery (such as I TOLD YOU I WAS SICK), or the shop sign explaining the Keys' philosophy of business hours (WHENEVER . . .). Open 9–1 daily. Free.

Red Barn Theatre

305-293-3035
www.redbarntheatre.com
319 Duval St., Key West 33040

Working with a local troupe of professional actors as well as national touring talent, the Red Barn Theatre, housed in the carriage house of the old Wreckers Museum, presents a half dozen shows each season, November to June. Recent offerings include *I Love You, You're Perfect, Now Change*, and *Sordid Lives*. $$–$$$.

Waterfront Playhouse

305-294-5015
www.waterfrontplayhouse.com
Mallory Square, 310 Wall St., Key West 33040

Home of the Key West Players, this small theater, converted from a wrecker's warehouse, is nearly three-quarters of a century old. Season runs from December through June. $$$.

Wyland Galleries of Key West

305-292-5240; 102 Duval St., Key West 33040
305-292-4998; 719 Duval St., Key West 33040

Here you'll see ocean art by Wyland, a famous environmental artist whose murals grace the Historic Seaport and buildings across the country, often as fund-raising projects for ocean education and protection. Open 9:30 AM–10 PM Sunday through Thursday and 9:30 AM–11 PM Friday and Saturday. Free admission.

SHOPPING

Emeralds International
305-294-2060
104 Duval St., Key West 33040

In case you're visiting Key West on a romantic whim or shopping for gifts for someone quite special, Emeralds International presents a large variety of beautiful stones from Colombia and around the world, duty free. Admire the 900-carat emerald sculpture on display when stopping by to purchase your gem. Open 10–6 Monday through Saturday and 11–5 Sunday.

Fausto's Food Palace
305-296-5663
1105 White St., Key West 33040

This semi-basic small grocery just on the edge of Duval and Old Town is a nice place to stock up on gourmet treats and basics for tubside treats at your bed & breakfast. Open 8–8 Monday through Saturday and 8–7 Sunday.

Key West Aloe
305-293-1885, 1-800-445-2563
540 Green St., Key West 33040

Homemade aloe and tropical-ingredient cosmetic treats are sold here. Open 9–9 daily.

Key West Chicken Store
305-294-0070
1229 Duval St., Key West 33040

This crazy shop of all things chicken celebrates Key West's famous wild fowl. Live chicks and chicken kitsch. Open 10–5 daily.

Key West Hand Print Fashions and Fabrics
305-294-9535, 1-800-866-0333
201 Simonton St., Key West 33040

Hand-printed fabrics and dresses, shirts, and more for men and women are sold here. Bright colors, comfortable styles. Open 10–6 daily.

Key West Island Bookstore
305-294-2904
513 Fleming St., Key West 33040

This tiny shop is packed with Key West–related titles as well as literary offerings from Key West residents. Bookworm heaven. Open 10–9 daily.

The Key West Winery
305-292-1717
www.thekeywestwinery.com
103 Simonton St., Key West 33040

How could you pass up Key Lime Wine? Here you can sample this and many other tropical wines and accompaniments. Open 10–6 Monday through Saturday and noon–6 Sunday.

Little Switzerland Jewelry
305-293-9771; 402 Duval St., Key West 33040
305-296-1998; 400 Front St., Key West 33040
305-293-8600; Hilton Marina

Little Switzerland sells Swiss timepieces, gifts, and unusual jewelry. Open 9 AM–11 PM daily.

Margaritaville Café and Store
305-292-1435
www.margaritaville.com
500 Duval St., Key West 33040

This gift shop, part of Jimmy Buffett's restaurant, is a must-stop for Parrot Heads. Open 10 AM–1 AM daily.

Waterfront Market
305-296-0778
Historic Seaport, 201 Williams St., Key West 33040

This is heaven for foodies. Make this your first stop for food supplies if you have a kitchen or a galley to stock. Choose from frozen organic fast foods; selections from the fresh caviar counter; fresh pink shrimp, lobster, and seafood; fresh produce; prepared sandwiches; and microbrews or wine. You can also eat at at the loft above the shopping zone or outside on the waterfront. Yum, yum, yum. Open 7 AM–6 PM Saturday through Thursday and 7 AM–8 PM Friday.

ANNUAL EVENTS

January
Art Under the Oaks
305-664-5241
San Pedro Catholic Church, mile marker 89.5, US 1 bayside, Islamorada

This free annual festival is held in mid-January.

Florida Keys Medieval Festival
239-839-8036
www.flkeysmedievalfest.com
Office at 1107 Key Plaza, #252, Key West 33040; event is held on Sugarloaf Key

This weekend festival of jousting, artisans, archery, a battle, and a royal feast is all presented in the flavor of medieval times. $–$$$.

Islamorada Waterfront Home Tour

305-664-4503, 1-800-FAB-KEYS

www.islamoradachamber.com

This is an opportunity to observe the very real lifestyles of the truly fortunate (and yes, probably rich, and maybe famous). The waterfront homes in Islamorada are fine island living at its most luscious. Held in mid-January. $$$.

Key West Literary Seminar

1-888-293-9291

www.keywestliteraryseminar.org

516 Duval St., Key West 33040

Held at the San Carlos Institute, the Key West Literary Seminar is a deliberately small group of writers from around the world who meet for workshops with internationally known professionals, literary discussions, and festive parties. The weekend-long seminar sells out a year in advance. $$$$.

Terra Nova Trading Key West

781-639-9545

www.premiere-racing.com

The largest international midwinter sailboat racing regatta in the world allows amateur sailors to compete against professionals and world-class competitors. Partake, or take in the view from oceanfront restaurants. Free for spectators; $$$$ for participants.

February

Old Island Days Art Festival

305-294-9501

Whitehead and Greene Streets, Key West

This weekend festival is part of a months-long celebration of Keys culture and history. Browse displays of fine art, including paintings, photography, glass, and sculpture. Free admission.

Pigeon Key Arts Festival

743-5176

Mile marker 47, oceanside, 1 Knight Key, Marathon 33050

More than 70 artists gather from around the country to display their fine art and craft wares on the historic Pigeon Key, where railroad builders bunked while building Flagler's rail to the Keys and where marine studies are conducted today. Live music and island food are also available. Shuttle service to the island from the Pigeon Key Visitor's Center, an historic railcar at mile marker 47, Oceanside. 10 AM–5 PM Saturday and Sunday. $.

April

Conch Republic Independence Celebration

305-295-7215

www.conchrepublic.com

Festival begins at 430 Duval St., Key West, but events are held throughout the Old Town area.

The Florida Keys seceded from the United States on April 23, 1982, after the U.S. Border Patrol put up a roadblock to search all vehicles exiting the Keys, stalling traffic for days and severely impacting residents' lives and the Keys' tourist-based economy. Federal officials claimed to be searching for illegal immigrants, although significantly more illegals entered through Miami than the Keys. Residents assume the real motive was drug enforcement and considered the search tactics harassment. The new nation called itself the Conch Republic, and the stunt, dreamed up by Keys' tourist czar Stuart Newman, generated national and international attention. The 10-day Key West celebration includes a drag race featuring the islands' famous drag queens, a Duval Street parade, and a battle of boats. Some events are free, while others require admission fees.

Seven-Mile Bridge Run
305-743-8513, 1-800-262-7284
Marathon Runners Club, P.O. Box 500110, Marathon 33050

At this annual race across the famous 7-mile bridge, 1,500 men, women, and children sprint, hike, and wheel themselves across the bridge en masse. Participants enjoy the quick, scenic run for its incomparably beautiful location as well as the slight rise of the

The Seven-Mile Bridge Run Monroe County Tourist Development Council

bridge, which creates a physical challenge. Entrants are asked to send a stamped, self-addressed legal-size envelope to the Marathon Runners Club to receive an application well in advance to participate in the run. More than ten thousand applications are received annually, but the race is limited to reduce traffic delays. Proceeds benefit local youth programs. $$$.

June
ChickenFest Key West
305-296-5596
www.cfkw.org
605 United St., Key West 33040

Key West has long been known for its red-feathered friends—chickens and roosters that stroll city streets freely along with Hemingway's six-toed cats. When the population began to grow rather unwieldy and competed with growing numbers of tourists for sidewalk space, a chicken catcher was hired to reduce the cock-a-doodle-doos. Last I heard he'd given up, but enterprising residents saw an opportunity to celebrate the fowl with four days of fun. Join a chicken run or chicken scratch golf tournament, a poultry-in-motion parade, and cooking contest. Some events have admission fees.

PrideFest Key West
305-292-3223
www.pridefestkeywest.com
513 Truman Ave., Key West 33040

This gay pride celebration week, pre-sented by Key West's Gay and Lesbian Community Center, includes parties, shows, and a service for those lost to AIDS. Free.

July
Hemingway Days
305-294-1136
www.sloppyjoes.com/lookalikes.htm

Help celebrate Ernest Hemingway's July 21 birthday with hundreds of Ernests at the look-alike contest, enter the Lorian Hemingway Short Story Contest conducted by the master's granddaughter, and enjoy the street fair, bull run, readings, and parties. Free.

Key West Food and Wine Festival
305-296-6909
www.kwrba.com/festival.htm

Sponsored by Key West Restaurant and Bar Association, events are held at several restaurants around Old Town. A week's worth of feasts and parties, from beer and wine tastings to champagne cruises to cooking classes and lobster feasts celebrating the broad span of culinary delights enjoyed in Key West. $$-$$$$.

Lower Keys Underwater Music Festival

305-872-2411, 1-800-872-3722
Looe Key Marine Sanctuary, 31020
Overseas Hwy., Big Pine Key 33040

Music is piped and played underwater for unique diving entertainment on the second Saturday of July. Free.

Reef Awareness Week

305-294-3100
www.reefrelief.org

Reef Awareness Week is a series of educational programs and films, educational snorkeling and diving expeditions, a marathon, an eco-shopping opportunity and a Jewel of the Sea Ball featuring hors d'ouevres and live music. Some are free, other events require admission. $-$$$$

September

Peterson's Poker Run Bike Week

305-235-4023
www.harleymiami.com
Peterson's Harley Davidson South,
17631 South Dixie Highway Perrine, FL 33157

Lower Keys Underwater Music Festival Monroe County Tourist Development Council

Contact Peterson's Harley Davidson South in Miami to sign up for the ride, which is hosted in Key West—at the end of the run—by Rick's Bar (305-296-4890; www.rickskeywest.com; 208 Duval Street, Key West 33040). Bikers may not have always had the finest of reputations, but today's Harley lovers also include white-collar executives out for a weekend ride. Started by Peterson's Harley of Key West more than 30 years ago, this event has some ten thousand motorcycles roaring down the Overseas Highway to spend a fun weekend in Key West, donating hundreds of thousands of dollars to local charities and millions to the local tourism industry. $–$$.

WomenFest

305-296-2491
www.womenfest.net
510 South St., Key West 33040

Lesbians and friends spend a week enjoying all Key West has to offer—sailing, snorkeling, and dolphin watching; cocktail galas; wet T-shirt contests; lesbian films; and more fun. Free.

October
Fantasy Fest
305-296-1817
www.fantasyfest.net
P.O. Box 230, Key West 33041

Ten days of bawdy fun for the most daring.
Masquerade parties culminate in the
Fantasy Fest Parade—the ultimate in New
Orleans risqué to the hundredth power.
Free.

November
American Power Boat Offshore World Championships
305-296-6166
www.apba-offshore.com
1323 20th Terr., Key West 33040

A float in the Fantasy Fest Parade Monroe County Tourist
Development Council

Considered to be the Indianapolis 500
of powerboat racing, this event includes three days of classes and racing, a boat parade, a
rock concert, and a boat show. $–$$$$.

Pirates in Paradise
305-296-9694
www.piratesinparadise.com
P.O. Box 1153, Key West 33040

This 10-day festival celebrates the Keys' pirate history with a series of events large and
small for big kids and little ones. Dress in your best pirate's cap and damsel bustier and
join the parties to hoist cold pints of ale on board a pirate ship or at one of several local
restaurants and museums. $–$$$$.

December
Key West Lighted Boat Parade
305-296-3773
Key West Historic Seaport, 202 Margaret St., Key West 33040

A holiday nautical display of lights and creativity in Key West Harbor. Free for spectators,
$$$ for participants.

EMERGENCY NUMBERS

In an emergency, dial 911.
Poison information: 1-800-222-1222
Key West police, nonemergency:
305-294-2511

HOSPITALS

Florida Keys Memorial Hospital
305-294-4692
5900 Junior College Rd., Key West 33040

Mariner's Hospital
305-434-3000
Mile marker 91.5, Plantation Key
91500 Overseas Hwy., Tavernier 33070

NEWSPAPERS

The Free Press
305-664-2266; 81549 Old Hwy.,
Islamorada 33026
305-743-8766; 6363 Overseas Hwy.,
Marathon 33050
www.keysnews.com

The Independent
305-451-1887
www.floridakeysnews.info
104300 Overseas Hwy., Key Largo 33037

The Keynoter
305-853-7103; 91655 Overseas Hwy.,
Tavernier 33070
305-743-5551; 3015 Overseas Hwy.,
Marathon 33050
www.keynoter.com

Key West Citizen
305-292-777
www.keysnews.com
3420 Northside Dr., Key West 33040

The Reporter
305-852-3216
www.upperkeysreporter.com
91655 US 1, Tavernier 33070

Solares Hill
305-294-3602
www.solareshill.com
3420 Northside Dr., Key West 33040

TRANSPORTATION

Bone Island Shuttle
305-293-8710
www.boneislandshuttle.com

Need a ride from your hotel to attractions
in Old Town Key West? Call Bone Island
Shuttle. It hits all the major stops. Kids
under 12 ride free. Runs 9 AM–11 PM daily;
call for route and pricing information.

Florida Keys Taxi
305-296-6666
6613 Maloney Ave., Key West 33040

Friendly Cab Co.
305-292-0000
800 14th St., Key West 33040

Greyhound Bus Lines
305-296-9072

Islamorada Taxi
305-664-4100

Keys Shuttle
305-289-9997, 1-888-765-9997
www.keysshuttle.com

Keys Shuttle provides door-to-door shuttle
service from the Florida Keys to the Miami
and Fort Lauderdale airports.

Key West Airport International
305-296-5439
3941 S. Roosevelt Blvd., Key West 33040

Key West Airport Shuttle
305-289-9997, 1-888-415-9997

Marathon Airport
305-743-2155
www.floridakeysairport.com
9400 Overseas Hwy., Marathon 33050

Mom's Taxi
305-453-4049, Key Largo
305-852-6000, Tavernier
305-852-888, Islamorada

TOURISM CONTACTS

Islamorada Chamber of Commerce
305-664-4503, 1-800-FAB-KEYS
www.islamoradachamber.com
Mile marker 82.5, P.O. Box 915,
Islamorada 33036

Key Largo Chamber of Commerce
305-451-1414, 1-800-822-1088
106000 Overseas Hwy., bayside,
Key Largo 33037

Index

N

(Continued)

DINING BY PRICE

LODGING BY PRICE

FOLLOW THE COUNTRYMAN PRESS
TO YOUR FAVORITE DESTINATIONS!

Explorer's Guide & Great Destinations Series

NORTHEAST

The Adirondack Book: A Complete Guide
The Berkshire Book: A Complete Guide
The Berkshire Hills & Pioneer Valley of Western
  Massachusetts: An Explorer's Guide
Cape Cod, Martha's Vineyard & Nantucket:
  An Explorer's Guide
The Coast of Maine Book: A Complete Guide
Connecticut: An Explorer's Guide
The Finger Lakes Book: A Complete Guide
The Hamptons Book: A Complete Guide
The Hudson Valley Book: A Complete Guide
The Hudson Valley & Catskill Mountains: An
  Explorer's Guide
Maine: An Explorer's Guide
The Nantucket Book: A Complete Guide
New Hampshire: An Explorer's Guide
New York City: An Explorer's Guide
Rhode Island: An Explorer's Guide
Touring East Coast Wine Country
Vermont: An Explorer's Guide
Western New York: An Explorer's Guide

MID–ATLANTIC

The Chesapeake Bay Book: A Complete Guide
Maryland: An Explorer's Guide
New Jersey: An Explorer's Guide
The Shenandoah Valley Book: A Complete Guide
The Shenandoah Valley & Mountains of the
  Virginias: An Explorer's Guide

SOUTHEAST

Blue Ridge & Smoky Mountains: An Explorer's
  Guide
The Charleston, Savannah, & Coastal Islands
  Book: A Complete Guide
Orlando, Central & North Florida: An Explorer's
  Guide
Palm Beach, Miami & the Florida Keys: Great
  Destinations
The Sarasota, Sanibel Island & Naples Book:
  A Complete Guide

WEST

Big Sur, Monterey Bay & Gold Coast Wine
  Country: Great Destinations
The Napa & Sonoma Book: A Complete Guide
Oregon: An Explorer's Guide
The Santa Fe & Taos Book: A Complete Guide
The Seattle & Vancouver Book: Great Destinations
The Texas Hill Country Book: A Complete Guide

General Travel

NORTHEAST

Adirondack High
Adirondack Odysseys
Big Apple Safari for Families
Chow Maine
The Colors of Fall
Covered Bridges of Vermont
A Guide to Natural Places in the Berkshire Hills
Dog-Friendly New England
Dog-Friendly New York
Dog-Friendly Washington, D.C. & the Mid-
  Atlantic States
Eating New England
Eating New Orleans
In-Line Skate New England
Hudson River Journey
Hudson Valley Harvest
Maine Sporting Camps
New England Seacoast Adventures
New England Waterfalls
New Jersey's Great Gardens
New Jersey's Special Places
Off the Leash
The Other Islands of New York City
The Photographer's Guide to the Maine Coast
The Photographer's Guide to Vermont
Shawangunks Trail Companion
Weekending in New England

MID–ATLANTIC

Waterfalls of the Mid-Atlantic States

WEST

The California Coast
The Photographer's Guide to the Grand Canyon
The Photographer's Guide to the Oregon Coast
Weekend Wilderness: California, Oregon,
  Washington

We offer many more books on hiking, fly-fishing,
travel, nature, cooking, and other subjects. Our
books are available at bookstores and outdoor
stores everywhere. For more information or a free
catalog, call
1-800-245-4151 or write to us at:
The Countryman Press, P.O. Box 748
Woodstock, Vermont 05091.
You can find us on the Internet at
www.countrymanpress.com.